DEADLY
BLUE

DEADLY BLUE

Battle Stories of the

U.S. Air Force

Special Operations Command

FRED PUSHIES

AMACOM

American Management Association

New York • Atlanta • Brussels • Chicago • Mexico City • San Francisco
Shanghai • Tokyo • Toronto • Washington, D.C.

Special discounts on bulk quantities of AMACOM books are
available to corporations, professional associations, and other
organizations. For details, contact Special Sales Department,
AMACOM, a division of American Management Association,
1601 Broadway, New York, NY 10019.
Tel.: 800-250-5308.   Fax: 518-891-2372.
E-mail: specialsls@amanet.org
Website: www.amacombooks.org/go/specialsales
To view all AMACOM titles go to: www.amacombooks.org

This publication is designed to provide accurate and authoritative information
in regard to the subject matter covered. It is sold with the understanding that
the publisher is not engaged in rendering legal, accounting, or other professional service. If legal advice or other expert assistance is required, the services
of a competent professional person should be sought.

Library of Congress Cataloging-in-Publication Data

Pushies, Fred
   Deadly blue : battle stories of the U.S. Air Force Special Operations command /
Fred Pushies.—1st ed.
      p.   cm.
   Includes bibliographical references and index.
   ISBN-10: 0-8144-1360-9
   ISBN-13: 978-0-8144-1360-9
   1. United States. Air Force Special Operations Command—History.   2. Afghan War,
2001—Aerial operations, American.   3. Iraq War, 2003—Aerial operations, American.
4. Afghan War, 2001—Personal narratives, American.   5. Iraq War, 2003—Personal
narratives, American. 6. United States. Air Force—Commando troops.   7. Special forces
(Military science)—United States—History—21st century.   8. Special operations
(Military science)—United States—History—21st century. 9. Close air support—
History—21st century.   I. Title.
DS371.412.P875   2009
958.104'7—dc22
                                                          2009010404

Printing number

10   9   8   7   6   5   4   3   2   1

To the Quiet Professionals of AFSOC

CONTENTS

★ CONTENTS

| F O R E W O R D |

On September 11, 2001, the nation's special operations forces were called upon as terrorists attacked our nation. Among the first units deployed were the Air Force Special Operations Command Air Commandos.

Since then, highly trained, rapidly deployable airmen from AFSOC have conducted global special operations missions ranging from precision application of firepower to infiltration and exfiltration, as well as resupply and refueling of special operations forces.

As of this writing, AFSOC aircraft have flown more than 25,000 combat sorties, amassing more than 75,000 combat hours since October 2001. Units have sustained combat and humanitarian operations 24 hours a day, seven days a week, 365 days a year. Albeit impressive, statistics don't portray the whole picture. The most important aspect of the story revolves around the people and the critical attributes they possess.

These are the stories of personal triumph and loss; they reflect selflessness, perseverance, and integrity. They are about the adaptability of each Air Commando who stands poised to combat today's threat.

War is nothing if not personal, and we are always mindful that our most valuable resources are the men and women who take an oath to support and defend with honor, who make the mission possible with skill, strength, tenacity, and determination. These twenty-first-century Air Commandos—from the boots on the ground battlefield airman to the air crews above—are an essential part of U.S. military missions around the globe.

It is the individual who embodies heroism and unselfish commitment to serve, for whom we pledge to protect. Our Airman's Creed personifies the AFSOC warrior: "I will never leave an Airman behind, I will never falter, and I will never fail." Keep these thoughts in mind as you read the stories of your AFSOC heroes, whose unwavering resolve and steadfast dedication to duty exemplify the Air Commando qualities that make this command the success it is today. I am a better person for having been associated with these heroes called Air Commandos and I love them very much!

Lt. Gen. Michael W. Wooley,

USAF, retired

Former AFSOC commander

Deadly Blue is a look into the often covert world of the U.S. Air Force Special Operations Command (AFSCOC). It is a collection of battlefield experiences of today's air commandos. From the first "boots on the ground" to the gunships overhead, these are the stories of the unsung heroes of America's war on terrorism.

During the course of this book, you will often read of CAS missions. CAS is an acronym for "close air support." The official Department of Defense definition, as stated in Joint Publication 3–09.3, *Joint Tactics, Techniques, and Procedures for Close Air Support (CAS)*, is "air action by fixed- and rotary-wing aircraft against hostile targets that are in close proximity to friendly forces and which require detailed integration of each air mission with the fire and movement of those forces." This publication further describes the fundamentals of CAS as being:

> conducted at any place and time friendly forces are in close proximity to enemy forces. The word "close" does not imply a specific distance; rather, it is situational. The requirement for detailed integration because of proximity, fires, or movement is the determining factor. At times CAS may be the best means to exploit tactical opportunities in the offense or defense. CAS provides firepower in offensive and defensive operations to destroy, disrupt, suppress, fix, harass, neutralize, or delay enemy forces.
>
> CAS may be used to mass the effects of combat power, in order to exploit opportunities in the offense and defense. Each Service organizes, trains, and equips to employ CAS within its roles as part of the joint force. As a result, a variety of aircraft are capable of performing CAS. The joint force commander (JFC)

**and his staff must be capable of integrating all CAS capabilities
into the operation plan.**

The rudimentary application of CAS goes back to 1911, when the
Italians at war with Turkey would drop hand grenades from airplanes. During WW I, the planes also served as an intimidating
weapon of war, albeit the dropping of hand-held bombs was far from
accurate. With the onset of WW II, the concept of close air support
became more viable, and air-to-ground fire crossed over to the prac-
tical. However, it was not until the Vietnam War that CAS became
the bread-and-butter mission for U.S. aviators. Pilots from the 1st
Air Commando Squadron, flying the A-1E Skyraider, referred to as
a "Sandy," and C-47 transports converted into AC-47 "Spooky" gunships, were on station. Fighters and bombers from the U.S. Air
Force, Navy, and Marines would drop so low to the deck that the
Green Berets on the ground could make out the artwork on the pilots' helmets.

With the advancement of today's sophisticated technology, including unmanned aerial vehicles (UAVs), gunships, and stealth
bombers, CAS has risen to a most deadly science. Fast movers are
great, bombers have the payloads, but there is no more lethal combination than an AC-130 gunship overhead and an AFSOC Special
Tactics Team on the ground. This is CAS at its finest, and the combat controllers have raised this to an art form.

Certain ground-combat capabilities are part of the airman's responsibilities, and so they require unique surface operations that are
integral to the application of air and space power. To provide those
capabilities, the Air Force has organized, trained, and equipped a
force of battlefield airmen with the distinctive expertise to deliver un-
equaled firepower with accuracy, responsiveness, flexibility, and persistence. The battlefield airman of the Air Force Special Operations
Command come from the Special Tactics Squadrons and consist of
combat controllers (CCTs), pararescuemen (PJs), and Special Operations Weather Teams (SOWTs). These highly trained professionals provide a skill set not commonly found across the Air Force,
and they typically operate in combat zones, outside the perimeter of
Air Force bases.

During Operation Enduring Freedom, in Afghanistan, Special Tactics Squadron team members routinely carried over 160 pounds of equipment. Some of this equipment was outdated, and occasionally they had difficulties communicating with one another. For this reason, the Air Force created an ongoing development program called the Battlefield Airman Operations (BAO) Kit. The purpose of the kit is to lighten the load of the STS team as well as provide them with state-of-the-art technology in radios, lighter batteries, integrated targeting devices, wearable computers, portable UAVs, plus the weapons, clothing, and other gear necessary to prosecute their vital missions. New tactics, techniques, and procedures are constantly being inserted into the BAO toolkit.

For example, as part of the SOF Warfighter Information Process Enhancements (SWIPE) Initiative, during the Joint Expeditionary Force Experiment (JEFX), the STT used Panasonic Toughbook computers—new information technology that enables the team to encompass a target from various positions. These wireless computers form a network through which team members can send information to the team leader, or "hub." The intelligence, digital photos or video, and reports that are gathered in the field can then be shared with other teammates or sent via burst transmission over SatCom to combatant commanders for review.

General Robert Holmes, who served as Deputy Commander, Joint Special Operations Task Force-South (Task Force K-Bar), was responsible for directing and conducting joint combat operations in southern Afghanistan. As testimony to the value of special operations, General Holmes reported that combat controllers were responsible for roughly 85 percent of all air strikes in support of Operation Enduring Freedom. Similarly, the Commandant of the Advanced Training Skills School at Hurlburt Field, stated that, for every one kill a Special Tactics operator made with his M4 carbine, he made 168 kills using close air support.

What does it take to be a member of the U.S. Air Force Special Operations Command? What kind of a person pushes himself beyond normal human endurance? What is it that drives that man to push on, no matter what the circumstances? It takes someone who places the mission before himself, the welfare of the team above his own welfare, and his love of freedom over life itself. These are the warriors of AFSOC, the aircrews in the skies and the Special Tactics Teams on the ground, who exemplify the traits worthy of the title Air Commando.

In these pages, I have tried to offer a limited window onto their world. It was indeed an honor to have been permitted to enter this world, if only via interviews. By recounting their experiences—in their own words—I have shone a light on a few of the many men who operate in the shadows—the covert world of special ops. Fittingly, some of their names have been changed, for purposes of operational security. But their stories of heroism and bravery, as well as quick reactions and solid thinking, are the afterglow of America's best efforts to bring peace and freedom to the world.

| A C K N O W L E D G M E N T S |

I would firstly like to offer my thanks to God, the author of liberty and freedom. May he continue keep our great nation in the hollow of his hand. I would like to offer my personal thank-you to all of the people who helped me with this project. To those who have shared their personal experiences in the following chapters, Thank You. It is because there are men and women like these deployed around the world that the rest of us can enjoy our freedom and sleep a little sounder at night. May God bless them, grant them victory, and keep them safe to return home to their loved ones.

Special thanks to Matt Durham (USAF Col–ret.) and Dawn Hart of the U.S. Air Force Special Operations Command Public Affairs Office (PAO), Hurlburt Field; 2d Lt Lauren Johnson, 1st Special Operations Wing, PAO, Hurlburt Field; 2d Lt Jennifer Richards, Nellis AFB PAO; Lt Col Susan P. Van Sloten, Deputy Chief of Staff, SOCJFCOM; Susanne Moore, Media Operations Chief, U.S. Joint Forces Command; Susan H. Meisner, Media Branch PAO, National Geospatial-Intelligence Agency; John Fristoe JPRA/J53; Ron Childress, Combat Controllers Association; Wayne Norrad, Special Tactics Recruiting, Hurlburt Field; Carol Darby, U.S. Army Special Operations Command PAO, Ft. Bragg; and Steve Dent, Imagery Coordinator, Australian Ministry of Defence.

Regional map of Afghanistan: Operation Enduring Freedom.
Courtesy of the U.S. Air Force.

Regional map of Iraq: Operation Iraqi Freedom. *Courtesy of the U.S. Air Force.*

DEADLY
BLUE

The Origin of the Air Force Special Operations

AFSOC crest. *Courtesy of the U.S. Air Force.*

What began as a noble attempt by the U.S. special operations forces ended in tragedy in the darkness of an Iranian desert. It was April 1980 when Special Forces Operation Detachment Delta, better known as "Delta Force," along with its Air Force and Marine aircrews, met with disaster. What Colonel "Charging" Charlie Beckwith did not know at the time was that the operation was headed toward disaster from the onset. Over the years there have been investigations, hearings, and countless articles written on why the mission ended in a debacle, so we will not belabor the issue here. All the Monday-morning quarterbacks had one conclusion in common, however: Operation Eagle Claw failed. This failure cost the lives of eight gallant troops, it cost the honor of the United States of America, and it hurt the credibility of U.S. special operations.

The Navy helicopters with Marine pilots proved to be the Achilles' heel of Operation Eagle Claw. One can only speculate on the compilations of mishaps that besieged the Sea Stallion helicopters. Some got lost in the desert and others malfunctioned, leaving the anxious force without the adequate airlift capability necessary to accomplish the rescue attempt. From the inception of the plan, they were "the" weak link. Were the pilots up to the task?

The Marine pilots, if we look at today's standards, had big boots to fill. They were being asked to fly at night. This alone was unusual practice for the "Flying Leathernecks." These pilots were now being asked to perform the extraordinary: launch off the deck of a carrier, at night, fly NOE (nap-of-the-earth), where radar could not detect them, and use no running lights. The pilots were issued PVS5 night vision goggles; however, they could be worn only for 30-minute intervals. This meant that the pilot and co-pilot had to alternate flying the huge helicopter every 30 minutes. The Marines had no pilots who had been trained in this type of flying. In fact, none of the service branches was prepared for such a contingency.

Following the disaster at Desert One, a review committee known as the Holloway Commission convened to look into problems within U.S. special operations. The outcome of this commission resulted in two major recommendations. First, the Department of Defense should establish a Counterterrorism Task Force (CTJTF) as a field organization of the Joint Chiefs of Staff (JCS), with a permanently assigned staff and forces. The JCS would plan, train for, and conduct operations to counter terrorist activities against the United States. The CTJTF would use military forces in the counterterrorism (CT) role. These forces could range in size from small units of highly specialized personnel to larger integrated forces. Second, the JCS should consider the formation of a Special Operations Advisory Panel (SOAP). This panel would consist of high-ranking officers to be drawn from both active service and retired personnel. The prerequisite for selection was a background in special operations or having served as a commander in chief (CINC) or on JCS level and having maintained a proficient level of interest in special operations or defense policy. The mission of the SOAP would be to review and evaluate highly classified special-operations planning to provide an independent assessment. Consequently, the progressive reorganization and resurgence of U.S. special operation forces began.

While this was occurring, the Air Force transferred responsibility for Air Force special operations from Tactical Air Command (TAC) to Military Airlift Command (MAC) in March 1983. The commander of the 23rd Air Force at Scott Air Force Base, Illinois, would assume all control of the Air Force special operations units. This new-numbered Air Force was tasked with the worldwide missions of special operations, combat rescue, pararescue training, medical evacuation, and training of HC-130 and helicopter crewmen.

Subsequently, on March 1, 1983, in response to the Holloway Commission report, all U.S. Air Force special operation forces were consolidated into the 1st Special Operations Wing (SOW) at Hurlburt Field, Florida. The 1st SOW would direct and coordinate active and reserve components of the Special Operation Squadrons (SOS). Active components consisted of the 8th SOS operating MC-130 Combat Talons and HC-130 Hercules Tankers, the 16th SOS operating AC-130 Spectre gunships, and the 20th SOS operating the MH-53 Pave Low and HH-53 Jolly Green Giant helicopters. The 1723rd Combat Control Squadron provided the combat control teams.

Reserve components of Air Force special operation forces included the 919th Special Operations Group (SOG) operating AC-130A gunships, the 302nd SOG operating the EC-130E command and control aircraft, and the Pennsylvania Air National Guard flying the Volant Solo EC-130E Psychological Operations aircraft.

In addition to traditional special operations skills, the 23rd conducted weather reconnaissance, security support for intercontinental ballistic missile sites, and training of USAF helicopter and HC-130 crewmen.

Operation Urgent Fury

In October 1983, the 23rd Air Force participated with other Caribbean forces in the successful rescue of Americans from the island-nation of Grenada. During the seven-day operation, centered at Point Salines Airport, the 23rd Air Force furnished MC-130s, AC-130s, and EC-130 aircraft, aircrews, maintenance, and support people.

During the Grenada operation, the 1st Special Operations Wing had two missions: the MC-130 Combat Talons were tasked with delivering U.S. Army Rangers to Point Salines, while Spectre gunships provided the air-to-ground support fire. Combat controllers were air-dropped in with the U.S. Army Rangers at Port Salinas Airport, making an unprecedented combat jump from only 500 feet. Each controller was laden with parachute gear and more than 90 pounds of mission-critical equipment. Upon landing, they quickly established a command-and-control radio net. They carried out air traffic operations for follow-on forces both at the airport and for other in-country missions. In addition to this, the combat control teams (CCT) performed as forward air control (FAC) for Air Force Spectre gunships, Navy fighters, and Army helicopter gunships. Throughout the operation, the crews of the 1st SOW continued in the tradition of the air commandos who preceded them. Flying in numerous sorties and fire missions, they performed mission after mission without sustaining any casualties during the entire operation.

The Grenada operation was not without its cost to the special operations community. Four U.S. Navy SEALs were lost at sea during a Rubber Duck insertion. This tragedy hit the SOF community hard. Operation Urgent Fury was also fraught with planning problems from the get-go; a lack of standardization of the special operations forces equipment contributed to making this plan gone awry. Though the special operations forces in Grenada did have a few rough edges, most of the planning problems were overcome because the special operations personnel from all three service branches excelled at what they do best: improvise, adapt, and overcome to achieve the mission's goals.

The Grenada mission became the springboard for the further consolidation of U.S. special operations forces. The Air Force particularly took a proactive stance by rebuilding a powerful special operations force. In May 1986, Congressman William Cohen, Senator Sam Nunn, and Congressman Dan Daniel introduced legislation that formed the basis for amending the 1986 Defense Authorizations Bill. This bill, signed into law in October 1986, in part directed the formation of a unified command responsible for special operations. In April 1987, the U.S. Special Operations Command (USSOCOM) was established at MacDill Air Force Base, Florida, and Army General James J. Lindsay assumed command. Four months later, the 23rd Air Force moved to Hurlburt Field.

In August 1989, General Duane H. Cassidy, MAC commander in chief, divested all nonspecial operations units from the 23rd Air Force. Consequently, the 23rd Air Force served a dual role, reporting to MAC but also functioning as the air component to USSOCOM.

Operation Just Cause

On December 20, 1989, at 1 P.M. local time, the United States launched an attack on Panama. The objectives of the attack were to protect U.S. personnel and installations, neutralize the Panamanian Defense Force, and capture General Manuel Noriega. During this operation the Air Force special operations units saw extensive use. Owing to their surgical firing capability, the Spectres were the ideal solution for the close-in urban combat environment with limited collateral damage. The Spectres were launched from the 16th Special Operations Squadron ("Ghostriders") at Hurlburt Field, Florida.

Other Air Force special operations assets included an EC-130 from the 193rd Air National Guard stationed at the Harrisburg Airport, Pennsylvania, to perform psychological warfare operations during the invasion. Pararescuemen and combat control teams (CCTs) participated in operations with the U.S. Army's 75th Rangers at Torrijos Airfield and Rio Hato Air Base. Combat controllers would also be attached to U.S. Navy SEAL Team 4 in support of the frogmen as they assaulted Patilla Airport and disabled General Noriega's personal jet.

In retrospect, Operation Just Cause served as a proving ground for the future 1991 war in the Middle East. The night tactics and stealth weapons battle-tested in Panama later accounted for many of the successes in Desert Storm. (While some of the issues that plagued the Grenadian assault in 1983 had been addressed, Operation Just Cause did have its share of problems as well. One of the major short comings resulted in four Navy SEALs being killed and eight wounded during the raid at Paitilla Airport.) The invasion of Panama also established a strategy for the way U.S. special operations forces would be deployed and used in the future.

The Birth of the Air Force Special Operations Command

On May 22, 1990, General Larry D. Welch, Air Force chief of staff, redesignated the 23rd Air Force as the Air Force Special Operations Command (AFSOC). Henceforth, AFSOC was responsible for the combat readiness of Air Force special operations forces. Headquartered at Hurlburt Field, Florida, the group would report directly to the Air Force chief of staff and be the Air Force's component of USSOCOM.

The new major command consisted of three wings—the 1st SOW, the 39th SOW, and the 353rd SOW—as well as the 720th Special Tactics Group, the U.S. Air Force Special Operations School, and the Special Missions Operational Test and Evaluation Center. The Air Reserve components included the 919th Special Operations Group (Air Force Reserve) at Duke Field, Florida, and the 193rd SOG (Air National Guard) at Harrisburg Airport, Pennsylvania.

AFSOC is the Air Force component of the U.S. Special Operations Command, or USSOCOM. Its mission is to provide mobility, surgical firepower, covert tanker support, and special tactics teams (STTs). These units will normally operate in concert with U.S. Army and U.S. Navy special operations forces, including Special Forces (SF), Rangers, Special Operations Aviation Regiment, SEAL teams, psychological operations (PSYOP) forces, and Civil Affairs units. AFSOC supports a wide range of activities, from combat operations of a limited duration to those of longer-term conflicts. They also provide support to foreign governments and their militaries. Subject to shifting priorities, AFSOC maintains a flexible profile allowing it to respond to numerous types of missions. CCTs provide qualified joint terminal attack controllers (JTAC) who are attached to SOF teams and control the majority of close air support (CAS) missions required in emergency situations.

From early August 1990 to late February 1991, AFSOC participated in Operations Desert Shield and Desert Storm, which involved the protection of Saudi Arabia and the liberation of Kuwait. It was the Green Hornets Pave Lows of the 20th Special Operations Squadron that began the air war in the Persian Gulf. In October 1990, U.S. Commander in Chief Central Command (USCINCCENT) General Norman H. Schwarzkopf had studied the multitude of maps, aerial and satellite imagery, and intelligence reports, and he pondered his next plan to action. It was the last week of the month when Colonel George Gray, commander of the 1st Special Operations Wing, met with the general. Col. Gray briefed Gen. Schwarzkopf on a plan called "Eager Anvil."

This plan included a flight of four MH-53 Pave Lows and an assault force of Army AH-64 Apache attack helicopters to execute the mission. The Pave Lows were equipped with forward-looking infrared radar (FLIR), terrain avoidance radar, a global positioning system (GPS), and other sophisticated electronics and navigational aids. The helicopters would cross into Iraq, leading the Apaches through the dark and over the featureless desert terrain to the target areas. Once on site, the Army pilots in their Apaches would "take out" two enemy radar installations simultaneously, with AGM-114 Hellfire laser-guided missiles. With these radar sites destroyed, a corridor would be opened for U.S. and coalition aircraft to begin the air campaign.

So critical was this operation to the commencement of Desert Storm that Gen. Schwarzkopf asked Col. Gray, "Colonel, are you going to guarantee me one hundred percent success on this mission?" Col. Gray looked at the general and answered, "Yes, sir." The USCINCCENT replied, "Then you get to start the war."

Lieutenant Colonel Richard L. Comer was a little taken aback at Col. Gray's commitment. Comer vowed that the mission would have to be perfect; he did not intend to make his boss a liar. He later commented, "This was the best joint helicopter flying operation I've ever seen." The Apaches were designed to shoot and destroy targets, and the Pave Lows were designed to get the AH-64s to the targets. It was a perfect match. The designation for the mission was "Task Force Normandy." There were two formations of two MH-53Js and two AH-64s. One group was assigned to the eastern site, the other to the westernmost installation.

At 2:12 P.M. local time, TF Normandy crossed the border and entered Iraq. All of the training that the 20th had under its belt was now paying off. The helicopters sped through the pitch-black night, flying no higher than 50 feet above the desert floor. Relying on the Pave Lows' computers and sensors, the Green Hornets' pilots zigzagged around Nomad camps, down into wadis (dry desert streambeds), flying nap-of-the-earth (NOE) to stay under the Iraqi radar. They staggered back and forth to avoid being observed by enemy observation posts.

The formations arrived on target, and at 2:38, the two sites were struck simultaneously by missiles. Within four minutes, the Iraqi radar installations ceased to exist. The air campaign had begun. Active-duty Air Force Reserve and Air National Guard components of AFSOC were deployed to Saudi Arabia and Turkey. The 1st SOW with its AC-130s, HC-130s, MC-130s, MH-53s, and MH-60s; the 193rd SOG with its EC-130s; and the 919th SOG with its AC-130s and HH-3s all deployed south of Kuwait. The 39th SOW deployed north of Iraq with its HC-130s, MC-130s, and MH-53s. Special tactics personnel operated throughout the theater on multiple combat control and combat rescue missions.

Air Force Special Operations Command combat control teams were responsible for the majority of air traffic control in the Persian Gulf theater of operation. In addition, the teams performed direct-action missions, combat search and rescue, infiltration, exfiltration, air base ground defense, air interdiction, special reconnaissance, close air support, psychological operations, and helicopter air refueling.

The Special Tactics Squadrons

The U.S. Army has the Rangers and the Special Forces (the Green Berets). In the U.S. Navy, the special operators are the SEALs. Rounding out the full force of U.S. special operations forces on the ground are the U.S. Air Force Special Operations Command Special Tactics Squadrons (STSs). A combination of combat control teams (CCTs) and pararescuemen (PJs) is referred to as a special tactics team, or STT. The STT is an integral part of the U.S. Special Operations Command (SOCOM) and its missions. The STT members frequently operate with the U.S. Navy SEALs, U.S. Army Rangers, and U.S. Army Special Forces units in special reconnaissance (SR), combat search and rescue (CSAR), and direct action (DA, as in airfield seizure), to name just a few of their capabilities. Every member of the STS teams is a volunteer. These highly motivated, proficient STTs are capable of being deployed by sea, air, or land (sound familiar?), often weighed down with 100 to 150 pounds of equipment, to execute their mission. These units are found regularly on missions alongside the U.S. Army and U.S. Navy SOF troops. Whether they fast-rope into an area with a company of Rangers, high-altitude low-opening (HALO) parachute in with a Special Forces A-Team, or lockout a submarine with a SEAL platoon, the STTs add a lethal element to U.S. special operation forces.

Operating under the AFSOC, the Special Tactics Squadrons comprise combat controllers, pararescuemen, and special operations weather teams. These men are proficient in sea-air-land insertion tactics into forward, nonpermissive environments. The combat control teams (CCTs) establish assault zones with an air traffic control capability. These assault zones could be a drop zone for a parachute deployment, a landing zone for heliborne operations, or a follow-on fixed-wing aircraft. They could also be for an extraction or low-level resupply operation.

In fact, the CCTs specialize in air traffic control. When given the go signal, they can place and then control numerous forms of lights—visible and infrared—as easily as you would use your TV remote on a home theater system. These combat control teams are also responsible for ground-based fire control of the AC-130 Spectre gunships and helicopters of AFSOC, as well as for all air assets, including Army and Navy aircraft. In addition to these capabilities, the CCTs provide vital command-and-control capabilities in the forward AO (area of operations) and are qualified in demolition procedures to remove obstructions and obstacles in the landing or drop zone. CCT -qualified JTACs are capable of directing air strikes from Air Force, Navy, or coalition fighters or bombers and AC-130 or helicopter gunships.

The ratio of CCTs to PJs varies with the mission profile and with whom the STT will be attached (for example, Rangers, SEALs, Special Forces). If the mission is a combat search and rescue, then the team will be pararescue "heavy"; if the task is to take down an airfield and hold it, the team is then made up primarily of CCTs. Each mission profile is unique and the special tactics teams are highly skilled in overcoming, adapting, and improvising to meet their objectives.

While the combat controllers are busy with their tasks, the PJs provide emergency medical care necessary to stabilize and evacuate injured personnel. The PJs are the ones who establish the overall combat search-and-rescue operations, as well as the planning and procedures. Also, the pararescue men of the STS provide triage and medical treatment for follow-on forces. To say that these individuals are highly skilled would be an understatement. They are instructed in the latest medical procedures in combat and trauma medicine. When they are not jumping into remote hostile environments or engaging in a joint task force field-training exercise (FTX), you might find them riding along with EMS units in urban areas. Large cities have high incidents of gunshot wounds and similar injuries, so these personnel gain further experience to take into the field.

During Operation Just Cause, the Special Tactics Squadrons were with the Rangers in the raid on Rio Hato. The CCTs performed air traffic control and special air assets fire control. The PJs were there to provide emergency medical assistance and triage evaluation. CCT members were also with SEAL Team 4 at Patilla Airport. CCTs also provided the air traffic control in Saudi Arabia and virtually ran the King Fahd International Airport during Operation Desert Shield. At the beginning of Operation Desert Storm, a four-man special tactics team was with the First Marine Division that opened the air corridor for U.S. and coalition aircraft. Likewise, three sergeants of the 24th STS were with the Rangers in Somalia.

In fact, the Somalia operation is a prime example of how the talents of members of the Special Tactics Squadrons are exploited. The CCTs called in air fire within meters of their position. They literally blew out one wall, then another, and thus were able to evade and escape (E&E), out of harm's way. For their actions during the firefight, TSgt. Tim Wilkinson was awarded the Air Force Cross for extraordinary heroism, while MSgt. Scott Fales and SSgt. Jeffery Bray received Silver Stars for gallantry.

During Operation Restore Democracy, while network news crews showed the U.S. helicopters settling into a landing zone in Haiti and being heralded as "the first Americans to land on Haitian soil," members of the AFSOC/STS had been on the ground for days already, surveying those helicopter landing zones and setting up lighting for the heliborne troopers.

There are six STS units worldwide, with approximately 360 combat controllers and 100 pararescuemen in the AFSOC. The 21st STS is stationed at Pope Air Force Base, North Carolina; the 24th STS is at Fort Bragg, North Carolina; the 22nd STS is at McChord Air Force Base, Washington; the 23rd is at Hurlburt Field, Florida; the 320th STS is at Kadena Air Base, Japan; and the 321st STS is at RAF Mildenhall, England.

The History and Development of Pararescue

Today's pararescuemen can trace their roots back to a remote jungle close to the China-Burma border, in the summer of 1943, during World War II. Here, twenty-one persons were forced to bail out of a disabled C-46 into an area so isolated that the only possible way to get to the survivors was with a parachute drop. Lieutenant Colonel Don Fleckinger, along with two medical personnel, volunteered to make the jump. From this mission, the concept of pararescue was born.

In the early fifties, with the formation of the Air Rescue Service, and subsequently in 1956, when it was reorganized as the Air Rescue and Recovery Service, the PJs, or para-jumpers, as the name implies, have been prepared to make the ultimate sacrifice to uphold their motto, "That Others May Live." In 1966, Air Force Chief of Staff General John P. McConnell approved for these pararescue forces the wearing of the maroon beret; the beret symbolizes the blood sacrifices made by the PJs and their devotion to duty in coming to the aid of others.

Trained in parachuting, mountaineering, and medical techniques, these men have come to provide rescue capability for both military and civilian situations. U.S. Air Force PJs have also been instrumental in the recovery of astronauts in the U.S. space program. In fact, pararescuemen have worked with NASA since the early *Gemini* programs of the sixties. They were present to support Skylab missions and they are currently on call to provide rescue support to the space shuttle program. The PJs gained even more rescue potential with the introduction of combined parachuting capability and scuba technique.

The pararescue forces operate at great risk to themselves. According to Master Sergeant Ron Childress (ret.), an instructor at AST (advanced skills training), "It is not uncommon for the PJs to put the survivor on the penetrator while they were under heavy fire and protect that survivor even at the risk of his own life." During the Vietnam War, PJs were considered part of the crew of the Jolly Green helicopters in the search and rescue of downed pilots. These men operated the jungle penetrators as well as the onboard weapons. The PJ might ride the hoist down to an injured pilot, with M-16 in hand, and secure the wounded man to the penetrator, then hold him secure as they rode back up to the relative safety of the hovering helicopter.

During Operation Just Cause, in 1989, pararescuemen were among the first U.S. combatants to parachute into Panama. The need for their medical expertise was continual during this short operation, as they recovered and treated the majority of Rangers who had taken the two Panamanian airfields in the first hours of the invasion. Speeding up and down the runway in their specially designed all-terrain vehicles equipped with litters, the PJs collected the casualties and brought them to a collection point. Then, at this location, the pararescuemen performed triage and provided the necessary medical attention until medical evacuation could be arranged. All this time, firefights were going on around them.

The PJs were on call during Operations Desert Shield and Desert Storm in the Persian Gulf, as well. It was during the Gulf War that pararescuemen penetrated into hostile territory on MH-53 Pave Low helicopters to recover a downed F-14 pilot, Devon Jones). After the war, pararescuemen also provided support for the airlift of Kurdish refugees fleeing into northern Iraq.

The training of pararescue personnel is a constant process. All the time, they endeavor to perfect current techniques while developing new procedures. Whether scaling the face of a mountain, doing a high-altitude, low-opening jump at 25,000 feet, racing down the tarmac of some foreign airfield, or being suspended from the cable of a CV-22 Osprey over a distressed vessel in the Pacific, PJs accomplish their tasks at all costs.

The Pararescue pipeline is as follows: Pararescue Indoctrination, Lackland AFB, Texas (twelve weeks); Air Force Combat Diver School, Panama City, Florida (six weeks); U.S. Army Airborne School, Fort Benning, Georgia (three weeks); Military Free Fall School, Fort Bragg, North Carolina, and Yuma, Arizona (four weeks); Survival School and Dunker training, Fairchild AFB, Washington (three weeks); Pararescue Medical Training, Kirtland AFB, New Mexico (twenty-two weeks); and Pararescue Rescue Training, Kirtland AFB, New Mexico (twenty weeks).

The Origins and Duties of the Combat Control Teams

The need for combat controller teams surfaced in the early air campaigns of World War II. During several major parachute assaults, the paratroopers fell short of their drop zone, resulting in troopers' being scattered as much as thirty miles from the intended zone. It became quite evident that effective guidance and control of the air transports were required. The Army created and trained a company-size group of scouts who were parachute qualified, and this unit became known as "Pathfinders." Their mission was to precede the main assault force to the drop zone. Once on the ground, they would use lights, flares, and smoke pots to provide a visual guide and offer weather information to the incoming planes.

Pathfinders were first employed in the fall of 1943, during the airborne reinforcement of Allied troops in Italy. Minutes before the main body reached the designated area, the Pathfinders hit the ground and established the drop zone for the follow-on paratroops. These forerunners of the combat control team (CCT) also proved instrumental in the D-Day invasion of Europe, preparing the way for elements of the 82nd and 101st Airborne Divisions to land.

The U.S. Air Force was officially established on September 18, 1947, and it assumed responsibility for tactical airlift support of U.S. Army forces. These Air Force Pathfinders were activated in January 1953, and by then were being called combat control teams. The teams provided navigational aids and air traffic control for the expanding airlift forces, but remained under aerial port squadrons until 1977. In 1984, the CCTs were restructured and assigned to the numbered Air Forces (for example, 21st Air Force, and so on), and in 1991 they were placed under the control of the host wing commanders.

Since their activation in the early fifties, CCTs have seen action worldwide. Combat controllers participated in the Lebanon crisis (July–October 1958), the Congo uprising (July–October 1960), the Cuban Missile Crisis (October 1962), the China-India confrontation (November 1962–September 1963), and the Vietnam War (1961–1975).

It was during the Vietnam War that the CCTs emerged as one of the Air Force's premiere units. Indeed, their exploits in Southeast Asia helped form the basis for current combat control operating methods. They were qualified as air traffic controllers, parachutists, and in emergency first aid; they also received training in communications, small-unit patrolling techniques, and ambush and counter-ambush tactics. In truth, it was the CCTs who established drop zones and landing zones.

Combat controllers occasionally could be found at isolated Army Special Forces camps scattered throughout Vietnam. On such occurrences these controllers called in air strikes to support the Green Beret camps or guided a C-123 Fairchild or C-130 Hercules down the airstrip for a much-needed resupply run. And these beginning operations helped establish the close bond between CCTs and other special operations forces.

From 1967 through 1972, for example, combat controllers assured mission safety, expedited air traffic flow, and coordinated activities with airlift control units. The CCTs were the last troops to be evacuated from the beleaguered outpost at Khe Sahn. Two U.S. Air Force combat controllers were among the last Americans to be airlifted from the U.S. Embassy when Saigon fell in 1975.

Prior to Operation Eagle Claw, a lone combat controller performed R&S (reconnaissance and surveillance) of Desert Site One. The mission planners had scores of aerial photographs, but they needed human intelligence (HUMINT), or someone on the ground. In early April 1980, Major John T. Carney, Jr., was delivered to the Iranian wasteland via a Central Intelligence Agency aircraft. The major pulled a small motorcycle from the plane. Equipped with a pair of night-vision goggles, a penetrometer, and some infrared lights, he began to survey the proposed landing site. Maj. Carney paused from time to time to take a core sample of the desert sand. This sand was later analyzed to determine if the location could support the weight of the Sea Stallions and Hercules that would bring in Col. Beckwith's rescue force.

It was for this mission that the "Box and One" lighting method was first deployed. Setting up his strobe lights in a box pattern approximately 90 feet apart, then placing the fifth light at the end of the landing zone 5,000 feet away, he had marked the end of the landing zone. Maj. Carney's team of combat controllers had given him a tool whereby five strobes would do the job normally requiring more than two dozen lights. With the battery casings of the infrared lights buried below the surface, Carney took one more survey of the area before loading his motorcycle into the CIA Otter and exiting Iran. When the aircraft containing the assault force arrived for the mission, the pilots hit the remote, and the five strobe lights lit up the landing zone below them. The mission of the combat controller was a success—one of the few successes of Operation Eagle Claw.

The birth of the STS concept grew out of the Grenada mission, not the Operation Eagle Claw, however. In 1983, combat controllers jumped with the Army Rangers into Grenada for Operation Urgent Fury in 1983, and again as the United States invaded Panama in 1989 in Operation Just Cause. While their PJ teammates tended the wounded, the CCTs, assisted by the Rangers, cleared obstacles from the runways, marked them with the "Box and One" method, and controlled the arrival of aircraft bringing the rest of the assault force. Worth noting here is that the gunships were actually controlled by TACPs assigned to those units during this operation.

So, whether it was on a trodden-down cow pasture in Europe in World War II where they lit smoke pots to mark the landing field, or an isolated Special Forces camp in the central highlands of Vietnam, or the all-out war of Desert Storm, combat controllers have been and continue to be an integral part of the success of special operations. Today, combat control teams are part of the ground combat forces assigned to the Special Tactics Squadrons of the U.S. Air Force Special Operations Command.

The combat controllers' roles and responsibilities are to plan, organize, supervise, and establish air traffic control at forward airheads. They select or assist in selecting sites and marking assault zones (drop, landing, or recovery) with visual and electronic navigational aids for day and night air-land and airdrop operations. The CCTs operate portable and mobile communications equipment and terminal and en route air navigation aids required to control and support the air traffic in these forward areas. These teams also evaluate and relay the status of assault zones to inbound aircraft as well as to headquarters. CCTs control vehicular traffic in the airport area, in the air and on the runway and taxiways. They also monitor air navigational aids and maintain qualification of primary assigned weapons.

These highly trained CCTs are organized and equipped to rapidly establish and control the air-ground interface in the objective area. Their functions also include special operations terminal attack control. In the event that the runway or airfield must be cleared of obstacles, the CCT units are trained in removal and are equipped with demolition materials that allow them to accomplish that task. Combat control teams may also be deployed with air and ground forces in the execution of direct action, special reconnaissance, austere airfield, combat search and rescue, counterterrorism, foreign internal defense, and humanitarian assistance operations.

On the ground, the CCT is "the" air traffic controller. He regulates en route and airhead air traffic and initiates, coordinates, and issues air traffic control clearances, holding instructions, and advisories to maintain aircraft separation and promote safe, orderly, and expeditious air traffic flow under visual or nonradar flight rules. Whether using the radio in his rucksack or the Tactical Air Navigation (TACAN) unit attached to the rear of a quad, he conducts ground-to-air communications; both visual and electronic systems are used to control and expedite the movement of aircraft while en route, arriving, and departing from the airhead. The CCT interfaces with pilots by issuing advisories on air traffic control, weather, and wake turbulence. He directs actions in handling aircraft emergencies during Special Tactics Team deployments to support contingency operations. Likewise, the CCT coordinates clearances, instructions, advisers, and air traffic movement with forward and rear area commanders.

Further, the CCT establishes and operates forward communications facilities and supervises and establishes high-frequency, satellite, or other long-range C4I links between forward and rear area commanders. The CCT develops terminal instrument procedures for assault zones, including gathering current ground intelligence in forward airhead areas, and coordinates with pararescue personnel on casualty and patient staging and collection point for expeditious medical evacuation.

Particularly in these emergency situations, the combat controllers may be deployed into forward-area and forward-operating locations in special operations missions, combat search and rescue (CSAR), and fire support duties. Along with the removal of obstacles with explosives, there may be an occasion when the CCT is called upon to "sanitize" a crash site. While the task of blowing up a downed aircraft normally is the responsibility of other operators (i.e., Rangers, SEALs, Special Forces, and so on), CCTs are fully capable of carrying out such a task if necessary.

Combat controllers may receive advance training and become

qualified as joint terminal attack controllers (JTACs), allowing them to provide close air support with the "fast movers." The Special Operations Tactical Air Control (SOTAC) is the actual school the CCTs go to in order to receive their JTAC qualification. In short, the special tactics CCTs are definitely one of the USSOCOM's most lethal weapons.

The Combat Controller pipeline includes the following: Combat Control orientation (two weeks); Air Traffic Control School, Keesler AFB, Mississippi (sixteen weeks); U.S. Army Airborne School, Fort Benning, Georgia (three weeks); Survival School and Dunker training, Fairchild AFB, Washington (three weeks); Combat Control School, Pope AFB, North Carolina (twelve weeks); Advanced Skills Training, Hurburt Field, Florida (fifty-two weeks); Military Free Fall School, Fort Bragg, North Carolina, and Yuma, Arizona (four weeks); and Air Force Combat Dive School, Panama City, Florida (six weeks).

Special Operations Weather Teams— Their Beginnings and Their Mission

Assigned to the 720th Special Tactics Squadron is the 10th Combat Weather Squadron (CWS). Its mission is to provide meteorological and oceanographic information in and for the special operations theater of operations. The functions of its members include tactical infiltration, data collection, analysis and forecasting, mission tailoring of environmental data, and joint operation with a host-nation's weather personnel. CWS personnel perform this job from a forward-deployed base or at times from behind enemy lines, using tactical weather equipment and an assortment of communications equipment.

Members of the CWS operate with subordinate units of the U.S. Army's Special Operations Command (USASOC), Special Forces Command (USASFC), and Civil Affairs/Psychological Operations Command (USACAPOC). The CWS personnel train and maintain the readiness of assigned forces to conduct special combat operations—anytime, anywhere, independently or attached to USASOC units.

✸   ✸   ✸   ✸

Today's Combat Weather Squadron can trace its lineage to 1943, with air and ground combat and special operations in the China-Burma-India theater of World War II. The volatile nature of the weather affecting wartime operations in this part of the world demanded the use of small teams of weather experts who could observe from deep within enemy territory. One of the earliest commanders of the squadron was Lieutenant Colonel (later Brigadier General) Richard Ellsworth. He and the 10th Weather Squadron (WS) operated with Colonel Phillip Cochran's 1st Air Commando Group, Brigadier Orde Wingate's Chindits (long-range penetration teams), and Brigadier General Frank Merrill's 5037th Composite Infantry Provisional ("Merrill's Marauders").

Then, in June 1966, the 10th Weather Squadron was reactivated at Udorn Airfield, Thailand, to conduct combat weather operations in Southeast Asia during the Vietnam War. The squadron also trained indigenous personnel and set up clandestine weather observation networks throughout the region. Tenth Weather Squadron personnel were key players in many successful special operations, including the Son Tay raid, which was America's attempt to rescue prisoners of war (POWs) from a prison camp in North Vietnam. The timing for the raid was advanced by 24 hours, based on the weather forecast submitted by the 10th Weather Squadron.

On April 1, 1996, the 10th Weather Squadron was redesignated the 10th Combat Weather Squadron (CWS), at Fort Bragg, North Carolina. This one squadron comprises five detachments located in the United States and two overseas locations. Special operations forces supported by the 10th CWS include U.S. Army Special Forces, U.S. Army Rangers, 160th Special Operations Aviation Regiment, special warfare training groups, and special operations support battalions.

In October 2008, the SOWT airmen received their own Air Force specialty code (AFSC), thus enabling trainees to enlist directly into this career field. Prior to this change, airmen wanting to join SOWT would have to serve in the Air Force before qualifying for special operations weather training. According to Chief Master Sgt.

Andrew Hopwood, AFSOC weather functional manager, "The new AFSC will provide special operations weathermen the right technical, physical and tactical training from day one. This will greatly enhance their battlefield observing, environmental reconnaissance and forecasting missions."

The Special Operations Weatherman pipeline is an abbreviated version of the CCT/PJ training pipeline. Trainees attend a two-week Special Operations Weathermen Selection Course at Lackland Air Force Base, Texas; initial-skills course at Keesler AFB, Mississippi (thirty weeks); Air Force Weather Course and Army airborne school at Fort Benning, Georgia (three weeks); Air Force Survival School at Fairchild AFB, Washington (three weeks); Special Operations Weather Apprentice Course at Pope AFB, North Carolina (thirteen weeks); and Advanced Skills Training (Phase 3 and 4), Hurlburt Field, Florida (twelve to fifteen months).

The Global War on Terrorism

Today, as America wages what former President George W. Bush termed the "Global War on Terrorism (GWOT)," members of the AFSOC are deployed around the globe. Before September 11, 2001, the AFSOC was conducting training missions, honing the skills of its staff. After the homeland attack, the Special Operations Command (SOCOM) went on high alert. While training of new operators still takes place, the operational tempo has increased exponentially, as the Special Tactics teams "jocked up" for the real-world missions of the GWOT. In Operation Enduring Freedom (OEF), members of the Special Tactics Squadron (STS) were among the first "boots on the ground" in Afghanistan, when combat controllers came in with various Special Forces (SF) operational detachments—Alphas, also known as A-teams," in the wasteland of Afghanistan. The mission of the SF soldiers was to link up with members of the Northern Alliance (a military-political organization of Afghan groups) and take the battle to the Taliban and al-Qaeda fighters. The combat controller provided close air support for those engagements, on Roberts Ridges and Tora Bora, bringing the fight to the terrorists. During Operation Iraqi

Freedom, they were among the first American operators across the border, preparing the way for Shock and Awe.

Today, airmen from AFSOC provide aerial surveillance using Predator unmanned aerial vehicles (UAVs). Very often, they are the first of the special operations community on the ground, as they prepare the area for follow-on forces. Typically, it will be a combat controller who is calling in close air support for fights against the Taliban in the mountainous terrain of Afghanistan, or a special operations weatherman who is forecasting the conditions for a drop zone in the Iraqi desert. From the special tactics operators on the ground, to the AFSOC pilots and aircrews in the air; these men and women of the U.S. Air Force Special Operations Command (AFSOC) stand poised, ready to answer freedom's call on a moment's notice. They are the quiet professionals deployed around the globe, and these are their stories.

2

The Fog of War

MSgt Alan Brady,
Special Operations Weather Team*

Weather is often as unpredictable and elusive as the enemy. Throughout history, weather has been the key factor for the success or failure of many military missions. During Operation Overlord, or the D-Day invasion of Europe, thousands of soldiers, ships, and airplanes waited seemingly forever for the decision to go, as headquarters monitored the weather forecasts. During the Battle of the Bulge, paratroopers of the 101st Airborne Division in Belgium's Ardennes Forest were surrounded by German soldiers, as the low cloud ceiling and fog prohibited any air support.

During Operation Eagle Claw, the aircrews flying into Desert One encountered an intense, mile-high sandstorm called a Haboob. For the MC-130 and EC-130 aircraft, the storm was a minor obsta-

*Name changed for security reasons.

cle. But the RH-53 helicopters that followed were overwhelmed, as pilots lost sight of each other and thereby dissolved the cohesiveness of their flight pattern. This weather anomaly resulted in the collective loss of three aircraft, caused the mission to be aborted, cost eight lives, and diminished the credibility of U.S. special operations capabilities.

In support of Operation Enduring Freedom, however, a Special Operations Weather Team (SOWT) was able to play an integral role in the successful completion of the initial incursion into Afghanistan. This mission, launched by the United States in response to the September 11 terrorist attack, took place in October 2001. Soldiers from the 75th Ranger Regiment conducted a nighttime air drop into Afghanistan territory. But prior to that deployment of Rangers, a Special Operations Weather Team was already on the ground, assessing the situation. As the MC-130 Combat Talons, laden with Rangers, headed for the Helmand Desert, the combat weatherman reported on local conditions at the drop zone: there was fog. Only an hour away from their destination, headquarters was considering the call to abort the drop. The special operations weatherman on the ground, however, radioed back the message, "Wait one. This will clear up in about fifteen minutes." With this information, the mission commander instructed the Combat Talons to continue heading to the drop zone. As the SOWT had forecasted, the fog lifted. The ramps were lowered on the MC-130 aircraft, and beginning at 1845 Zulu, the Rangers exited the Talons, dropping them onto Objective Rhino—a Taliban compound located in Khandahar.

The Special Operations Weather Team (SOWT) is defined by the Department of Defense as a task-organized team of Air Force personnel organized, trained, and equipped to collect critical weather observations from data-sparse areas. These teams are trained to operate independently, in permissive or semi-permissive environments, or to augment other special operations elements in nonpermissive environments, in direct support of special operations.

Master Sergeant Alan Brady served as a member of the 10th Combat Weather Squadron (CWS), which is under the command of the 720th Special Tactics Group (STG). He was one of the first combat weathermen on the ground in Afghanistan; he has served six rotations in support of Operation Enduring Freedom and two rotations in Iraq in support of Operation Iraqi Freedom.

As the air commandos of the twenty-first century prosecute America's global war on terrorism, what does SOWT bring to the table? MSgt Brady answered that question as follows:

"'Combat Weather' is a big term; most of the guys that are in SOF are Special Operation Weather Teams. Our mission is to enable air power on the battlefield. The way we do that is by providing ground truth and environmental information from anywhere, be it permissive, semi-permissive, hostile, or austere locations. We provide that information within the commander's decision cycle so [that] he can make a decision as to whether to execute the mission based on the weather, or to push it or take advantage of weather that is poor for the enemy but good for us. Those are the types of things we bring to the fight.

"Straightforward ground-truth information. A lot of time we deal with computer models and all those things you see on the news, where they show everything. You see it on the news every day—you see the weather forecasts . . . someone says it is going to rain and it doesn't. We're those guys who go out to make sure that we *know*—no kidding—what it is going to do, either at or near the objective area of the target, for that evening, day, or week. We go out and collect that information in time for [the commander] to make his decision based on actionable weather intelligence."

The special operations weathermen, though capable of operating independently, normally are inserted with a team of special operations forces (SOF). This team could consist of an Army Special Forces Operational Detachment Alpha (ODA), a Navy SEAL platoon, or other teams, depending on whoever is going to be in the area and will need this data. Sometimes the mission of the SOWT has the priority and the other SOF assets serve as security for the team. However, the majority of times the special operations weathermen are attached to a reconnaissance element going into the location, and they offer an additional piece of information that is proved from that target location. That is, each element of the team has its part in the reconnaissance mission, and SOWT is the weather element. Though their skill set focuses on the meteorological aspects of the mission, the special operations combat weathermen are fully equipped and trained to operate as SOF combatants.

The primary missions of the SOWT are strategic reconnaissance (SR). According to MSgt Brady, "We get in, get out, and hopefully no one ever knows [we] were there. In our mission, if someone knows we are there, we're doing something wrong and that becomes a big deal, real quick." MSgt Brady explained, "If we are standing there prior to a mission, and we are getting on the aircraft at the same time as everyone else, [and] if you were to look at us, you wouldn't be able to tell the difference between us—Air Force, Navy, whatever . . . we are all pretty much kitted-out the same way. On our first insertion into Afghanistan, we wore standard BDUs [battle dress uniform] and looked like one, big team. Later on, I grew a beard . . . I think everyone did—it comes with the territory, it's part of the culture. When you look at the multiple cultural realities of the region, because part of the SOF mission is to win the hearts and minds of the people, part of the way we did that . . . was to grow a beard, which is a sign of manhood in these countries, a sign of wisdom. If I go in there clean shaven, they are going to look at me like I am a young kid. If I go in there with a full-grown beard, they are going to look at me different—not necessarily like a tribal elder, but definitely like somebody who knows what he is talking about."

The Special Operations Weather Teams are trained in the same insertion and extraction methods as are other SOF units. MSgt Brady is a prime example of having the myriad skills required: he is qualified as a static-line jumpmaster, free-fall jumpmaster, scout swimmer, fast-rope master, rappel master, "helo" cast master, and numerous other skill sets that he and other SOF need for SOWT operations. MSgt Brady added, "Whatever SOF insertion and extraction system you can imagine, [we] were . . . involved [in]. Our insertion/extraction methods are pretty much the same as everyone else's."

Referring to the initial phases of Operation Enduring Freedom, MSgt Brady related: "I was part of the reconnaissance team that was put in to sit right on a major route where we were going to have a lot of aircraft flying through the area. I was put in there about three days ahead of this force that was going to come through with a lot of helicopters—an aerial refueling type of scenario. My job was to pass along the ground truth—the no-kidding, 'What is really happening here?'—[information]. In those opening stages of [the operation], it was known that Afghanistan did not have a good history of providing weather information, let alone while we were at war with them, so anything they were providing would be shut off. In this case, when you compared the ground truth to what the computer models were saying, the [ground truth] was approximately fifteen to twenty degrees Celsius off the temperatures the models were forecasting. This [difference would have had] a huge impact on fuel expansion, how much the helicopters and airplanes could lift while flying through that area, bases on density, altitude, and things like that. I got on the ground about three days before this mission was to kick off, and the information I provided allowed the commander to change his plan.

"By changing his plan, [the commander] was able to add aircraft, add refueling points, so that this mission could be carried off successfully. That [change] was just based on the temperature. The . . . computer model said it was going to be a lot uglier—that is, visibility and cloud ceiling—than it ended up being. . . . We did not think [the computer forecasts were] going to be that far off . . . however, because I was on the ground, I was able to provide other information that we had not even considered. That ground truth allowed this mission to be carried out, and it was very successful."

In short, if the commander had not received this up-to-the-minute, more precise weather data, the mission might have failed, because the aircraft would not have been able to make to their planned insertion positions. The pilots would have had to discretionary-land somewhere else, as the temperature and fuel consumptions would have been higher than they had anticipated. Getting refueling assets to them to make that mission happen might have required too much extra time; they might have had to land and idle, waiting for the refueling aircraft to show up before they could take off again and hit the target. Also, this was a rather long-distance mission, and if the helicopters were forced to land and idle, they would have been subject to enemy attack.

★   ★   ★   ★

The varied skills of the special operations weathermen rapidly become obvious. MSgt Brady recounts the insertion of his first mission: "We inserted, via fast rope, with an SOF team. Our primary way of going in was to air-land, with fast rope as our secondary. But when we hit the objective area, again ground truth presented itself as a team player: the area was a sand-dune desert, with everything that went with it— swirling dust and brown-outs, which limited the visibility. [Conditions] made it extremely difficult to air-land . . . so the team went into fast-rope mode. The helicopter went into a hover, [they] threw the ropes, and out we went . . . about sixty feet to the ground. Then, we did a seven-kilometer movement that, I tell you, about two kilometers of which was straight up."

"Fast rope" is military shorthand for what is officially called "fast rope insertion and extraction system," also know as FRIES. This is a technique to get an entire team on the ground within seconds, and it begins with small, woven wool ropes that are, in turn, braided into a larger rope. This larger rope is then rolled into a deployment bag, and the end is secured to the helicopter. Depending on the model of chopper, it can be located just outside the front hatch on the hoist mechanism or attached to a bracket off the back ramp. Once the helicopter is over the insertion point, the rope is deployed. Even as the rope is hitting the ground, the team members are jumping onto it and sliding down as easily as a firefighter goes down a pole. Once the team is safely on the ground, the gunner or flight engineer on the helicopter pulls the safety pin, and the rope falls to the ground. (In the event of a covert insertion, the rope can be retrieved and brought back into the aircraft.)

This rope system is extremely useful in the rapid deployment of SOF personnel, though it does introduce a higher level of risk. But MSgt Brady suggests that it has further benefits: "There are often other reasons to fast-rope—for example, if you have to land on a ship or building roof, where the helicopter cannot land. When you look at the Mog [Mogadishu, Somalia] operation, the streets were narrow and the only way to get to ground was to rope in. Fast-roping is faster than rappelling—you use a single rope, you reach out and grab it; there are no extra carabineers to connect . . . just get on and go. Once you are on the ground, you are down and free from the rope."

As with all SOF teams, the special operations weathermen carry mission-specific equipment. When asked what types of special gear the SOWT use, MSgt Brady responded: "I carry a lot of weight, but I would not say it is the weather equipment that weighs so much. It is actually the comm[unications] equipment. I carry a lot of the same communications systems as everyone else—that is, the AN/PRC-117F, with a computer system that I can connect to do text messaging.

"I find when I'm with the Special Forces, SEALS, or whoever, I carry a big radio—that is, a 117F, with a computer satellite antenna, and I carry it everywhere with me. When I am with an SF ODA, they may have one or two of those 117Fs on the entire team, but they are not *all* carrying one. On the other end of the scale, I am *always* carrying that heavy equipment. It is not . . . that we are better; it is part of our regular life, carrying the radio gear and everything else, whereas [this] is not [the case] for every one of the other SOF individuals.

"I carry communications batteries, water, food . . . just like everyone else. But my weather equipment, [compared to] when I went in during this initial stage in Afghanistan, has obviously progressed significantly. I now carry a Kestrel 4000 weather sensor, which is about the size of a computer mouse. The Kestrel sensor can provide barometric pressure, altitude, density altitude, temperature, humidity, wind speed, wind chill, dew point, wet bulb, and heat index. When I first went in, the equipment was considerably larger and had a few more pieces to it than just this one, nice small sensor. The old saying [is that] every ounce counts, but when you put the entire kit together and measure it, it would probably total only four or five pounds, and that includes the spare batteries. The one thing that is a little heavier is the hand-held laser ceilometer, which measures ceiling height and visibility distances—that thing by itself weighs three to four pounds. That is the only [equipment] that would be considered heavy—from a 'weather guy' perspective."

☆　☆　☆　☆

Regarding his mission in Iraq, MSgt Brady related: "At the time we were doing the mission planning, one of the reasons this was a weather-centric mission—meaning why we [SOWT] were there—was [that it would be] weather specific. They were seriously contemplating . . . alternative options . . . to execute this mission . . . because [the] models were forecasting this to be a very ugly time to be trying to fly helicopters and airplanes through this particular region. That is why they decided they were going to put us on the ground. They understood that weather models are not 100 percent accurate, and without the data needed to make them accurate, they continue to be inaccurate.

"In this case, it was a weather-centric mission for us to confirm or deny the model information and give a 'No kidding, good time, good thumbs up' from someone on the ground who was in the region—to say conditions are favorable, 'go ahead and launch this mission.' At the time, we were looking at some pretty ugly sandstorm-type concerns and a full frontal-passage fault that would bring rain, which would have brought along with it fog and some other issues, such as tracking on the ground. There were some definite weather considerations, and that is why this was a weather-centric mission."

Mountainous terrain, and the environment that goes with, it can wreck havoc on military operations, especially when they involve a small SOF team. For this reason, the Special Operations Weather Teams (SOWTs) provide a vital tool to the strategic planners and SOF commanders. From the mountains of Afghanistan to the deserts of Iraq, the men of the SOWT step up to meet the challenges. MSgt Brady was among the first SOF teams to cross into Iraq prior to Operation Iraqi Freedom. His team prepared the way for what would become known as the "Shock and Awe" invasion of that country. The mission for his team was to scout their area of operations.

Indeed, this is where you primarily find the special ops weather guys, typically doing reconnaissance, gathering information so the bosses in the rear can decide what the best course of action is. How does this fit the overall battle plan? The official term for this job is "Intelligence Preparation of the Battlefield," or IPB. This intelligence-gathering is a systematic, continuous process of analyzing the threat and the environment in a specific geographic area. The process is designed to support staff estimates and military decision making, and it helps the commanders selectively apply and maximize their combat power at critical points in time and space on the battlefield. The commanders do this by determining the threat's likely course of action (COA); course of action is a possible plan open to an individual or commander that can accomplish or is related to accomplishing the mission.

A COA is initially stated in broad terms, with the details determined during staff wargaming. To develop COAs, the staff must focus on the key information and intelligence necessary to make such decisions. Course of action includes five elements: *what* (the type of operation), *when* (the time the action will begin), *where* (boundaries, axis, etc.), *how* (the use of assets), and *why* (the purpose or desired end state), all of which involve describing the environment your unit is operating in and the effects of that environment on the unit. Thus, IPB is a continuous process of *defining* the battlefield environment, *describing* the battlefield's effects, *evaluating* the threats, and *determining* the course of action. The IPB is conducted prior to and during the command's initial planning for an operation, but it continues during the operation as well. Each function in the process is performed continuously to ensure that the results of the IPB remain complete and valid. In short, the team provides support to the commander and direction to the intelligence system throughout the mission and into the preparation for the next mission.

MSgt Brady recounts his special reconnaissance (SR) mission in support of Operation Iraqi Freedom. He was armed with an M4 carbine. He started off with a Leupold 7x10 scope, but eventually moved to a Trijicon ACOG 4x32. While he did not carry an M203 on his weapon, other members of the team were armed with the 40 mm grenade launcher. His secondary weapon was an M9 carried in a holster and ready to go, while in his pack he stashed an HK P7 pistol. "We were some of the first groups across the border into Iraq. We were vehicle-mounted, traveling around 'reccing out' locations for potential re-supply air drops, a helicopter landing zone, and even an airplane landing zone, if the need came down to that. We were working with some pretty interesting folks on that one, which I cannot get into. We traveled all over the place, setting the [mission's] condition or success by finding these places and getting them figured out, so [that] as [the] follow-on forces came in, they [would have] a way to receive re-supplies, and so on. We found our way pretty far north after a time."

Of the weather techniques employed during a reconnaissance (RECCE, pronounced REK-ee) one is to use weather balloons to measure the mean effect of wind, or MEOW. MSgt. Brady explained the process: "In reference to re-supply air drops, [we have] to assure the accuracy of the drop so it [will] land where we need it, and not somewhere in the hills, where we have to go and track it down. We track a balloon, knowing the known ascension rate of helium [and] the height that the airplane is going to release the equipment at, and then we take the reverse heading on that [in order to] tell the airplane how far they have to offset to deliver the load to the appropriate point of impact—normally it is at night, with IR [infrared radar] and NVGs [night-vision goggles].

"This could be done during the day, but rarely—unless the hostiles know we are there and we are engaged. It has been known to happen, but usually it is done covertly, at night. . . . One of the other things we still [sometimes] carry [is the] MEOW kit, which can include a pretty hefty helium bottle—imagine a pony bottle for scuba diving, but a little bigger. When I was mounted in Iraq, I had three or four of those with me, carried in a rucksack. On multiple occasions, I did MEOW to support a re-supply. Once we were out for several weeks. There were a couple occasions [when] we had the opportunity to air-land the aircraft and get supplies right off the ramp, but most of the time it was just—airplane flies through, drops the supplies—and we were re-supplied."

On the subject of theaters and compromised missions, MSgt Brady explained: "It depends on the mission. One of my rotations into Operation Iraqi Freedom was a staff job, and I thought that was more grueling. Neither AOs [areas of operations] are real picnics: Afghanistan has the cold, which you don't get in Iraq. There is a great deal of traveling in the mountains and hills; it's higher up, so you need a lot of training and work-up to operate in those higher elevations.

Miserable conditions at times—one minute it's raining, the next it starts to hail, then sleet, then sunshine; you are sweating and then you are freezing again. It is a difficult place to do weather forecasting.

"[On the other hand,] Iraq is a sandbox—period. Out west, it is a little green—actually a nice place, except that that is where all the bad guys are hiding. Iraq is basically flat—some hills and valleys, but nothing like Afghanistan. Afghanistan is so big. You could be going around one rock, and the enemy could be going around the other side and you would never see him. In some of those mountainous regions you could count out probably fifty different trails on the side of the mountain within the same one square kilometer area . . . from goat paths, to normal human traffic, to vehicular traffic. It could be motorcycles or those Toyota Hi-Lux pickup trucks, or whatever. Yes, you could definitely hide. You may be hiding and the enemy is coming up at you twenty-five meters away, and they never see you."

Was MSgt Brady ever compromised? He explained that there are various levels of compromise, firefight close. He said that the enemy was engaged with other units and did not know he was there. And because of the small size of his element, he did not want to get in the middle of the mix. But he added that there were nomads all over the place. "They will surprise the hell out of you . . . where they come from. Like I said, you've got fifty different goat paths, and you have been watching the area for days on end—satellite imagery and everything going on—and then, ten minutes after you get on the ground, here comes a guy with his goats. He has not been there for five to seven days, and there you are on the ground, and this guy just shows up. Everyone in the team tries to make himself look like a rock, or dig himself into a hole, because he doesn't want to be compromised. If we get compromised, our options are: get out, or move to a new location. If we move to a new location, that usually changes the mission parameters . . . and then you take the chance of running into another goatherder, or even just a family out for a stroll."

Brady provided another example: "Intel says there are now dogs in the area. You land, and you find a bunch of scraggy feral dogs barking at you. You don't want to shoot them, and you don't want to feed them, 'cause then they'll hang with you and give away your position. You know [that] no one owns them, and you try to separate yourself from them the best you can. 'Mr. Murphy' has a prominent place in SOF missions."

*   *   *   *

MSgt Brady emphasized that, of all of the Special Tactics Squadron operators, the Special Operations Weather Teams (SOWT) seem to be the most under-advertised folks. Combatant commanders are always trying to get more of them on site when missions get underway. And MSgt Brady's story is testimony to their importance, as well as the daunting challenges of their work.

| C H A P T E R |
3

Boots on the Ground

MSgt Calvin Markham,
23rd Special Tactics Squadron

Master Sergeant Calvin Markham would officially be the first AFSOC combat controller with boots on the ground in Afghanistan, in support of Operation Enduring Freedom. He joked: "I think my bosses were trying to get rid of me." Markham was attached to a Special Forces (SF) Operational Detachment Alpha (ODA) from the 5th Special Forces Group (Airborne). The veteran combat controller had been with the ODA-555, call sign "Triple Nickel," for less than a week when their op order came down. MSgt Markham and the SF A-team loaded on two MH-47E Chinook helicopters of the 2nd Battalion of the 160th Special Operations Aviation Regiment (SOAR Airborne), better known as the "Night Stalkers."

The MH-47E is a heavy assault helicopter, specifically designed and built for the type of missions carried out by the 160th SOAR. It has a completely integrated avionics subsystem, which combines redundant avionics architecture. Gone are the old steam-gauge indicators, replaced by the latest digital avionics; the cockpit was now referred to as the "glass cockpit." The new avionics includes dual-mission processors, remote terminal units, multifunction displays, and display generators, all of which improve combat survivability and mission reliability. To facilitate in-flight refueling, the aircraft is fitted with an aerial refueling probe. Two L714 turbine engines power the helicopter, with full authority digital electronic controls providing more power during hot or high-altitude conditions. Two integral fuel tanks replace the internal auxiliary fuel tanks commonly carried on the MH-47D, providing 2,068 gallons of fuel with no reduction in cargo capacity. The modification of design to incorporate these integral fuel tanks is evident in the wider stance of the aircraft over the D models.

On the evening of October 19, 2001, the pair of MH-47E helicopters lifted off into the night sky, for MSgt Markham's insertion into Afghanistan. The treacherous flight would push the limits of the aircraft, as the pilots flew over the 16,000-foot-high mountains. To lighten the helicopter, the aircrew had stripped away as much of the equipment as possible. Traveling from their staging base, the crew made their infiltration from Karshi Khanabad (K2), Uzbekistan, into the Hindu Kush Mountains. They were to rendezvous with the Northern Alliance to coordinate battle efforts, taking the war to the Taliban and al-Qaeda fighters.

The air war of Operation Enduring Freedom had begun on October 7, 2001, as President George W. Bush announced: "The United States military has begun strikes against al-Qaeda terrorist training camps and military installations of the Taliban regime in Afghanistan. These carefully targeted actions are designed to disrupt the use of Afghanistan as a terrorist base of operations, and to attack the military capability of the Taliban regime." With their orders in hand, American bombers and carrier-based aircraft, as well as Tomahawk cruise missiles from U.S. and British vessels, pounded enemy locations within Afghanistan. However, the targeting data relied heavily on satellite imagery and other intelligence sources, and the initial targets were large fixed facilities such as airfields. The commanders decided that it was time for real-time ground truth—eyes on the targets as well as bomb damage assessment—and that meant boots on the ground.

Filling a pair of those boots would be MSgt Markham. His task was to provide the ODA with close air support (CAS) for the mission. While the Special Forces soldiers are trained in the science of calling in CAS, it is the AFSOC combat controller who raises the bar—elevating the tactics, techniques, and procedures to an art form. These skills can be likened to the difference between calling in one aircraft and orchestrating the operation of an air battlespace with multiple aircraft. As retired AFSOC Senior Master Sergeant Philip Rhodes stated, "A Special Tactics Team on the ground and a gunship overhead are a most lethal combination." Within twenty-fours of being on the ground, MSgt Markham would have the opportunity to apply those skills.

MSgt Markham was the lone combat controller with the Special Forces team. When asked about this arrangement, he explained: "During the first two weeks of the war, starting on October 17, 2001, I was the only Air Force guy with twelve Army guys. We were kind of a test team, to see how this was all going to work out. Once the commanders saw our success in putting a serious 'slaying' on the enemy, they started putting in more teams. The next couple of teams that went in did not have a combat controller with them. Everyone in the military has a specialty, and ours is air-to-ground skills—airmanship. The Army teams that had subsequently infiltrated did not have success; in fact, they were having a hard time with the close air-support piece. So they then installed another combat controller. They flew him in by himself, just so he could do the CAS effectively for the team."

Sitting in the back of the helicopter, it would be difficult to pick out the combat controller from the other soldiers of the ODA. Markham looked like any of the other SF team members. He was armed with an M4 carbine, along with about eighty pounds of gear, including a laser target designator, GPS, night-vision equipment, food, and of course, his radios. Being one of the first SOF teams to go in and exercise the "unconventional warfare" aspect of their mission, they had gone native—that is to say, they had some latitude with uniform and modified grooming standards.

As the helicopters settled down in the landing zone, MSgt Markham and the others dashed off the rear ramp. Hitting the ground, they immediately established a 360-degree perimeter as the MH-47E helicopters exited the insertion point. The SOF team was positioned in a ravine, with mountains that rose above them upward to some 10,000 feet. As the sounds of the Chinooks faded, the America special operations team watched hordes of men began approaching their position with flashlights. Markham commented, "It was like ants pouring out of the woodwork."

The question on everyone's mind was, "Were these guys friend or foe?" As it turned out, they were members of the Northern Alliance, come to greet the Americans and welcome them to their country and their fight. The Northern Alliance was a multiethnic group comprising members of three non-Pashtun tribes: Tajiks, Uzbeks, and Hazaras. The alliance was formed in opposition to the Taliban, which they had been battling since 1996.

Markham explained what happened in the next few hours: "We got inserted by helos and were greeted by the Northern Alliance, where we walked on foot for a few kilometers to a safe house. Once there, we started our planning with them. The alliance commanders knew why we were there. We would not have been there if it hadn't been because of September 11. I'm sure other government agencies had been promising them the world in their fight against the Taliban, but they had not been able to deliver. Now, here we were, this ragtag group of Americans offering help to the Northern Alliance, which was facing an enemy two to three times its size. I am sure they were thinking, 'Great, what can twelve men do against such an enemy?' The next day, we pushed south from the Panjshir Valley down into the Bagram area. We got out to Bagram the next day, and started calling the first ground-controlled air strikes of the war. During our time in country we moved around on everything from trucks, to horseback, to foot. It just depends on where we were and what type of terrain we had.

"That first day, in calling in our CAS [close air support] on the enemy, we eliminated more Taliban than the Northern Alliance had killed in ten years—so, we were pretty lucky. We built instant credibility with them, and from that point on they did everything above and beyond what a soldier does. They protected us, they fed us, they treated us better than one of their own. In fact, during one of the heated battles, when we were engaged in trying to take Kabul, we were taking serious ground fire and artillery and mortar fire. The Afghan general and his colonels jumped on top of me and my men to protect us from the incoming fire: they were afraid [that] if something happened to us, the airplanes and all the support would go away; but if something happed to them, it was not as big a deal, because their next-in-command would step in and take over. I don't know how many generals from a host-nation's army [would try to] keep us alive at their [own] peril—that was incredible."

With the SOF team on the ground, the war was about to take a giant turn in favor of the Northern Alliance forces. The alliance fighters would pick a target and MSgt Markham would mark it with the laser acquisition marker (SOFLAM). A short time later, a laser-guided bomb would fall from the sky and destroy the target. On one occasion, the Northern Alliance fighters pointed to a tank that they had been trying to take out for three years. The combat controller identified the target, vectored in a fast mover, painted the target, and destroyed the tank—all within twenty minutes. The alliance forces were amazed at the accuracy of the laser's aiming device—so much so, that they seemed to avoid the device as if it were some type of death ray.

This vital piece of equipment was the special operations forces laser acquisition marker, or SOFLAM—officially called the Ground Laser Target Designator (GLTD II) by the manufacturer, Northrop Grumman. The SOFLAM is a compact, lightweight, portable laser target designator and rangefinder. It is capable of exporting range data via an RS-422 link and importing azimuth and elevation. Designed to enable special operations forces to direct laser-guided smart weapons, such as Paveway bombs, Hellfire missiles, and Copperhead munitions, SOFLAM (or AN/PEQ-1A) can be part of a sophisticated, digitized fire-control system with thermal or image-intensified sights. (STANAG refers to the Standards and Agreements set forth by NATO, for the process, procedures, terms, and conditions under which Mutual Government Quality Assurance of Defense products are to be performed by the appropriate national authority of one

NATO member nation, at the request of another NATO member nation or NATO organization. PRF is the number of pulses per second transmitted by a laser.)

In the country for almost a month, MSgt Markham, ODA-555, and the Northern Alliance made their main push into Kabul. Markham explained the importance of the city of Kabul: "This was the center for the Taliban—the command and control. If it fell, then that would be it. We had about 5,000 Northern Alliance troops against 10,000 Taliban fighters, but through close air support, we completely annihilated them. The night of November 12, we pushed all the remaining Taliban forces south."

Markham recalled the battle: "We were on the Shomali Plain, a sixty-kilometer front line and thirty-kilometer-deep battlefield. The Taliban were dug in to their positions with tanks, artillery, mortars, and their headquarters buildings." From these positions, the Taliban could attack the small American team and the alliance forces with everything they had. Markham recalls, "We took enormous amounts of fire: small arms fire, tank rounds—you name it. They also had ZSU-23s, an anti-aircraft weapon, and turned those on us. It looked like flaming footballs, from our position."

When the call came in for close air support around Kabul, one of the Air Force F-16 pilots was surprised to hear an American's voice on the radio. The Falcon pilot could not believe there were American teams already on the ground, with equipment prepared to call in CAS. The "fast mover" let the bombs drop on the target. The small team of Americans was outmanned and outgunned, but MSgt Markham continued to call in CAS, orchestrating the massive air power against the intense Taliban attacks. At one point, he brought in a B-52 bomber, which dropped its ordnance dangerously close but with devastating results. "The targets were being destroyed," Markham said, "You could feel the concussion of the explosions from their position." Each time a target was destroyed, the Northern Alliance cheered and General Sharriff hugged MSgt Markham. The war planners in Washington, D.C., estimated that it would take the ODA six months to accomplish its mission; Markham and his team successfully completed the mission is just over three weeks.

Reopening the Embassy in Kabul

The first U.S. personnel to enter the American Embassy in Kabul were combat controllers of the 720th Special Tactics Squadron. MSgt Markham related the event as follows: "We were sitting in Kabul for about two weeks, getting some of the smaller Taliban cells—going against them, getting them out of Kabul. We were waiting for permission to go to the Embassy. Basically, headquarters said no, not yet—the State Department will take care of that. Finally, on November 30, 2001, we were authorized to go and open up the Embassy.

"There was myself, another combat controller from the 21st Special Tactics Squadron, TSgt Markus, and Lt "Billy," who was with another SF team. Our teams had all come together and we met at the Embassy. We cleared it, cleared the grounds, and talked to the Northern Alliance and the Afghan family that had been securing the Embassy since the closure in 1989. They provided us with the equipment and everything else to get into the Embassy on that day. The Taliban had briefly broken into the Embassy and had occupied the building for three days. But the Embassy had been locked up pretty well, so they did not have a whole lot of rooms to get in to—some of the main common rooms and the main barracks area.

"We had an Air Force K-9 specialist there with us; they went in and cleared the building of any booby traps or explosives. Then, we went ahead and did a search of the Embassy and secured it that day. We met no Taliban resistance; prior to going in . . . we had pushed them out of Kabul, so the day we got there we did not meet any resistance."

MSgt Markham continued his story: "On December 13, 2001, the Marines and the State Department officially opened the Embassy. We . . . discovered [that] the Taliban had tried to burn or destroy some things in the building. I found an American flag that was in what I believe was the ambassador's bathroom. The inside of the bathroom was all done in marble. The Taliban had taken the flag and stacked it on some grass . . . to get it to burn; they must have closed the door, and since there was no means of ventilation, the fire went out. So we had this flag that had char marks on it and some discoloration. We took

MSgt Calvin Markham (center), along with another combat controller from the 21st Special Tactics Squadron (right) and a U.S. Army Special Forces soldier (left), in front of the U.S. Embassy in Kabul. The actions of these SOF teams put the Taliban on notice: the Americans were back in town. *Courtesy of the U.S. Air Force.*

the flag—me, TSgt Markus, and Lt "Billy"—and had a small ceremony. We folded it up and gave it to Markus because he was going to be on a flight back to Uzbekistan. We wanted to present the flag to our commander for giving us the opportunity to secure the Embassy."

With pride in his voice, MSgt. explained what happened next: "Markus wrote a letter and attached it to the flag, and sent it home. As it turned out, he was not able to get back to Uzbekistan, so the flag and note were placed in a box and handed to a load master. TSgt. Markus told him, 'Hey, man, protect this with your life. This thing goes back to our boss.' Later that night, the package got to Uzbekistan. So, that was quite an honorable moment for all of us. Today that flag is on display at the headquarters of the 23rd Special Tactics Squadron."

Opening Bagram Air Base

Combat controllers really earned their pay at the beginning of Operation Enduring Freedom. MSgt. Markham related how the SOF teams transformed a wasteland into an operational airfield: "Our team opened up Bagram Air Base. That was the first airfield under permissive environment to be opened. . . . [it] would serve as the gateway to Afghanistan. I left Bagram about October 14, 2001, and that was when Lt "Billy" took the airfield over from me. We pushed into Kabul, and two months later [Bagram] was an air base [again]. Bagram was a pretty popular Russian base, so it was a well-established airfield. It was one of the things we looked at while we were in the Bagram area, and I sent reports back saying that this airfield was good to go—that we could stage a lot of logistics out of there, once we took it.

"The night of November 15, we brought in the first U.S. and British C-130s; by November 17 to 20, we started bringing in C-17s. We pushed our efforts forward, and [these were] not only combat operations. You hear that SOF does a lot of combat ops, but even more incredible [was that] after those ops were the humanitarian missions— bringing in food, medical supplies, and clothing to people who needed them. As soon as we got Bagram and Kabul opened, the greatest thing we could do was to help the children and the people displaced because of the Taliban. We were able to accomplish a number of CA [civilian affairs] and madcap missions out of the base."

Concerning the close working relationship between SOF units, MSgt Markham stated: "The most important thing that I hope anyone takes out of this is that SOF came together—Air Force, Army, and Navy— and we executed a mission on the enemy. What people thought would take us from six months to a year, or probably never even accomplish, my particular team . . . made it happen. As SOF warriors, that is what we do. We do the nonsexy jobs—the ones no one wants to do—and we got out there and we make it happen.

"It takes everybody working together; it is not one person. I could never say 'me . . . by myself, I did this.' It took every person working together on the team to make this happen. Even today, we have excellent guys—just studs—out there doing the jobs . . . doing the stuff no one else wants to do. They are working together with their Army or Navy counterparts, making that happen. It is just incredible, with the things that our guys are expected to perform, and the expected level of performance, that they make this happen."

The Silver Star

The following is the citation to accompany the award of the Silver Star to William Markham.

The President of the United States takes pleasure in presenting the Silver Star Medal to William "Calvin" Markham, Master Sergeant, U.S. Air Force, for conspicuous gallantry and intrepidity in action while serving with the 23d Special Tactics Squadron in support of Operation Enduring Freedom, near Kabul, Afghanistan, from 14 October to 30 November 2001. On 21 October 2001, within forty-eight hours of the detachment's arrival in Afghanistan, Sergeant Markham planned, organized, and led a close air support reconnaissance mission to within two kilometers of the Taliban front line in order to identify potential observation posts from which his team could execute missions. Almost immediately upon arrival, Sergeant Markham's team came under direct enemy fire from tanks, mortars and artillery. Despite heavy incoming fire, in which numerous rounds impacted within fifty to seventy-five meters of his position, Sergeant Markham instinctively and success-fully directed multiple close air support sorties against key Taliban leadership positions, command and control elements, fortified positions, and numerous anti-aircraft artillery sites. Throughout this highly successful mission, Sergeant Markham skillfully directed multiple air strikes involving over one hundred seventy-five sorties of both strategic and attack aircraft resulting in the elimination of approximately four hundred and fifty enemy vehicles and over three thousand five hundred enemy troops. The resulting close air support operations were decisive in supporting the Northern Alliance ground offensive, which resulted in the successful liberation of the capital city of Kabul and led to the eventual surrender of hundreds of al Qaeda and Taliban ground forces. Master Sergeant Markham's valor and calmness under enemy fire were a constant source of inspiration to his detachment and General Fahim Khan's Northern Alliance forces. By his gallantry and devotion to duty, Sergeant Markham has reflected great credit upon himself and the United States Air Force.

4

SatCom and Saddles

MSgt Bart Decker,
Operation Enduring Freedom

Following the terrorist attacks on September 11, 2001, the U.S. military shifted into high gear and the special operations units went into overdrive. MSgt Bart Decker, a combat controller with the 23rd Special Tactics Squadron (STS), based out of Hurlburt Field, Florida, was on the first chalk into Uzbekistan at the beginning of October 2001. MSgt Decker, along with a handful of other AFSOC Special Tactics Squadron team members, would be among the first combat controllers inserted into Afghanistan.

    An abandoned Soviet air base located near Karshi Kandabad, in the south-central part of Uzbekistan, became the U.S. special operations forces' base of operations in the initial phases of Operation Enduring Freedom. The air base, which was known as K2, would be the jumping-off point for the insertion of special operations forces into Afghanistan. The base became the home of the Joint Special Operations Task Force-North, which was designated "TF Dagger." The core element of the task force was the 5th Special Forces Group (Airborne), under the command of Colonel John Mulholland. Along with the 5th SFG, the task force included members of the 160th Special Operations Aviation Regiment (Airborne) and the 720th Special Tactics Group of the Air Force Special Operations Command. Along with these units was an assortment of operators from other government agencies and the Australian Special Air Service Regiment (SASR). In addition to units of the special operations forces, soldiers from the 1st Battalion, 87th Infantry, 10th Mountain Division (Light) were also deployed to provide base security and serve as a quick-reaction force, if needed. The task force would carry out the orders of the commander in chief: "To bring the terrorists to justice, or bring justice to them."

The war planners determined that the best course of action was to establish contact with three influential leaders within the Northern Alliance: Generals Abdul Rashid Dostum, Mullah Daoud, and Fahim Khan. Special Forces ODAs would be split among the three warlords, with the purpose of establishing a base of operations for follow-on SOF missions in Afghanistan. On the night of October 19, 2001, the members of ODA-595, code name "Tiger 02," loaded aboard two MH-47E helicopters. Their mission was to link up and work with General Dostum in the area of Mazar-e Sharif.

General Abdul Rashid Dostum, born in 1954, was one of the powerful warlords and the current leader of the Uzbek-Afghan Northern Provinces. During the Soviet invasion of Afghanistan, Dostum joined the Afghan military and fought alongside the Soviets against the mujahideen, or Afghan insurgency. He eventually left his Russian comrades, switched sides, and joined the mujahideen. When America's war on terrorism was initiated, Dostum again switched sides to fight along with the special operations forces against the Taliban.

The Chinooks were piloted by aircrews of the 2nd Battalion, 160th Special Operations Aviation Regiment (Airborne), known as the "Night Stalkers." These pilots pushed the limits of their aircraft as they navigated over the mountainous terrain, flying higher than they had ever previously flown. During the perilous insertion, the helicopters also carried out aerial refueling with an MC-130P Combat Shadow from the 9th Special Operations Squadron.

Flying escort for the Chinooks would be a pair of MH-60L Direction Action Penetrator (DAP) helicopters. The MH-60L DAPs are variants modified to accept a wide assortment of weapon systems. These DAPs are used for armed escort and fire support and to conduct close air support employing precision-guided ordinance in the support of infiltration or exfiltration of small units. Capable of mounting two M-134 7.62 mm mini-guns, two 30 mm chain-guns, two 19-shot 2.75-inch rocket pods, sixteen AGM-114 Hellfire missiles, and air-to-air Stinger missiles in a wide range of combinations, the DAP is a formidable weapon in the SOAR arsenal.

The standard configuration of the DAP is one rocket pod, one 30mm cannon, and two mini-guns, but this configuration is changed based on mission, enemy, troops, terrain, and time. The time needed to reconfigure the aircraft is minimal from either the armed version to the utility version or back again. The MH-60L DAP has the capability to perform both the assault and the armed missions; the 7.62 mini-guns remain with the aircraft regardless of mission. Though the DAP was equipped for flight in adverse weather, the environment in Afghanistan was so bad that the Black Hawk helicopters were forced to return to K2. The MH-47E helicopters continued the insertion using their advanced avionics. At 0200 on October, 20, the ODA-595 made their insertion onto landing zone Albatross.

On November 2, MSgt Bart Decker grabbed his gear and loaded aboard a MH-47E helicopter for his insertion into Afghanistan. "We were semi-native. We wore sterile BDUs [battle dress uniforms], but did have longer hair and beards. I was armed with an M4, a 9 mm pistol, and a radio, which is our biggest weapon. We could communicate if the need arose. We had a Harris 117F and M148 MBITR as well."

For long-range communications, the AN/PRC-117F covers the entire 30 to 512 MHz frequency range while offering embedded COMSEC and Havequick I/II ECCM capabilities. This advanced-software, reprogrammable digital radio supports transmission power with Havequick I/II capability. The 117F is fully compatible with the KY-57 TSEC in voice and data modes for secure transmissions. The radio supports both DS-101 and DS-102 fill interfaces and all common fill devices for Havequick word-of-day (WOD) and encryption key information. This device supports the Department of Defense requirement for a lightweight, secure, network-capable, multiband, multimission, antijam, voice/imagery/data communication capability in a single package.

The Thales Communication AN/PRC-148 Multiband Inter/ Intra Team Radio (MBITR) is a powerful tactical hand-held radio designed for the Special Operations Command (SOCOM). The MBITR exceeds the tough SOCOM requirements and provides a secure voice and digital-data radio with exceptional versatility, ruggedness, and reliability. The immersible unit weighs less than two pounds and includes a keypad, graphics display, and built-in speaker-microphone. Typical of the advanced designs of Thales radios, the MBITR uses digital-signal processing and flash memory to support functions that are traditionally performed by discrete hardware in other manufacturers' equipment. The power output is up to 5 watts.

The combat controller was attached to a Special Forces Operational Detachment Command element (ODC 53), under the command of Lieutenant Colonel Max Bowers. Regarding the ODC, Decker commented, "They had not had that organization since Vietnam." A Special Forces ODC is one of the detachments of operational Special Forces officially called a Battalion Headquarters Detachment. The detachment is commanded by a lieutenant-colonel, with a command sergeant major as leading NCO, and comprises the battalion headquarters, the S-1 Section (personnel), the S-2 Section (intelligence), the S-3 Section (operations), the S-4 Section (logistics), the S-5 Section (civil-military operations), the S-6 Section (communications), and the medical section. The detachment is responsible for the command and control of the activities of the Special Forces battalion, including isolating, launching, controlling, sustaining, recovering, and reconstituting Special Forces ODAs. The capabilities of the detachment, also know as C Detachment or C-team, is to provide command and control, staff planning, and staff supervision of battalion operations and administration. The detachment plans, coordinates, and directs Special Forces operations separately or as part of a larger force; provides command and staff personnel to establish and operate a forward operation base (FOB); and supplies advice, coordination, and staff assistance on the employment of Special Forces elements to a joint Special Operations Command, Joint

Special Operations Task Force, Security Assistance Organizations, or other major headquarters.

Upon his insertion into Afghanistan, MSgt Decker and the members of ODC 53 met up with ODA-595. Over the next eight days, their paths would cross as they all established the forward operating base (FOB 53) in the city of Mazar-e Sharif. One of the largest cities in Afghanistan, Mazar-e Sharif is the capital of Balkh Province. It is linked by roadways to Kabul in the south and Uzbekistan in the north, and was a major trading area for the region.

Mazar-e Sharif had two airfields. During a Pentagon briefing, the commander of CENTCOM, General Tommy Franks, referred to the city as being so close to the Uzbekistan border that it could serve as a land bridge into Afghanistan—a reason it was considered so critical in the fight against al-Qaeda.

MSgt Decker related: "Me and another controller came up the Dara-e Suf Valley—which translates as "River of Caves"—and that was true. You felt like you had stepped back in time. We met up with the Northern Alliance, there in the valley. They had some tents erected, but we ended up living in a cave for the first two nights. Along this area . . . there were small caves scattered throughout the valley. Me and my team stayed in one of these caves; the walls were lined with dried horse crap as insulation; it served its purpose, as it would be about ten degrees at night when we pulled guard duty, but [when we] got back into that cave and it was fifty to fifty-five degrees in there.

"We maneuvered up north. There was a combat controller with another ODA on one flank and another combat controller with a different Special Forces team on the other flank, [and we were in the middle]. Together, [we] three teams made our way up the Dara-e Suf Valley. We got up to Mazar-e Sharif, and liberated the town around November 10."

The Northern Alliance provided horses for the Special Forces team and combat controllers, and horses became the standard mode of travel at this time. Decker described his experience on this old-fashioned means of transportation: "The only way you could get through the mountains was on horseback—there was no other way. There [certainly] was no way you could have put a chopper on the top of the mountain, as it was occupied by the enemy. We would be riding those

Combat controllers were among the first U.S. special operation forces on the ground in support of Operation Enduring Freedom. Within a month of the 9/11 attacks, MSgt Bart Decker, along with several members of the 720th Special Operations Group, was operating from a forward-deployed base in Uzbekistan. MSgt Decker on horseback rides into battle with members of the Northern Alliance. *Courtesy of the U.S. Air Force.*

horses on narrow mountain trails, where to the left side of the ledge was a five hundred- to one thousand-foot drop-off, and to the right of the ledge was a sheer cliff that went up about three hundred feet. The ledge we were riding on was four to six feet wide, and we were doing that at night. We kept pushing and pushing our way up this valley. We had to clear the mountain top before we could occupy it.

"Riding the horses was one of the biggest challenges for us. We went in pretty heavy with equipment; I carried a day pack and our other gear was transported by mule. That was challenging, because the other controller with me had never been on a horse, and I did not have all that much experience with them, either. And these horses—what we [had] were . . . not like those cowboy saddles you see in the westerns. These were wooden [saddles] and it was not a comfortable ride. We did get some regular saddles air-dropped in later on, but by then we were in vehicles—good intentions, but they came in a little too late. Luckily, the weather was outstanding. It was around fifty degrees during the day and then dropped down into the teens at night. But we had the gear to take care of that, so it was not an inhibiting problem—we were prepared for that.

"We used the Mark-One eyeball for a lot of those nights during the insertion, as we had a lot of [natural] illumination—we did not have to rely on night-vision devices. We did have night-vision capabilities, and we would use the goggles from time to time to see what was up ahead or to check for enemy presence. We had our GPS units with us, too, but we were pretty much being guided by the Northern Alliance. As we traveled, we did have air cover on call. I did not work any fighters, thought the two teams on the flanks worked a lot of the fast movers."

MSgt Decker continued: "We traveled in a reverse wedge formation, so the two teams on our flanks were both to our front right and left." The wedge formation is used when contact with the enemy is possible; it provides excellent firepower to the front while still maintaining good firepower to the flanks, offers good flank security, and can be used with all of the movement techniques.

"We were miles apart, but we did see each other from time to time. As we traveled, I did not work any fighters until the night before we moved into Mazar-e Sharif. We all had our procedures for getting air overhead. At this phase of the war, it was not a problem getting air; we were pretty much the only action in town at that time." MSgt Decker and the Special Forces team spent eight days on horseback as they traveled from their insertion point to Dostum's base camp. Decker explained: "We stayed in that valley for the first two days, then we moved for a couple days, then we stayed on another mountaintop for two days. We actually got left up there and had to walk down on foot, which was a seven-hour jaunt. This happened because Dostum, his leaders, and a couple other leaders, went down for a meeting and they never came back up. We had pushed the Taliban out of the valley so quickly that we ended up walking back down the mountain to join Dostum. We had to rent some mules and walk out of there with all our gear. Then we met up with them, and it was back onto the horses again. . . . We walked down to another town to meet back up with Dostum and the Northern

Alliance guys. From that point, we moved the next day to another mountaintop and that was the final push. We met back up with one of the Special Forces teams that had been on my flank on that mountain. The controller with the ODA was already calling in close air support that afternoon."

The fall of Mazar-e Sharif would be the first major victory for the Northern Alliance. Elements of the U.S. special operations forces, British and NATO forces, and combined Northern Alliance forces under General Dostum and General Ustad Atta Mohammed, an ethnic Tajik, captured the Taliban stronghold. "From atop a mountain we had a good vantage point overseeing Mazar-e Sharif," MSgt Decker continued. "We were doing the final push. As night fell, you could see all the headlights of the vehicles of the Taliban and al-Qaeda forces, leaving the city. That is when I brought in two F-15s and two F16s, and took out most of that enemy convoy.

"With the fall of Mazar-e Sharif, we were going to Konduz to negotiate a surrender of Taliban and al-Qaeda fighters. On our way out of town, we [passed] the Qala-i-Jangi Fort. The name means "House of War." [The building] is a nineteenth-century fortress located roughly forty kilometers from Mazar-e Sharif. It had been under the command of Dostum, until the Taliban ran him out in the nineties. The fortress was then serving as a makeshift prison for the Taliban and al-Qaeda fighters who had been captured. This fort was also where six hundred or so Taliban and al-Qaeda fighters held their prison uprising, at which CIA agent Johnny "Mike" Spann was killed. We were not in town when the uprising happened, and that presented a problem. Everyone who was TAC-qualified was up in Konduz, which was a seven-hour drive [away]. They brought in a quick-reaction force because all of us were gone. There were a few Special Forces staff at the FOB, roughly a ten-minute drive [away], but [there was] no one qualified to call in the air strikes. The uprising ended with close air support from an AC-130 gunship.

"Mazar was our nickname for Mazar-e Sharif, our area of operations. All those people who did not get taken out that night ended up going to the city of Konduz. The next day, we moved into the city itself. The streets [of Mazar-e Sharif] were lined with people, clapping and cheering their liberation. We set up at the fort for about two weeks, and then we moved to another building that used to be a girls' school. We started renovating the building, and that eventually is where we set up our FOB [forward operating base]." A forward operating base is used to support tactical operations without establishing full support facilities, and it might be in operation for an extended time. Backup support by a main operating base is required.

"Once the FOB was established, we started buying vehicles. The 'green guys,' which is to say the ones with the money, came down for us to buy vehicles. We did not have any military vehicles the first time I was there—they were all indigenous, a mix of vehicles, mostly Toyota High-Lux models. We had everything, including minivans that we used as our air traffic control vehicle for running the airfield. We put in a little table; had our radios set up, and used [the minivan] as a mobile tower. Then, we had two brand-new Nissan pickup trucks that had been brought to the operations base at K2 by helicopter. All the other vehicles we bought out of the local economy. We also employed some of the locals. We had local mechanics who took care of the vehicles. To fix the school, we hired janitors, plumbers, and the like. Immediately, the United States got the locals involved in rebuilding their city. They were vetted, cleared, and happy to be working with us.

"Meanwhile, our team went over to a place called Konduz and negotiated the surrender of twenty-five hundred to three thousand Taliban and al-Qaeda forces. When we went to Konduz, we had a SOFLAM set up when these guys [the Taliban] were capitulating. Prior to that, the enemy leader would come up and speak to the leader of the Northern Alliance; afterwards he would go back and talk with his people. One of the Taliban guys came up and saw the SOFLAM. General Dostum told him it was a vaporizer, and if we shot a guy with it, he would just melt. Of course, they believed it. That was around Thanksgiving time. After that, we came back and just worked the airfield in Mazar-e Sharif for the remaining month. We ended up leaving there in January 2002. It was basically a four-month tour, and then our squadron [the 23rd] went back in May 2002—to Kandahar that time."

MSgt Decker continued with this story: "Once we had come back from the Konduz mission, which was about four days, it is almost into December. For the next forty-five days, we worked the airfield there at Mazar. The airfield had been bombed at the beginning of the war, so it was very challenging landing C-130s in between bomb craters.

"We had some engineers from the 823rd Red Horse Squadron with us, and they were working with the locals to patch the holes in the airfield. We would get one end patched and use it with the C-130, while they were working on the other end. With all of the air traffic [we had], that would start rutting the runway again, so we had to continually move the runway." "Red Horse" stands for Rapid Engineer Deployable Heavy Operations Repair Squadron Engineers. It is an Air Force equivalent of the Navy Construction Battalion, better known as the Sea Bees.

From the time of his insertion into Afghanistan to his setting up the forward operation base, MSgt Decker did not engage the enemy with his M4. He recalls, "I never shot a round. It was all radio and close air support. The radio is our primary weapon, and it is the most lethal."

MSgt Bart Decker spent approximately four months down range, or as he says, "From Hurlburt Field, wheels up, back to Hurlburt, was roughly four months." He served another tour in support of Operation Enduring Freedom, and then another four months, as the United States pushed into Iraq in support of Operation Iraqi Freedom.

5

Tora Bora, Closing in on bin Laden

SSgt Dale Stockton*

Operation Enduring Freedom was only two months old, but by the middle of December 2001, the Taliban and al-Qaeda fighters knew what it was like to be pursued by the only military superpower in the world. The massive deployment of U.S. and coalition special operations forces (SOF) was unprecedented. The SOF teams were indeed the "tip of the spear" and that spear was poised at the throat of the terrorist. These special operations units, working in conjunction with other government agencies and the Northern Alliance, took the war to the enemy's back yard. With General Abdul Dostum's victory at Mazar-e Sharif, and the fall of Kabul and Kandahar, the terrorist forces retreated toward the Afghan/Pakistani border. There, at Tora Bora, the enemy hid in the complex cave systems that permeate the

---

*Name changed for security reasons.

region. It was believed that the enemy had built substantial fortifications and had filled the anterooms with ammunition, weapons, food, and other war-fighting supplies to sustain a battle.

In addition to the large number of enemy fighters present, U.S. intelligence located two "high value targets" (HVTs) at Tora Bora: Usama bin Laden and Abu Musab al-Zarqawi. Tora Bora would become the focal point for an assortment of special operations forces in the area, both U.S. and coalition, as well as other special mission units. The special mission units (SMUs) are defined by the Department of Defense as a group of operations and support personnel from designated organizations that is task-organized to perform highly classified activities. These are the "tier one" operators whom no one talks about, so we will not elaborate on who may be in these units. Suffice it to say that Colonel "Chargin' Charlie" Beckwith would be proud.

Assigned to one of the ARSOC teams would be Staff Sergeant Dale Stockton, a combat controller with the 720th Special Tactics Group. Regarding the disposition of the HVTs, SSgt Stockton explained, "U.S. intelligence placed Usama bin Laden in the area at this time, and he was held up with a large number of al-Qaeda forces. Our mission was to go in there and capture or kill."

In addition to SSgt Stockton, there were two other combat controllers from the 23rd STS working with ODA-572 and General Hazrat Ali, a commander of the Northern Alliance forces. Another combat control team (CCT) was assigned to a separate unit, and a fifth controller operated with another government agency team.

Using the Bagram Air Base as a base of operations, SSgt Stockton deployed with the team en route for Tora Bora. He described the journey: "We inserted by vehicle, driving in using Toyota pickup trucks. The Japanese vehicle was commonly used by Taliban and al-Qaeda forces indigenous to the region. The roads were real rough, similar to a two-lane dirt roadway—we called it the 'Devil's Highway.' We headed out of Kabul, and spent the first night in Jalalabad, Afghanistan. Leaving there early the next morning, we arrived on site by mid-afternoon. We began planning the next morning, and were going to insert the evening of night two with our mujahideen subcommanders. Based on the different types of assets we had with us, we determined [that] we were close to the enemy.

"Once we became situated on site, this was a straight, unconventional warfare mission. Our team linked up with the mujahideen and headed up the mountain. We split up our team members with the different mujahideen subcommanders, who controlled separate battlespaces. Our mission was mainly to provide command and control, as well as close air support."

The term "battlespace" is a concept that combines what we think of as a battleground (actual terrain) with the air/space dimension and all the effects that combination brings (radio communications, radio frequency spectrum—lasers, GPS signals, etc.—aircraft, unmanned aerial vehicles, satellite imagery, and so on)—everything that directly impacts a tactical event. The Joint Forces Department of Defense definition encompasses all the environmental factors and conditions that must be understood to successfully apply combat power, protect the force, or complete the mission. This includes air, land, sea, space, and enemy and friendly forces; the facilities; the weather and terrain; the electromagnetic spectrum; and the information environment within the operational area and area of interest.

Another term related to "battlespace," often used by the combat control teams, is "de-confliction of aircraft." This is an air-traffic controller's term that combat controllers use as well. In order to not create conditions favorable for a mid-air collision between aircraft (manned or unmanned), air traffic controllers issue instructions to the pilots that preclude those air assets from being at the same point at the same time; they do this via time separation (spacing the units apart by minutes) or spatial separation (lateral separation by several miles, as plotted on maps, or altitude separation by thousands of feet). As SSgt. Stockton explained, "The end result is deliberate air effects on the battlespace, where we need it, when we need it, without our planes crashing together in the air."

SSgt Stockton made initial contact with the enemy on his second day on site: "Around noon, the mujahideen had been pinned down with a three-way crossfire by al-Qaeda mortars and DShKs." The DShK, pronounced "DUSH-ka," is a Soviet heavy anti-aircraft machine gun that fires 12.7 x 108 mm ammunition. This large gas-operated, belt-fed, air-cooled weapon is fed by a top-mounted thirty-round detachable drum magazine. The ammunition feed uses nondisintegrating steel belts, from the left side. The DShK machine gun fires from an open bolt and in automatic mode only. The gas piston and chamber are located below the barrel; the gas piston is attached to the bolt carrier. The rate of fire is six hundred rounds per minute. Stockton continued: "[I] and one of the Army team leaders headed up in a single vehicle to help bail out those guys. I was equipped with a SOFLAM a Mark VII laser rangefinder, a 117 Foxtrot radio, and an M4."

The laser rangefinder, officially called the MK VII Target Locator, provides fire support teams and forward observers with daylight and night-vision capability, so as to observe and accurately locate targets. This information is then transmitted to the fire support command, control, and communications, to computers, and to the intelligence system. The MK VII Target Locator can be hand held or mounted on a lightweight tripod, laser, or target locator, incorporating a Class I eye-safe laser rangefinder and a digital magnetic compass to determine range, azimuth, and vertical angle from the observer to the targets of interest. When targeting data is sent to a GPS PLGR (receiver), the system can compute and display the target location. The precise target location can then be transmitted digitally, using the RS-232 digital interface, to a compact, lightweight handheld device. This system is ideally suited for calling in close air support. The Mark VII can range to tactical targets out to five kilometers, with good visibility; an internal image intensifier is incorporated for night operations. The day optic is a 7.25-power monocular, while the night optic is 4-power. The hand-held device weighs four pounds, with the entire system only six pounds.

Sergeant Stockton continued: "We got on site and established where the enemy was located. At this time, we called in F-18s on the al-Qaeda mortar and DShK positions. This was the first incident when I called in air strikes, during the first and second weeks of December 2001." Sergeant Stockton further explained about the events of that night: "The mujahideen did not fight at night like we do; they fought during the day and then stopped at night; so we were left alone up on the mountain.

"When al-Qaeda started a counterattack that day, we [began to] move down the mountain on foot, [to be] picked up by a quick-reaction force [QRF]. There were just the two of us up there initially to stage the fight. This movement was [back] to the mujahideen positions; they had anti-aircraft guns shooting up at the Taliban and al-Qaeda. And 'AQ' was shooting back at them with 12.7 millimeter DShK and 82 millimeter mortars. We were basically moving back through friendly lines. As night fell, we found we were the only two left in the observation post still fighting. We could see the DShK positions moving around and we felt like we were being flanked. [So] we headed on down the mountain and called for a pickup from the QRF. The QRF was from within our unit—that is an SOF asset, a reserve we had available to us. We . . . headed back down to the little base camps we had set up, and received a debrief from Intel and an update on the battlespace, including new information on enemy positions.

Driving in the Tora Bora region on the Devil's Highway, one can see the vastness of the Afghanistan countryside. U.S. SOF teams would use indigenous vehicles such as this Toyota pickup to blend in with the locals. Combat controllers assigned to Tier One units and Special Forces ODAs used this method of travel to close in on al-Qaeda high-value targets. *Courtesy of the U.S. Air Force.*

We modified our plans and would re-insert the next night. This [next] time, we split up into three teams and headed back up the mountain."

Over the course of the next week, Sergeant Stockton continued working with the mujahideen fighters, calling in air strikes. He related how the Afghan forces were amazed at the capabilities of the American special operations teams: "When we initially linked up with them, their aggressiveness [level] was definitely boosted. You could tell the difference with just a couple hours of close air support. Those guys were just getting back into the fight. This capability really helped them out."

As the battle for Tora Bora raged, Stockton would be the sole combat controller calling in air support. "When we initially got on site, there were two other combat controllers operating with the 5th SFG. They had the battlespace, but were more on the flanks and not really in the battle; they were holding onto the battlespace until we showed up. We tagged off and they handed over the battlespace, and exfiled the area.

"I was lucky enough; well, let's say I was inserted in the best position to call in close air support. The other controller, unfortunately, was just not in the best position to call in the air strikes. . . . I was using the MK VII laser rangefinder hooked up to a PSN-11." The precise name for the PSN-11 unit is PLGR+96 (Precise Lightweight GPS Receiver), hence the nickname "Plugger." The PLGR+96 is an advanced version of the U.S. Department of Defense hand-held GPS units. It addresses the increasingly demanding requirements of the special operation forces. The secure (Y-code) differential GPS allows the user to accept differential correction without zeroing the unit. Other features of the Plugger include wide area GPD enhancement for autonomous positioning accuracy to four meters circular error probability (CEP), jammer direction finding, targeting interface with laser rangefinder, remote display terminal capability, and advanced user-interface features. Weighing in at a mere 2.7 pounds (with batteries installed), the GPS unit is easily stowed in the cavernous ruck-sack that the Special Tactics Squadron troops carry. In addition to hand-held operation, the PLGR+96 unit can be installed in various vehicles and on airborne platforms. The Plugger is an integral part of the close air support (CAS) mission, sending GPS coordinates for the bomb runs.

Over the course of the next ten days, Stockton would continue to call in air strikes on Tora Bora. During a three-day period alone, he averaged thirteen hours of uninterrupted CAS. Regarding such an ac-complishment he related: "The majority of the CAS was JDAM [Joint Direct Attack Munition]. On a few occasions, I did use the SOFLAM for the F-16s, but mainly I used more of the JDAM-guided munitions. A B-1B bomber can carry twenty-four JDAMs, eight in each of its three large weapons bays."

The JDAM is a guidance tail kit that converts existing unguided free-fall bombs into accurate, adverse-weather "smart" munitions. It is a guided air-to-surface weapon that uses as the payload either the 2,000-pound BLU-109/MK 84, the 1,000-pound BLU-110/MK 83, or the 500-pound BLU-111/MK 82. The JDAM enables employ-ment of accurate air-to-surface weapons against high-priority fixed and re-locatable targets from fighter and bomber aircraft. The guid-ance is facilitated through a tail control system and a GPS-aided in-ertial navigation system. The navigation system is initialized by transfer alignment from the aircraft that provides position and veloc-ity vectors from the aircraft systems.

Once released from the aircraft, the JDAM autonomously navi-gates to the designated target coordinates. The target coordinates are loaded into the aircraft before takeoff, manually altered by the aircrew before weapon release, or automatically entered through target desig-nation with onboard aircraft sensors. In its most accurate mode, the JDAM system provides a weapon circular error probability (CEP) of five meters or less during free flight, when GPS data are available. If the GPS data are denied, the JDAM can achieve a thirty-meter CEP or less for free flight times up to 100 seconds, with a GPS-quality handoff from the aircraft. The CEP is the radius of a circle within which half of a missile's projectiles are expected to fall. As such, it is an indicator of the delivery accuracy of a weapon system. The JDAM can be launched from very low to very high altitudes, in a dive, toss, or loft and in straight and level flight, with an on-axis or off-axis delivery. The JDAM enables multiple weapons to be directed against single or multiple targets on a single pass.

For the CAS mission over Tora Bora, SSgt Stockton had a wide variety of aircraft to choose. He described his situation: "We had everything from gunships, every type of fighter, except the A-10s, because they were not there yet. You name it, we had it, fighters to bombers—B-52s and B-1s. We also had several AC-130 gunships, which we utilized. Basically, at nightfall I would check a gunship in on all the friendly positions and then get them working in the engagement areas and have them watch our area to make sure we were not getting flank by the al-Qaeda and Taliban forces."

Unaware of the capabilities of the AFSOC gunships, the enemy fighters would build fires to keep warm during the cold winter nights. Using thermal imaging, CAS missions were called in and the AC-130 gunships would pinpoint these locations, and rain down fire from the night sky. Sergeant Stockton remained modest about his accomplishments at Tora Bora: "The majority of the CAS mission was not me, specifically, finding a target and engaging it. A lot of it was intelligence-driven targets. I was there to de-conflict aircraft and make sure we were not dropping bombs on friendlies." While his Silver Star citation notes 600,000 pounds of ordnance, Sergeant Stockton was certain to make it clear: "I was not the guy who was actually finding six hundred thousand pounds worth of targets to engage. I was managing the battlespace to keep aircraft from crashing into one another. I was definitely up there lasing targets for a good number of targets; I did find, fix, and designate a good number of targets. However, that is a lot of ordnance. I cannot say I, personally, found and fixed six hundred thousand pounds worth on my own."

While Stockton was calling in close air support on the Taliban and al-Qaeda fighters, the mujahideen were closing in on the enemy. He recalled: "The 'muj' were doing the exploitation of the caves and closing in on their areas. We were linked up with the 'muj' subcommanders on the battlespace areas. They would bring back intel—passports, etc.,—and hand them off; in turn, we would pass them off and they were processed thorough our channels.

"Toward the end, there was not much resistance. When I first got there, there were surface-to-air missiles going off on a regular basis. The most evident piece of defeat I saw toward the end was an RPG [rocket-propelled grenade] being fired at a B-52, up at 30,000 feet in the air. He [the enemy] had no way of actually engaging the target; it was a last act of desperation on the part of the al-Qaeda fighter."

By mid-December, the intensity of enemy fighting had declined. Word was that the Taliban and al-Qaeda had wanted a ceasefire to bring people off of the mountain. There was the possibility of surrender by the enemy to the Northern Alliance, but this never occurred. Was this just an enemy ruse to allow Usama bin Laden and other al-Qaeda leaders to escape? In the end, most of the Taliban and al-Qaeda fighters had been killed; those left had slipped away through mountain passages into Pakistan.

Stockton commented on the conclusion: "I was working an op on the western area of the battlespace I was in the area, at the OP in the engagement area that we were clear to engage the enemy, while they were doing all the de-confliction of the battlespace and coordination of the ground forces. I don't know why stuff happens, but one day they called and said to stop any CAS and come back down the mountain—the purpose of our mission was not met. We loaded into the trucks and headed back to base camp. All of this happened well above my pay grade. . . .

"We came off the mountain, to that base camp in Jalalabad, and I set up a landing zone there. We landed a bunch of fixed-wing and rotor-wing aircraft. Loaded the Toyotas on the aircraft, and took them all with us when we exfiled. I never fired a shot with my weapon; I never got any good shots. The best weapon was my radio."

The Silver Star

The following is the citation to accompany the award of Silver Star to Dale Stockton.

Staff Sergeant Dale Stockton distinguished himself by gallantry in connection with military operations against a manned enemy of the United States near Tora Bora, Afghanistan, from 6 December 2001 to 20 December 2001. During this period, Sergeant Stockton excelled in multiple missions where he was directly engaged in combat actions against Taliban and Al Qaeda forces. He provided surgical terminal attack control of close air support aircraft at a volume and accuracy not yet seen until this major offensive in the Tora Bora region of Afghanistan.

Sergeant Stockton volunteered to move to the forward most lines of battle to assist the local Afghan opposition group's assault on the key enemy fortified stronghold. While moving to the front, he came under heavy machine gun and eighty-two millimeter mortar fire as close as twenty-five meters. Though the other government forces stopped, he continued to press forward with complete disregard to his own personal safety.

Positioned in front of the most forward troops, Sergeant Stockton directed numerous close air support missions against the enemy dug in positions while under intense two-way direct and indirect fire. His actions rallied the other government forces and directly resulted in their most successful single day advance of fourteen hundred meters, seizing the previously impenetrable key enemy stronghold. Sergeant Stockdale expertly controlled well over three hundred close air support aircraft sorties of multiple F-15, F-16, B-1, B-52, F-14, AV-8B aircraft, and the full combat munitions expenditure of five AC-130 gunships. He skillfully ensured the pinpoint delivery of an incredible 600,000 pounds of munitions on enemy targets. In this three-day period he averaged thirteen hours of uninterrupted close air support control daily, an amazing display of dedication, expertise, and deadly destruction. By his gallantry and devotion to duty, Sergeant Stockton has reflected great credit upon himself and the United States Air Force.

Diggers and Yanks

TSgt Eric Neilsen, Operation Iraqi Freedom

In his radio address to the nation in March 2003, President George W. Bush stated,

> My fellow citizens, at this hour, American and coalition forces are in the early stages of military operations to disarm Iraq, to free its people and to defend the world from grave danger. On my orders, coalition forces have begun striking selected targets of military importance to undermine Saddam Hussein's ability to wage war. These are opening stages of what will be a broad and concerted campaign. More than thirty-five countries are giving crucial support—from the use of naval and air bases, to help with intelligence and logistics, to the deployment of combat units. Every nation in this coalition has chosen to bear the duty and share the honor of serving in our common defense.

To further emphasis this commitment, a White House report confirmed, "Coalition forces have made important contributions in the war against terrorism across the spectrum of operations. Particular contributions include, but are not limited to, providing vital intelligence, personnel, equipment and assets for use on the ground, in the air and at sea. Coalition members also have provided liaison teams, participated in planning, provided bases and granted over-flight permissions—as well as made sizable contributions of humanitarian assistance."

The following was reported in an Australian communiqué. "The terrorist attacks on the United States on 11 September 2001 were viewed by both the United States and Australia as an abhorrent assault on the core values of democracy and freedom, which both nations hold dear and have fought to defend." As a staunch supporter of the United States, Australian Prime Minister John Howard announced on March 18, 2003, that the government had committed Australian Defense Force elements in the Middle East to join the coalition of military forces prepared to enforce Iraq's compliance with its international obligations to disarm. Australia's contribution to the coalition was known as Operation Falconer. As part of this support from "down under," approximately 150 members of the Australian Special Air Service Regiment (SASR) based out of Perth arrived in the country on February 11, 2003.

Assigned to the Combined Joint Special Operations Task Force–West were four Special Tactics Squadron (STS) members of the U.S. Air Force Special Operations Command (AFSOC). The senior combat controller was Tech Sergeant Eric Neilsen of the 21st Special Tactic Squadron, out of Pope Air Force Base, North Carolina, who was attached to elements of the Australian Special Air Service Regiment (SASR). The mission of the SASR was to perform reconnaissance and surveillance operations deep into western Iraq. Troops from the Holsworthy-based 4th Battalion, a commando element from the Special Forces task force, served as part of the quick-reaction force for the regiment. TSgt Neilsen's tasks would be to support the "Aussies" as the U.S. and coalition forces prepared for Operation Iraqi Freedom. He was there during the initial push of

Shock and Awe, the invasion of Iraq. The story put out about the mission was that it was a Scud hunt. The operation was to neutralize Iraqi's theater ballistic missiles in western Iraq and deny the enemy the ability to launch their missiles.

☆ ☆ ☆ ☆

The STS members would prove anew the old adage, "Whoever controls the air, controls the ground." Sergeant Neilsen related: "I was attached to a coalition unit; we ended up doing a forty-seven-day patrol. What happened that day was, we were supposed to be taking out Saddam's second line of early warning systems. We were supposed to go to each one in our area and clear them out. Stop them from doing what they to. We go to the first one. As it turned out, it was exactly like Intel said it was suppose to be: there were a couple of people at it who did not really want to be there. Unfortunately, we were looking at the places we were supposed to go next, and they were not quite fitting the description that we were given of very small buildings. The next two looked like large compounds.

"The other issue that happened during that time [was this]: I was giving up some air from our ambush. When we got ambushed within the next thirty to forty-five minutes, the other teams ended up getting into firefights as well. They were on the net asking for air. Since I already had air support, both U.S. and coalition, I was picking and choosing who was in the second- and third-worse situation.—trying to divvy [up] the air, splitting up the aircraft that they had already given to me, and give it to the other teams. We have the MBITR, but I still prefer the big radio; I don't mind being a pack mule if it means I have more power on my back. Since I was operating from a vehicle, I was using the 117 to call in air.

"From that point on, we cleared that compound and we were a few minutes from being done, to move to the next one. Our guys were pulling security on the northeast and west. We spotted vehicles moving at us pretty fast which matched the description of their counter-SOF vehicles that we had been dealing with ever since we went into the country; at that point, they surrounded us and ambushed us, and we had to fight that one out."

The Iraqi counter-SOF vehicles were compact sport utility vehicles (SUVs) equipped with heavy machine guns mounted in the beds, as well as additional mortar support. Their tactics were to outmaneuver and overwhelm the allied SOF units. Although the Iraqi vehicles did present a threat; the Iraqi plan failed abysmally, as the SASR teams with their AFSOC combat controller would call in close air support (CAS) and decimate the enemy vehicles.

"It took us between six and eight hours to get to the point where we could get the upper hand and maneuver around them. The problem was [that] they hit us from three directions, and from the south we had the largest compound, which we had left a few of our guys watching so we could not retreat south, or we would have pulled them right in on our other team. . . . Plus, the other team radioed and reported [that] they had another hundred enemy fighters coming out of the compound—that they were watching . . . coming toward us. The biggest problem we had was that it was daylight; it was flat-out desert, and the enemy was using pretty much everything on us, from mortars to heavy weapons to AAA [anti-aircraft artillery] pieces."

There were no HMMWVS for these combat controllers, working with the SASR; they rode in the Australians' six-wheel Long Range Patrol Vehicle [LRPV]. Sergeant Neilsen commented: "The coalition vehicles were theirs; the only thing that was ours was what we brought in our two rucks." The American combat controller would be assigned a position on the LRPV. Neilsen described, "I was manning the .50 caliber for forty of the forty-seven days of the patrol. The .50 was pretty much my primary weapon during the patrols. I did have an M4 with an ACOG, and a. 9 millimeter in my bag, but that was my backup to my back up at that point."

According to the Australian Ministry of Defence, the Land Rover six-wheel drive, two-ton chassis has been adapted by the Australian Special Air Service Regiment to serve as an armed long-range patrol vehicle. This early version mounts two 7.62 mm general-purpose machine guns. Greater firepower is now available with the aft GPMG being replaced by a quick-change-barrel .50 caliber heavy machine gun. A trail bike is carried in a cradle mounted at the rear of the vehicle. The Long Range Patrol Vehicle is purpose-built for deep-incursion missions. It can carry sufficient fuel, water, ammunition, rations, and equipment to

A group soldiers from the Australian Special Air Service Regiment take a break. Their mode of transportation is a 6x6 long-range patrol vehicle. TSgt Eric Neilson, 21st STS, was attached to the SASR in support of Operation Iraqi Freedom. *Courtesy of the Australian Ministry of Defence.*

support its crew on long patrols in hostile territory. As such, it continues the regiment's long history of using armed Jeeps and Land Rovers to create mayhem behind enemy lines. Long Range Patrol Vehicles are currently on active service with the SASR in Afghanistan.

"We maneuvered around—that took a while between the case and the guys using the Javelin missiles, and pure luck. What it came down to was [that] after six hours, we got them pushed back into one of the compounds, except for a few of them, while our other guys were dealing with them. The boss actually asked me if I thought I could get the planes to disappear for about thirty minutes. He wanted to sneak up behind them, making it look like we had retreated."

The Javelin is a man-portable, highly lethal, and survivable medium anti-tank weapon system for the infantry, scouts, and combat engineers. Weighing fifty pounds and measuring 3 feet 6 inches, the Javelin is a "fire-and-forget" shoulder-fired anti-tank missile fielded to replace the Dragon. The Javelin's unique top-attack flight mode, superior self-guiding tracking system, and advanced warhead design allow it to defeat all known tanks out to ranges of 2,500 meters. Its two major components are a reusable command launch unit (CLU) and a missile sealed in a disposable launch tube assembly.

The CLU's integrated day/night site provides target engagement capability in adverse weather and countermeasure environments. The CLU also may be used by itself for battlefield surveillance and reconnaissance. The system is fielded with no specific test measurement or diagnostic equipment, thus allowing forces to deploy rapidly and unencumbered. The Javelin's fire-and-forget guidance mode enables gunners to fire and then immediately take cover, greatly increasing survivability. Special features include a selectable top-attack or direct-fire mode (for targets under cover or for use in urban terrain against bunkers and buildings), target lock-on before launch, and a very limited back-blast that enables gunners to safely fire from enclosures and covered fighting positions.

Sergeant Neilsen continued: "I sent the planes back to the tanker, telling them what we were planning on doing. So, the Australian officer and I worked out the timing and we faked that we were retreating. We pulled a giant loop all the way around them to where they could not see us, and we literally pulled up behind their compound. Me and a couple other guys got out of the vehicle and moved up to the top of one of the berms, about 400 to 500 meters from them, and just sat there and watched them until the planes came back in. It was funny: we were watching them and they were watching where we used to be, almost like storytelling with each other, how they beat off the infidels.

"Then, all of a sudden, when the A-10s reappeared, coming from behind me, the enemy turned and saw the planes coming in, then looked down and saw all our vehicles lined up right behind their compound, waiting for them. From that point on, we had the A-10s start taking out the vehicles so they could not get away, then following the guys while both of my guys were hidden in a couple of places.

"I was manning the .50 cal on my vehicle when the firefight started. As soon as it started, I called back that I needed some air pushed to me, and I told them what was going on. With the CAS I hit one target approximately two kilometers away, but most of the targets were within one klick. The enemy closest to us that we had engaged was about 250 meters away. Some of the other coalition vehicles engaged guys that were closer.

"It was not the first time we had fought with this enemy force, so we did not want to get too close. They had the heavy weapons, such as mortars, in the compounds, which was a pretty good advantage over our having .50 cals and 7.62 millimeter machine guns. I don't think they were expecting the Javelins; between the anti-tank missile and the CAS, after a while they simply stood no chance. What Intel told us afterward, which was contrary to what they told us prior to the mission, was [that] they figured about 200–240 enemy troops had been in the compounds. We had only a couple dozen on our team.

"That ambush was the fourth or fifth firefight we had been in. From there, we continued to clear out our area. We were out in the field for forty-seven straight days. By the time we were done, we had cleared out our whole area of responsibility. Plus, we ended up seizing Al Asad Airfield, Objective Weber, while we were out there on the move, never having returned to the fire base. It was just one of those things they told us to do while we were out on the move."

Located in northern Iraq, Al Asad Airfield is the second largest air base in the country. It is positioned roughly 108 kilometers west of Baghdad. Modeled after the Russian air bases, the airfield is supported by two primary runways measuring 14,000 and 13,000 feet, respectively. Similar to other Iraqi air bases, Al Asad included an assortment of hardened shelters and hangars, with multiple runways and taxiways. The SASR discovered over fifty MiG aircraft at the air base and nearly 8 million kilograms of explosive ordnance.

According to the U.S. Air Force "Gulf War Air Power Survey," the Iraqis had built nearly 600 shelters on various airfields. Al Asad had thirty-three of the super-hardened shelters. These hardened aircraft bunkers (HABs) had sufficient strength to take overpressures even from nuclear weapons. The HABs were often referred to as "Yugos," since they had been constructed by Yugoslavian contractors using a Belgian design. The HABs typically had three layers. The innermost was a concrete shelter; the second layer consisted of several feet (and possibly more) of rock, dirt, or sand on top of the shelter; and the third layer, the "blaster slab," was usually made up of reinforced concrete blocks installed like a layer of bricks over the soil layer. The function of the blaster slab, of course, was to cause bombs to explode before reaching the shelter itself.

TSgt Neilson related: "One of the roughest parts of the mission was the sandstorms. We got hit three times; the worse one lasted around twenty-four hours. Our team actually had to put the vehicles into a box to make sure no one walked out [into] it. Our visibility was down to less than ten feet. The static from the sand blowing in the midst of the antennas was frying our computers, and shocking us, so we had to break everything down. The worst part was, after sixteen to eighteen hours, we all thought it was letting up. At first it started to rain, and then it turned into a mud storm for the next six hours, which in turn caked everything in desert mud. The sandstorm was orange, and when it went to a mud storm, it turned more of a red.

"On another occasion, a storm came up as we were about to perform a DA [direct action] mission. That pretty much canceled the op, and we had to sit there and ride it out. We picked it up where we left off, after [the storm] went by, which was about eight hours later. There was no hiding from it. You can cover up, but you are still going to eat dust. We left a couple of guys on security to keep an eye out, and the other guys hunkered down, stayed where they were, so we would not lose anybody. We made sure nobody walked away, because they probably would not find their way back if they did."

Even in the harshness of war there are times when the troops find moments to look at the lighthearted nature or the strangeness of their circumstances, if no other reason than as a way to relieve tension. I would hazard a guess that even Hannibal's men made jokes about getting elephants over the Alps. Sergeant Neilsen related: "Lighthearted things happened almost every day. Everyone knew you had to make jokes, ya gotta laugh. I was in college when Desert Storm happened, so I got to see the triple-A going up in the sky. Now during OIF, one time we were driving close to one of the cities at night a bomber went through and dropped their load and every gun in the city seemed to open up on them. We just stopped and watched. [It] would be the little things people would say, or [we'd] see how lucky we would be sometimes. During an ambush, one of our guys had set up a mortar tube a little too close to us. We don't think he saw it, but he tried to shoot at a guy who was setting it up, and one round actually hit the tube as he dropped the round into the weapon, knocking it backward and causing the weapon to fall back and fire on our own guys. Things like that we would laugh about later.

"There was one time when we were running out of Javelins so we would grab a captured RPG [rocket-propelled grenade] out of the back of the vehicle to save the Javelins for other targets. On the days we got to stop, we would, refit, rearm, and *sleep*. In forty-seven days, there was not a day when I got more than four hours of sleep. You [keep] moving, pulling security—it is just go, go, go! We did not stop for the first five days.

"The weirdest was [encountering] the toughest man I [have] ever seen in my life. During the ambush, we went around behind the enemy. We hit the vehicle first. Two guys were hiding in it and lived through a five hundred pound bomb that took out their vehicle. They then ran over to a triple-A pit; they ended up having thirteen guys in a pit that was about twenty feet across. I brought the A-10s back around and talked them onto it. They put down two more five-hundred-pound bombs; one hit just outside the pit and the other hit the middle of the pit. I was about to call in thirteen enemy KIAs on that pass. As soon as I had the key up, we saw this head pop up and the guy got up and ran away. They ended up capturing him; he was bleeding from his mouth and ear from a concussion, but he was not torn up. We couldn't believe that he had survived.

"Four hours earlier we were trying to hit one of the compounds, and I brought an F-16 across. The Iraqis were shooting heavy weapons and AAA. I watched a lot of vehicles going toward the compound, so I thought I would go after that one first. One of the F-16s put a JDAM through the roof, but it dudded. It was annoying, but at least I knew my coordinates were good. So they sent me another plane. He put another one through the same spot, and every one just stopped. We had no idea what was in that building, but whatever the JDAM hit, it picked up the building and flipped it over. It charred the entire compound, and we didn't see a single person move in that compound again. It was just a massive explosion, like it had hit a fuel storage or ammo cache—the whole thing went up as soon as the bomb hit. Everyone looked over at me, 'Yeah, dude, do that again!' That was an accident of some sort, but I'll take it. We had some young guys with us who had never been in a firefight before because they had been with another part of the group. After the fight, we would tell them, 'I can't believe you did not get hurt; you had RPGs going off about ten feet over your head.' They argued that no one had even shot at them . . . until they saw a photo of an RPG airburst going off right over their heads. Then they started to believe us."

"After the capture of the Al Asad air base, we stayed out a little longer. Our boss told me he wanted a runway, so we spent the next couple of days at the base. We were still pulling patrols and were trying to get an infrastructure going, but it was not happening—right off the bat. We pulled security and ran patrols to continue clearing the area. Another Control and I started searching the runways and the [surrounding] area, trying to figure out where we could make a workable runway to start bringing in planes. Finally we found a spot. The guys we were with helped us clean it off, and two of us sent back three surveys of the runways. After a few days we got approval to start bringing in planes.

"Units that were close to our location were driving to the airfield so they could do exfiltration; and we finally worked our exfil, as well. We kept the airfield open for twenty-four hours. Of all the controllers out there, all but one of us were level seven, which allowed us to work the runways on our own. We would take turns; when we were not working the runways, we were more than likely out on patrol with the team, going to different areas and continuing the mission of clearing out our AO [area of operations]. I got taken out on the final 130 for our task force. Actually, this was an AFSOC MC-130; I worked their landing, and they took off with me on board."

The Bronze Star

The following is the citation to accompany the award of the Bronze Star (First Oak Leaf Cluster with Valor) to Eric Neilsen:

Technical Sergeant Eric D. Neilsen distinguished himself by heroism as Primary Terminal Attack Controller, Combined Joint Special Operations Task Force-West while engaged in ground operations against the enemy near western Iraq, on 24 March 2003. On that date, Sergeant Neilsen was the primary terminal attack controller attached direct support to an elite coalition Special Operations Force headquarters element, tasked to conduct the counter theater ballistic missile mission during Operation Iraqi Freedom.

While conducting this critical mission, Sergeant Neilsen's vehicular mounted team became engaged in close combat with Iraqi counter Special Operations Forces units. Enemy soldiers ambushed Sergeant Neilsen's unit with rocket propelled grenades, heavy automatic weapons, mortars and small arms fire. While he and his team battled wave after wave of a numerically superior Iraqi force, which had outflanked them, Sergeant Neilsen rapidly established communication with air assets and requested close air support. Sergeant Neilsen and his team successfully repelled the initial attack and continued to engage the enemy now dug into two fortified compounds. With complete disregard for his exposed position, Sergeant Neilsen directed the multiple sets of arriving fighter aircraft in lethal close air support onto both of the compounds, destroying numerous command building and guard posts. The attack killed over fifty enemy personnel and led to the capture of an Iraqi Republican Guard Colonel and two other officers, and save the lives of his collation teammates. Sergeant Neilsen's employment of airpower, despite withering enemy fire, was the key to victory. The coalition commander stated that such a degree of success would have been unattainable without him. By his heroic actions and unselfish dedication to duty, Sergeant Neilson has reflected great credit upon himself and United States Air Force.

7

Austere to Operational

SSgt Brian Loudermilk, Operations Enduring Freedom and Iraqi Freedom

Operation Iraqi Freedom began on March 19, 2003, as the United States and coalition aircraft and cruise missiles pounded the city of Baghdad. The initial campaign was referred to as "Shock and Awe." As explosions roared through the capital city of Iraq, tracers from enemy gun emplacements lit up the night sky in answer to the devastating ordnance raining down on the city. Intelligence provide by the CIA placed Saddam Hussein and high-ranking members of his regime at a complex in the southern part of the city, called the Dora Farms. President George W. Bush ordered an airstrike and cruise missile attack aimed at the complex. While the high-explosive detonations destroyed the complex, the information provided by the CIA had been wrong. Hussein and other leaders were not at the complex.

The operation was less than a few hours old, and it was already being plagued by "Mr. Murphy." Depending on which version you have, it had been his by Murphy's Law of Combat Operations, rule

The combat controllers of AFSOC use a wide assortment of transportation, from the HMMWV to motorcycles, the latter as seen here secured to the front of the vehicle. These vehicles allow the operators to swiftly recon an airstrip or movement to a FOB. *Courtesy of the U.S. Air Force.*

16: "No OPLAN ever survives the initial contact." The original plan had called for a twenty-four-hour period for special operations forces and CIA paramilitary teams to carry out their covert missions prior to the invasion. The flawed information from the CIA, and the order to attack the complex, threw the schedule off by twenty-four hours. On March 20, the invasion began, and three weeks later, on April 9, 2003, Baghdad fell.

During the initial phases of Operation Iraqi Freedom, members of the AFSOC Special Tactics Squadron (STS) would be positioned at the airport. SSgt Brian Loudermilk, a combat controller with the 720th Special Tactics Group (STG), was among this combat control team (CCT). He related: "My team was tasked with the air traffic control portion of the Baghdad airfield in the initial assault when Operation Iraqi Freedom kicked off in 2003. We air-landed on the bad airfield, using the taxiway as the main runway. We worked the airfield and air traffic control for the next thirty days at the Baghdad airfield, bringing in supplies and troops. This was the heaviest traffic at the time, as we were running both rotary- and fixed-wing aircraft into the airfield. In addition to the military aircraft, we were also bringing in civilian aircraft providing medicine and assistance of a humanitarian nature. We had three runways going, and at times we would be landing three aircraft simultaneously. The aircraft were mainly re-supply—both helicopters and fixed-wings—bringing in supplies and equipment." Baghdad International Airport (BIA), as it became called, was previously Saddam International Airport. It is the largest airport in Iraq, located roughly sixteen kilometers west of downtown Bagh-dad. The BIA has a primary runway that is 13,000 feet long and a sec-ondary runway located on the military side of the airfield that measures 8,800 feet. According to the "Gulf War Air Power Survey," there were eight hardened aircraft shelters at the airfield.

Another popular mode of travel used by the Special Tactics teams is the all-terrain vehicle. This pair of ATVs is loaded with equipment and communications gear that the combat controller will need, whether in setting up ATC for an airhead or calling in CAS against the enemy. The battlefield airman of the AFSOC is equipped, trained, and ready to give the enemy every opportunity to give their lives for their cause. *Courtesy of the U.S. Air Force.*

Sergeant Loudermilk continued: "Once the airport had been secured, we were allowed to come in on the first air-land. We were brought in by an MC-130 Combat Talon and we established the airhead. Our main mode of transportation when we got there were ATVs; that is how we got around. We had HMMWVs, but we mainly used the four-wheelers and the mini-bikes. From then on, AFSOC was in control of the air traffic control [ATC] at Baghdad Airfield. Our combat control team was put in control of that portion of the ATC at the airfield—which, at the time, was unusual for our career field, based on the nature of our operations. We are usually in for the first three or four days of the operation, then we normally move on, allowing more structured air traffic control personnel to come in. [That's because] they would have more fixed navigation aids and items of that nature; our equipment is more portable and temporary. However, based on the situation at the time, the call was made that we were the best choice [to stay]. Even though there were some Army air traffic control personnel on the ground, who had come in on the original ground assault of the airfield, they stood by and we took over. For our level of air traffic control, it was pretty outstanding for the [number] of days and . . . the volume of aircraft. These actions happened approximately twenty-four hours prior to taking the capital city of Baghdad."

The Department of Defense definition of an airhead is "a designated area in a hostile or threatened territory which, when seized and held, ensures the continuous air landing of troops and materiel and provides the maneuver space necessary for projected operations." Normally, the airhead is the area seized in the assault phase of an airborne operation. Also, it can be a designated location in an area of operations used as a base for supply and evacuation by air.

Sergeant Loudermilk described the activity at the airport: "The outlying areas around the airport were hostile. There were still battles going on, and periodically the Iraqis would take shots at the aircraft. We had Apaches flying security that occasionally ran into some skirmishes along the perimeter of the landing zone. On one occasion, there were people on the landing zone who were taken into custody. They were carrying bags, but it was never clarified if they had explosives or not. [Conditions were] still hostile at the time—

to the point where we had to pull security during our stay on the airbase."

Regarding the equipment specific to running an airport, SSgt Loudermilk explained: "We had TACANs [Tactical Air Navigation] available, but they never were necessary, based on the weather and the GPS coordinates that the pilots were using. The Army had brought in PAR [Precision Approach Radar] equipment for approaches and things like that for the aircraft, and they never got utilized, either. We were basically bringing the aircraft VFR [visual flight rules]."

Tactical Air Navigation (TACAN) is an ultra-high-frequency electronic air-navigation system that is able to provide continuous bearing and slant range to a selected station. Precision Approach Radar (PAR) is radar equipment in some ATC facilities operated by the FAA and/or the military services, at joint-use civil/military locations and separate military installations, to detect and display azimuth, elevation, and range of aircraft on the final-approach course to a runway. This equipment may be used to monitor certain nonradar approaches, but it is primarily for a precision-instrument approach, whereby the controller issues guidance instructions to the pilot based on the aircraft's position in relation to the final approach course (azimuth), the glidepath (elevation), and the distance (range) from the touchdown point on the runway, as displayed on the radar scope. Visual flight rules (VFR) govern the procedures for conducting flight under visual conditions. The term VFR is also used in the United States to indicate weather conditions that are equal to or greater than minimum visual flight requirements. In addition, the term is used by pilots and controllers to indicate a type of flight plan.

Here's what happened, according to SSgt Loudermilk: "We had six guys on the initial push, and then on the second night, we had an additional six combat controllers come in. Over the course of the next week, it started to build up and we ended up with about twenty [controllers]. We were pulling twenty-four-hour shifts working ATC. That was for the first thirty days, until the airfield was operational, then it was taken over by the Australians. The Aussies were more of the standard air traffic controllers than the combat control teams [CCTs]. The CCTs . . . our skills are air traffic control, but that is not the only thing we do. [We are as] proficient [in these skills] as some of the people sitting in the tower, doing it everyday. As far as the story goes, for us to have that [opportunity] to work that long and to get that experience . . . was pretty outstanding."

What made this mission so special was the amount of time the STS members actually ran the airbase. Sergeant Loudermilk elaborated: "The CCT ran the airfield for more than just an initial two- to three-day task; they ran the *entire* air operation for thirty days. The fact [was] that, while we were working air traffic, our team was carrying out other tasks as well. About three weeks into the op, we had opened up three runways. We had a dedicated fix-wing runway, a rotary runway. We had a civilian runway where we landed a lot of civilian airplanes to keep them away from the military operations that were going on. . . . The civilian airplanes were like the Red Cross aircraft bringing in medicines and humanitarian items. This is also unique for our abilities."

Running the air traffic control for an international airport was a mission for which the combat control teams were, indeed, aptly qualified. However, the point at which the combat controllers of AFSOC are different from their ATC comrades is when they are placed in adverse environments, under austere conditions, and in enemy territory.

Late in 2003, SSgt Loudermilk was deployed to Afghanistan in support of Operation Enduring Freedom, where he used these skills exceptionally well. He described his mission in the mountainous region of Southwest Asia: "On my first couple of deployments, I was mainly running with the landing-zone survey team. We were tasked to survey various landing zones throughout Afghanistan. When I say 'survey' I mean that we would check the [areas] to make sure they were suitable for landing. For the most part, the areas were non-hostile, but there was always a threat.

"During one particular mission, was there an actual hostile event. That was in the western part of Afghanistan, on the Iranian border near Shindand Airfield. There was a clash between warlords, and we were there to bring in some ANA [Afghan National Army] troops to defuse the situation, which they did after five days." Shindand Airfield is in the eastern province of Farah, and it is the largest air base in Afghanistan. The base was retaken from the Taliban by the Afghan National Army, and U.S. aircraft began flying in September 2004.

Loudermilk expanded his description of this mission: "I was by myself when we went into Shindand Airfield. We had about fifty ANA with us when we set down. A lot of times, when we do surveys, we may just have the helo that brought us in—or perhaps an Apache overhead providing security. But a lot of places we go to today are fire bases that are manned by American forces. In that case, we go in to access the airfield to make sure it is still good to go, or if they want to build one, we go in for the survey."

A landing-zone survey includes physical inspection and documentation of the site. The survey is done to identify and evaluate any potential hazards to aircraft and personnel. The team ascertains if the area is suitable for operational and safety standards, determined by taking measurements, noting GPS coordinates, calculating the size, obtaining maps, and creating diagrams. SSgt Loudermilk explained the process: "We do some general field tests. We can do soil sampling, but we would have to send anything in to get an exact reading. From our training and experience, we can determine [whether it's] sand, silt, or gravel. With our equipment, we can say [whether] this field can take a C-130 or not."

SSgt Loudermilk described his mission in the winter of 2003: "Jalalabad Airfield was one of the landing-zone surveys I worked, which was a pretty big operation for Mountain Resolve. It was primarily a re-supply route and refueling area—in other words, a FARP [forward area refueling and re-arming point]. When we hit the ground, there was nothing there but a bare base—an Afghani in the tower of the building. We came in with some army personnel, and at that time I was the lone combat controller on the ground."

A forward arming and refueling point, or FARP, is a temporary facility, organized, equipped, and deployed by an aviation commander and normally located in the main battle area. It is closer to the area where operations are being conducted than the aviation unit's combat service area. The FARP provides the fuel and ammunition necessary for maneuvering the aviation units in combat—

that is, to permit combat aircraft to rapidly refuel and rearm simultaneously.

Whether they are setting up FARPs in the valleys of Afghanistan or the deserts of Iraq, or they are the air traffic controllers for the largest air base in the theater, the combat controllers of AFSOC live up to their motto, "First There."

8

Green Hornets
over Fallujah

SSgt Donald Christianson, 20th Special
Operation Squadron, Operation Iraqi Freedom

The aircrews of the 20th Special Operations Squadron, known as the "Green Hornets," fly the Sikorsky MH-53J Pave Low helicopter. The aircraft is used to carry out low-level, long-range, undetected ingress into denied or hostile areas. This is done in day or night, even under the worst weather conditions for infiltration, exfiltration, and resupply of special operations forces. The 92-foot, extremely maneuverable Pave Low is the largest and most powerful helicopter in the U.S. Air Force inventory, powered by two General Electric T64-GE/100 engines. Equipped with forward-looking infrared (FLIR), inertial GPS, Doppler navigation systems, terrain-following/avoidance radar, an on-board computer, and integrated advanced avionics,

The MH-53 Pave Low helicopter, which served with distinction over four decades, will be retired. On September 27, 2008, the Pave Low helicopter flew its last combat mission in support of special operations forces. *Courtesy of the U.S. Air Force.*

its pilots can achieve precise, low-level, long-range penetration without detection.

The Pave Low with the Interactive Defensive Avionics System/ Multi-Mission Advanced Tactical Terminal (IDAS/MATT) modification, termed the M model, provides aircrews with a heightened level of readiness and efficiency. This system is a color, multifunctional, night-vision-compatible, digital map screen. Located on the helicopter's instrument panel, the display gives the crew a more concise view of the battlefield and instant access to real-time events. The helicopter's flight path, manmade obstacles such as power lines, and even hostile threats "over the horizon" are depicted in an easy-to-read manner.

This advanced system receives its data from a satellite, directly into the unit's computer. The signal is then decoded and the data are displayed in 3-D color imaging of the surrounding terrain, including contour lines and elevation bands. At the push of a button, the crew can visualize a digital navigational course and bearing information, in addition to the map display. Designed to give crew members priority ranking in consolidating the many functions, the easy-to-control instrument panel processes information efficiently. Much better suited for operations in Iraq than Afghanistan, the Pave Low is limited to a ceiling of 16,000 feet.

All of this high technology results in what the Air Force calls the "crew concept": the pilot of the MH-53J gets assistance from the co-pilot and flight engineer. These three individuals are crammed into the flight deck, smaller than an average-size closet. Each has responsibility for managing a section of the controls, but together they can maneuver the Pave Low in a way that staggers the imagination—and sometimes the stomach. The Pave Low has a speed of 195 miles per hour and a range of 600 statue miles, but unlimited with air refueling. Offering protection to the crew is armor plating as well as its weapon systems. Just aft of the flight deck are two 7.62 mm mini-guns and at the rear of the helicopter, on the exit ramp, is a .50-caliber machine gun. These guns are manned by two aerial gunners and one of the additional flight engineers.

SSgt Donald Christianson, a flight engineer, recounted a fateful mission on April 13, 2004: "At the start of the day, we had a mortar attack that hit right near our tent, in the base where we were staying. During the crew brief, we were joking around [about] how we wanted to get up and go fly that night, because it was safer in the air than in our compound, with all the mortar fire. We briefed up for our flight. Our mission that night was to do an ammo re-supply, and then we were supposed to pick up a guy who was KIA [killed in action]."

The mission called for a pair of Pave Low helicopters to make a run to Fallujah, where the crew was to delivery supplies to a Special Forces ODA in the desert city. From Fallujah, the crew was then to pick up the remains of a Special Forces team member who had been killed in Mahmudiyah, a town south of Baghdad. Aboard the helicopters were Special Forces soldiers sent to retrieve the body. Sergeant Major Michael Stack had been killed in action while his ODA was conducting combat operations in Al Anbar Province, Iraq. A Special Forces team from Company C, 2nd Battalion, 5th SFG, had been traveling from Baghdad to Al Hillah when they were ambushed by insurgents. SGM Stack's vehicle had been pulling rear security when the convoy came under attack. Manning the .50 caliber machine gun, he covered the team's movement so they could escape the enemy fire. The convoy continued toward Al Hillah, where again they came under heavy enemy fire. During this ambush, SGM Stack was killed in an explosion.

Sergeant Christianson continued: "We took off, and we constantly had a problem . . . landing, with helicopters fouling the landing zone. We would fly into the landing zone, and there would be various helicopters in there. So we would have to circle around and wait for them to move [out] and then land. That happened several nights. Where we were was not the kind of place you want to be trolling around. Once again, that night, we went in to deliver the ammo [and] the same thing happened: the landing zone was fouled. We went around, and our comment was, 'Let's get out of here—we don't want to be hanging out here.'"

The helicopters were flying approximately 180 feet off the ground when an insurgent, positioned 300 feet in front of the lead aircraft, stood up and launched an RPG [rocket-propelled grenade] straight at the nose of the large helicopter. Christianson described the situation: "In the lead aircraft, the flight engineer had just looked down to punch in some coordinates into the navigation system, to go to a different landing zone. There was a blast from the ground, and an immediate impact on the chalk lead as it was hit by the RPG. We were in a tight formation, flying just to the left of them. When the RPG exploded, it hit the nose and blew the top off the cockpit. It blew all the throttles off, and injured the pilots and flight engineer." The blast blew the helmet and night-vision goggles off the head of co-pilot Captain Tom Lessner. Flight engineer Tech Sgt Christian MacKenzie was hit with multiple shrapnel wounds, flash burns, and injury to his left eye. The aircraft immediately pitched up and almost came to a stop in the middle of the air.

Christianson said: "We broke left, and once they regained control of the helicopter, they broke left and almost hit us. We immediately called out 'Break right!' While I was doing that, I was also punching out flares, as we were not sure if it was a manpad or something else that shot as us." A "manpad" is the term used for a man-portable air-defense system, which is a shoulder-launched surface-to-air missile, such as a Stinger. These missiles typically use an infrared guidance system and are a serious threat to low-flying aircraft, especially helicopters.

The enemy fired a second RPG that sailed between the two helicopters. The first helicopter pitched nose up approximately 80 degrees, and then began to fall from the sky. Captain Steve Edwards, the pilot, had been able to keep his night-vision goggles on during the attack, and although he was wounded, he managed to regain control of the crippled Pave Low and land the aircraft. The RPG had totally blew the top of the cockpit away, so the controls were gone. The only way the lead helicopter could shut the [engine] down once on the ground was by yanking on the control cables attached to the throttles.

Though the first helicopter was down, the [crew] was far from safe. Close to fifty insurgents began to close in on their position. Sergeant Christianson continued: "While we were doing [our own] breaking maneuvers, the insurgents shot an RPG right across the nose of our aircraft and another across our tail. The tail gunner saw where the [insurgents] were and started to return fire. At that time, we could not find [the] lead [helicopter]. Doing all our breaking maneuvers, descending, we almost ran into some wires as we got down to about seventy-five feet, trying to get away. We avoided the wires, and by that time we had no idea where [the] lead was. We tried to get them on the radio; the only way we could tell where the incident took place was [by seeing] a big ring of smoke in the air. That was the only area we thought they could be. We flew by once, still getting shot at.

"We went around, and [thought], 'Hey, we're going to get ourselves shot down if we don't think about what were doing.' Our pilot says, 'We're not leaving them. We are going to do one more fly-by and see if we can find them. If that doesn't work, then we'll land at the LZ [landing zone] and try to get them on the radio.'

"We did one more fly-by and were still taking fire. We were discussing what . . . to do next when the pilot, still, is saying, 'I don't want to leave them.' It had been about six minutes now that we [had been] circling around, and still we had no radio contact with the other helicopter. We didn't know if they had crashed bad . . . or what happened. So, the pilot said we were going to do one more check. We did one more fly-by and the tail gunner spotted the aircraft in a field with about five-foot-[tall] grass. Our pilot whipped the Pave Low around and landed next to the downed helicopter. We had a couple of Special Forces team members on board, and we sent them out to assist. We then gathered all the classified stuff and helped the injured. After about five minutes, we were starting to get really nervous. The area we were in . . . the grass was so high you did not have a good field of view around you . . . we knew [that] the people who [had] shot down the lead helicopter were very close to the area."

"In the mean time, we called in an AC-130 gunship on the radio, and they arrived overhead to give us some assistance. They had a visual on the insurgents who were slowing creeping up on us. At this time, the gunship did not have clearance to engage, so the enemy kept creeping up on us. Finally, we got everyone on board our helicopter, and as we were taking off, they shot an RPG right off our tail. That was very close. Once again, our tail gunner returned fire. The footage from the gunship showed [that] the insurgents were about a hundred-fifty to two hundred feet behind our helicopter when we took off—that's how close they were. We did some maneuvering and got those guys out of there. Once we returned to the base, we got medical attention for them and that was the gist of the mission."

"They sent some Marines in later to secure the helo, but they came under attack so badly. They were able to get on the helo and retrieve some stuff we could not get off when we had landed the night before. They came under heavy mortar attack, killing one of the Marines. Then they said 'Forget this!' and called in an air strike. By the tine the air strike arrived, some of the insurgents had boarded the helicopter and were killed when the helo was destroyed."

☆ ☆ ☆ ☆

Rather than have the Pave Low fall into enemy hands after it was shot down on April 13, 2004, U.S. military officials called in two Air Force F-16s to destroy the damaged helicopter. SSgt Christianson's final comments were: "Normally, it is safer to be in the air. We get shot at quite a bit. A lot of times, they're just shooting where they think they heard something, so it's not real accurate. The biggest things we are concerned about are the manpads. That night, we were flying really low. It was really dark, and I don't know how someone with an RPG could have shot that helicopter down. I don't know, but they did get pretty lucky. That night, being in the air was just as dangerous as being on the ground."

CHAPTER
9

Vintage Aircraft and Modern Techniques

MSgt Paul Lawson and TSgt Olivia Seise, 6th Special Operations Squadron

Foreign internal defense, or FID, is one of the core missions of the special operations forces. Involving participation by U.S. civilian and military agencies, the goal of FID is to protect a foreign society from subversion, lawlessness, and insurgency. Commensurate with U.S. policy goals, the focus of all of our foreign internal defense efforts is to support the host-nation's program of internal defense and development. The FID programs attempt to build viable internal institutions that can respond to the needs of that society. The most significant manifestation of these needs is likely to be a combination of economic, social, informational, and political factors. The United States, therefore, generally employs a mix of diplomatic, economic, informational, and military means to support these objectives. Military assistance is often necessary in order to provide the secure the environment for these efforts to be effective.

The mission of the 6th Special Operations Squadron (SOS), according to the AFSOC, is to serve as a combat aviation advisory unit. It is to assess, train, advise, and assist foreign aviation forces in their employment, sustainment, and forced integration of airpower. That is, these squadron advisers help friendly and allied forces employ and sustain their own airpower resources, and when necessary, integrate those resources into joint and combined (multinational) operations. Lieutenant Lauren Johnson, 1st Special Operations Wing, summarized AFSOC's FID mission: "The main goal behind the FID is to enable the foreign force to operate and employ their own air power by themselves. Then we will assist and provide guidance if needed, but the primary objective is for them to be self-sufficient in those operations. It is not that they are tagging along with our forces and helping us out." The squadron was reactivated in 1994 and was expected to handle a full range of military operations, from small military-to-military contact events and contingency operations to major regional conflicts.

The combat aviation advisers of the 6th SOS possess specialized capabilities for foreign internal defense, unconventional warfare, and coalition support, such as the ability to integrate foreign airpower into the theater-campaign, promote safety and interoperability, facilitate airspace de-confliction, and upgrade host-nation aviation capabilities. Imparting such capabilities to the host-nation's armed forces is particularly important in the fight against terrorism. This is especially applicable when the host-nation has to fight alongside U.S. forces or when allied forces have to carry the tactical initiative with U.S. training and advisory assistance.

When deployed to a host-nation, the squadron executes its mission by using theater-oriented, Operational Aviation Detachments Alpha and Bravo teams, referred to as OAD-A and OAD-B. The purpose of OAD-A is to serve as the tactical training and advisory team. The task of OAD-B is to provide command, control, and communications; logistics; and administrative and medical support to multiple OAD-A teams deployed in the field. The deployed teams are tailored in both size and capability to meet specific mission requirements. Typically, the teams comprise a dozen individuals, led by a captain or master sergeant.

A standard deployed OAD-A and OAD-B normally would have the following organization: OAD-A—rotary-wing pilot, two transport pilots, navigator, flight engineer, transport loadmaster, two maintenance crew chiefs, engine specialist, special tactics, security police, survival specialist, and medical technician; OAD-B—mission commander, operations officer, regional specialist, logistics officer, intelligence officer, information management, communications specialist, aircrew life support, supply, and flight surgeon. The tempo of current operations against terrorism has affected the 6th SOS, as MSgt Lawson explained: "We do have STS teams assigned to the unit on occasion. They are heavily tasked throughout AFSOC. But we do, on occasion, augment with additional member from the STS community. Normally, when our teams go down range, they comprise primary air crew members, some maintenance, and then, depending on the type of trip it is, we can add in logistics trainers—whatever we may need for the mission."

One of the unique aspects of the 6th SOS is the selection process and unique training. This is not a case of just throwing a bunch of guys into a plane and sending them to some Third World nation; there is a big effort made to get them to this stage. The teams receive all types of intensive training, covering a number of aspects, so they are proficient in many areas and can perform their duties in the partner nations. This training can take up to a year to accomplish.

TSgt Olivia Siese elaborated on the training: "Regarding the training and the selection process, each person does apply to be accepted into the unit. That includes aircrews, maintainers, combat personnel, and security police, so [selection] is [in] a variety of career fields. Currently we have about thirty-two different career fields. [People from] each of these [fields] make up the teams that go out to the partner nations. Initially, before they become combat aviation advisers, they go through an intense training [to grow] familiar with whatever culture they are going to be working in. Even though they may work with interrupters, every member receives training, in [foreign languages] including Russian, Polish, German, Korean, Arabic,

Spanish, French, and Thai. A lot of times, the training will include force protection and personal survival training."

On the subject of foreign languages, MSgt Paul Lawson added: "We do a language training program and everyone does [his or her] best to keep up with what is required. Depending on the country, you generally find, down range, [that] the majority of the pilots speak English fairly well. This is [because] most of the pilots' training is conducted in European flight schools or even in America, hence the working language is English. Where we usually find the most [problems] with languages is with enlisted aircrew members or ground crews. Most of our guys, depending on the language in use, have fairly good skills with the foreign units. We have improved over the years, although [for] some of the more difficult languages, like Arabic, we usually have to rely on interrupters."

Personnel assigned to the 6th SOS are required to complete a demanding curriculum that produces language-proficient, regionally oriented, politically astute, and culturally aware aviation advisory experts. The curriculum for the combat aviation adviser includes extensive indoctrination in advanced field-craft skills (including force protection and personal survival), instructional skills, risk management, and safety. Training covers such topics as the dynamics of international terrorism, weapons (M9 and M16), cross-cultural communication, theater orientation, basic and advanced survival, and other courses pertinent to their area of operations.

Member of the 6th SOS also receive survival, evasion, resistance, and escape (SERE) training. The SERE instructors teach the squadron members to survive under any conditions, anywhere in the world. The training emphasizes survival aids and hazards with respect to plants, wildlife, climate, and terrain; identification of sources of food and water; how to obtain and prepare food; purification of water, building of fires, land navigation; and other field skills. All airmen receive entry-level, or A-level, training. Additionally, B-level is provided to those with a moderate risk of capture, and C-level training is reserved for those with a high risk of capture. The B- and C-level training is applicable primarily to aircrew members— those traditionally with higher-risk duties. In addition to aircrews, advanced SERE training is provided to battlefield airmen—those with the responsibility—for combat control, pararescue, tactical air control, and combat weather.

MSgt Lawson explained about the training: "We do our own training; which is a little different [from] most [other] Air Force units. Our specific unit trains its own personnel, with its own pipeline training, whereby we train our combat aviation advisers to be proficient. It is a combination of SERE training—we [run] the gamut. Obviously, the aircrews come here with the basic survival schools. We send, or attempt to send, everyone from the unit—and that includes maintenance and everyone else—to the basic survival school. Once they get that accomplished, we try to take it up the next couple of levels. Sometimes we find ourselves being the only Americans in the country, outside of Embassy personnel, so our training gets a little more extensive and in-depth than most units."

So how does this translate to operations? The squadron's tactical flying activities encompass both fixed- and rotary-wing operations, including combat search and rescue, close air support, and airlift/aerial delivery—that is, infiltration, exfiltration, re-supply, and air drop. Assistance is provided in the sustainment area, which includes aviation maintenance; supply; munitions; ground safety; life support; personal survival; air base defense; command, control, and communications; and other sustainment functions in support of combat air operations. The OAD-A/B teams assist the theater combatant commanders and subordinate commands in operational-level planning and joint combined-force integration in fixed- and rotary-wing operations. This assistance may include assessment of foreign aviation capabilities, liaison with foreign aviation forces, and assistance in planning theater air campaigns for combined operations. The squadron also performs safety and interoperability evaluation of foreign aviation capabilities prior to commencing any combined operations and exercises. Once the 6th SOS signs off on the proficiency and safety levels of the foreign aviation unit, it then serves as a force multiplier, fielding advisory teams and drawing foreign units into joint and combined operations. The squadron also serves in a direct-execution role.

Members of the 6th Special Operations Squadron specialize in foreign internal defense. Such vintage aircraft as the Mi-8 "Hip" and Huey helicopter are common in Third World nations. Providing these countries with FID support today can furnish an ally in conflict tomorrow. *Courtesy of the U.S. Air Force.*

MSgt Lawson relates his experience with the 6th SOS during an FID mission in December 2004: "We were conducting a foreign internal defense mission in the Middle East; working on the foreign helicopters over there. Basically, FID is all about teaching partner nations how to fight lawlessness and insurgency within their own borders. We were doing that with several different units, and were [also] doing quite a bit of flying; both day and night.

"At this time, we were toward the end of our exercise. We usually end the training with a final exercise. We pulled all the players together to pick a location and set up a scenario. This was so they could utilize all the tools we [had] provided them. In this particular case, we decided to try for an airfield that we had previously seen during our training.

We were flying in a Mi-17 HIP helicopter. We flew to the location early in the day to do a quick look-through to show it to our mission commander, so we [we would have] good eyes on where we had decided to do the exercise. [In] the middle of the day, we went back in there and discovered some tribesmen had moved into that particular area. They had not been there before, when we had gone by. We really did not think much of it. We went in to do an approach of the airfield, and subsequently were fired upon.

"We took eight to ten hits of 7.62 millimeter rounds. In the course of evading the incoming fire, and getting away from the airfield, we suffered some injuries. My engineer who was flying with us took a round in the arm and two of the others with us for the training also were hit fairly severely. We ended up flying back to our airfield. During this time, we had additional medical personnel on board so we were treating the wounded all the way back to the airfield. We got back to our airfield, got them off-loaded, and transferred them to a MedEvac fairly rapidly. Thankfully, we were at a location that had some MedEvac personnel on site. We had gotten them out in time, and everyone survived to tell the tale afterwards."

Lawson continued: "For our particular missions, we generally work by our selves. On occasion, we have worked with additional ground-based SOF units to integrate the training. For example, during our final exercise, we may include other SOF-trained host-nation forces—it depends on the setting and what our mission is. In the past, when we did some of the exchange training, there were some ground units in the area at the same time. If our time in the country coincides, we may try to wind things up so we can get the maximum training participation on both sides of the house."

Being sent to a host-nation can bring with it unique circumstances. For instance, the combat aviation advisers find their own living arrangements—even their eating habits are far from the norm. MSgt Lawson commented: "In the past, prior to 9/11, we normally would live with those partner nations, either in their barracks or at least on their air base. As the threats have increased over the past few years, it really just depends on the security situation and how comfortable we feel with the bases; occasionally we stay in State Department-approved hotels.

"I have not had anything really weird to eat; most things are just common to the region. If you are in the Middle East, you are going to eat some hummus, tabbouleh, and the usual fare. My experience has been with the CENTCOM area. I'm sure if we asked some of the guys from other parts of the world, they [would] have some strange things [to say], but part of this deal is that you just have to work through it. You do not want to offend a host-nation, so if you have to eat goat, you eat goat . . . and lots of different types of lamb."

"We do see some surprising things. On one occasion, we were flying tactically in one of the helicopters, so we were about a hundred feet off the ground. We usually make the limits a little higher when flying with the partner nations. In the middle of the flight, one of the [host-nation] backenders decided to pull out a tray of candy and serve it to the pilots. At the time we did not find it so humorous, because we were busy scanning the mountainous terrain. Afterwards, we found it amusing. The guy was just trying to be hospitable at a very inopportune moment, but that's okay."

One of the unique characteristics of the 6th SOS mission is the aircraft on which they train. When you travel across the tarmac at Hurlburt Field, Florida, you can observe the latest and greatest in technology—the CV-22 Osprey. You will pass the MH-53 Pave Lows, plus some airframes dating back to the Vietnam War. When you come to the hangers of the 6th SOS, though, you definitely feel nostalgic. It is as if you have stepped back in time to the cold war. The stock aircraft of the 6th SOS are previously owned planes and helicopters of Soviet origin. At one time, there was even a C-47. When it comes to flying old foreign planes, MSgt Lawson said, "They are not so much old as archaic, by American terms. You could say that we specialize in the Russian models since those are the aircraft predominantly in use in the countries we train. These aircraft are cheaper and fairly reliable. A lot of the Russian helicopters are like John Deere tractors with blades—very reliable. They just keep running and running."

"The squadron has made slight modifications to the aircraft, but nothing cryptic. We are still flying with steam gauges, as opposed to the digital cockpits of the newer aircraft. We have added some avionics so we can do some instrument flying and to be safer in the weather. Predominantly, all the aircraft at Hurlburt are used for training purposes; we generally fly on the host-nation's aircraft. We do not deploy with our aircraft, as do the other units."

On the topic of pilots and aircrews, MSgt Lawson makes an interesting observation: "I am rotary engineer by trade; however, I have been associated with the mission for a while so that I have gotten familiar with some of the fixed-winged assets. We tried to find the more experienced, older aircrews. Although this is getting more difficult, as with our OpTempo, everyone is competing for the same level of experience. In the time we've done this, we have found it is easier to have someone who has a lot of experience, so that by the time they come to us they are fairly good at what they do for a living. When we throw a different aircraft at them, it does not take them as long to acclimate . . . as it would a new guy to figure out the new bird."

To answer the question as to where FID fits into the U.S. mission to combat terrorism, MSgt Lawson explained: "When you really think about it, the GWOT [Global War on Terrorism] is so broad [that] it is going to be difficult for America to fight this on its own. What FID brings to the table is [that] we go in and we train the partner-nation up to a certain skill level, depending on what is [needed]. When we get to [that] level, they can assist us in the mission.

"The forces of the host-nation can then work predominantly in their own area, either as a member of a coalition or on their own with specific guidance. Realistically, if we had been much larger. . . . We have done a fairly good job [considering] the size we are, in comparison to other units, but we operate globally and it has been difficult because of our [low] numbers. But if you think about it, if we have been operating in a country for the past five to seven years, and suddenly we have an outbreak and something needs to be accomplished, we already have some inroads with the partner-nation—militarily and usually [also] with some civilian authorities. So, that really sets the stage for interaction and use of their facilities as well as their personnel.

"We get direction from our commanders on what they want to accomplish, and we stick pretty close to the plan. We stay in the sphere of air power. Normally, we have a five- to ten-year strategic plan for each of the countries we work in. We know the direction we want to go, and we work hard on getting there. . . . We have had some really great successes that, at times, seem fairly small, but on a more strategic stage [they] are very significant. I've been in the Air Force over nineteen years, and this has probably been the most challenging mission, but also the most rewarding. So it has been a good ride."

10

The Quick Reaction Force

TSgt Brad Reilly, Combat Controller, Operation Enduring Freedom

This would the second tour "down range" for TSgt Bradley Reilly, this time operating with the Combined Joint Special Operations Task Force-Afghanistan, in support of Operation Enduring Freedom. As a member of the elite AFSOC 23rd Special Tactics Squadron, Combat Controller TSgt Reilly was assigned to a Special Forces (SF) Operational Detachment Alpha (ODA) 163. The ODA was from the 1st Special Forces Group (Airborne), code name, "The Beast."

On April 11, 2005, intelligence came in that General Khil Baz had been traveling through the Khowst-Gardez Pass in Paktya

---

Names of Special Forces members in this chapter have been changed for security reasons.

Taking a moment during a patrol in Afghanistan, TSgt Brad Reilly remains alert and ready for action. While his radio and headset are his constant companions, he is armed for bear. Personal weapons are M9 9 mm Beretta semi-automatic pistol, M4A1 5.56 mm carbine, and M240B 7.62 mm machinegun mounted on the team's vehicle. *Courtesy of the U.S. Air Force.*

Province, known as the K-G Pass, when he and his forty fighters were ambushed by anti-coalition militia (ACM) forces. ACM is the new name for the Taliban and al-Qaeda fighters—that is to say, the bad guys. The general picked up his iridium phone and called back to get American help. The ODA was part of a quick reaction force (QRF) responding to the call of General Khil Baz, who was the border battalion command and a new ally in the fight against the ACM. The Khowst-Gardez area was historically identified as a porous border, with large numbers of enemy fighters transiting back and forth between Afghanistan and Pakistan. TSgt Reilly commented: "It is a busy area to be in."

The QRF comprised nine Special Forces soldiers, one combat controller (TSgt Reilly), eight Afghan fighters with two interpreters, and two members from other government agencies. The force was spilt in half, with TSgt Reilly riding in Chalk 2, flying in the second of two UH-60 Black Hawk helicopters. They traveled from Forward Operating Base (FOB) Salerno to FOB Chapman, and from there on to the K-G Pass area. As the Black Hawks traversed the 50 to 60 kilometers to the ambush location, they were escorted by a pair of AH-64 Apache gunships. Additionally, two A-10 Thunderbolts or Warthogs, depending on which school you come from, were heading for the ambush site.

TSgt Reilly told his story: "We had not been to this area that often. The road in Khowst had been ambushed a thousand times. Some of the maps of the area were older Russian maps; for our mission we used those from Falcon View. Falcon View is a program allowing access to all sorts of maps; we can pick the scale and the area, and it provides the type of map we need. We . . . get a map or imagery up to one meter. When we see what we want, we print it out and tuck it into our gear, and away we go.

"So we flew into the K-G Pass and identified the vehicles. There was a long line of vehicles on each side, with normal traffic going down the pass 'cause they weren't going through this ambush site. By the time we got there, about forty-five minutes had elapsed and there was nothing going on. My helicopter sat down, [and] we walked around, surveying the site of the ambush. The vehicles were shot up, with bullet holes and RPG [rocket-propelled grenade] rounds, but there were no casualties and nothing was going on. Additionally, the general had placed his guys at the base of the hill, where they [had] ascertained was where the ambush had originated. While we were doing this, the SF team sergeant, Sgt Dave Hooper, linked up with General Khil Baz, The SF guys were thinking about extracting the general, [but] doing that would have pushed a couple of the SOF operators off the helicopter.

"Seeing everything was okay, we got back in the helicopters and took off due west, looking at mountaintops, wadis, whatever, trying to get a trace on the guys who pulled off the ambush. At the top of the hill about two kilometers away, we found this guy—a single ACM fighter. It took me a while; the point man was saying 'He's right there,' and kept pointing behind the tree. Finally I picked him out—he was in the fetal position, lying under some trees in a pretty good hiding position. We observed [that], approximately ten feet away from the guy, there was a backpack with three RPGs sitting on top. So, we knew this was not some sheepherder out there, wandering around with an RPG.

"We could have shot him right then, but he was not doing anything hostile. Our helicopter did a couple of circle passes around him and he still did not respond—he did not do anything. So the team leader said, 'We're putting in Chalk 2 [Reilly's bird] and I want you to go and capture this guy.'

"The Black Hawk leveled off and we set down about four hundred meters northwest of him. I had two AH-64 gunships loitering a little farther out from our insertion point. In addition to the Apaches, I had an A-10 at about seventeen thousand feet; which is not that high, because on the mountain site, I was at eighty-three hundred feet. As soon as we got off the helicopters, I went to radio 'comms,' and I was talking with all the players. All of a sudden, this guy started shooting at us. Instinctively, we started shooting back at him—really, just to put some rounds on him. You know, if someone is going to shoot at you, you shoot back just to put some rounds on them.

"Immediately, I got the AH-64 to start making attacks on his position while the team maneuvered around. This was kind of a long way around, which took them about ten minutes to get there. We were moving pretty fast, maneuvering along the hillsides, which were like fingers on the ridgeline. Once we got within fifty meters, we called off the helicopters because we were going to hit the target ourselves. Me and Nick continued to lay down fire while the team Sergeant and the team chief and medic came in for a flanking movement. Our line of attack was not two distinct groups; it was more like everyone [had] spread out in an arc, closing [in] on the target.

"The farther guys, [with] Sgt Hooper, performed a flanking maneuver on the ACM. We threw a grenade. Nick had two or three grenades, and we launched them over toward the position. I pulled out a fragmentation [frag] grenade, and threw it into that position; right about the same time, the SF team sergeant also threw a 'frag' into the position. As the dust settled, we swept through and found the guy was dead. One of the operators pulled the guy's weapon and we consolidated on the top of the hill.

"I was looking down this eastern finger of the mountain, just scanning the area. You know, there was one guy here for sure, so maybe there [were] more. There, right down from me, about ten feet away, was some clothing—the type typically worn by the fighters. It was just lying on the ground. I was on the radio monitoring my team and on their other frequency, I was monitoring the air in a Peltor headset. So I told them [that] I saw some clothing, [that] I was going to check it out. I got to where the clothing was laying, and probably twenty feet in front of me, there was a guy behind a tree. He popped up and began to fire on me; I returned fire him and killed him. It happened pretty fast.

"I moved farther down the ridge, drawing nearer to the downed ACM fighter. Along with our chalk were four Afghan fighters, and two of the coalition soldiers followed me down to the dead ACM. When we got to him, they started pulling off his gear and such. One of them removed his radio and was trying to give it to me. I told them, 'Don't mess with that; there could be more guys down there.' No sooner had I uttered those words than two more guys began shooting at us from two different spots. I engaged one of the guys—pretty much found him fast enough—shot him before he could shoot us. Because of the amount of fire, I got on the radio and told Dave [that] there were more guys down there.

"Sgt Hooper immediately came down toward our location. He was close . . . we were separated by a mere ten feet . . . and we were engaging these two targets. One was now dead and we were trying to locate the other. At this point, I began working the air to bring in the Apaches to find these guys. However, every time I'd find one, or get close enough to identify the target and get ready to talk an aircraft in on him, we would close the distance and shoot the guy ourselves. From our insertion to this point was about twenty-five minutes. We continued moving down the mountain; about halfway down, we ran into more guys, who fired on us.

"By this time, the Apaches were low on fuel and they had to return to the forward operation base, so the pair of AH-64 gunships returned to FOB Salerno. I rolled the two A-10s down to two thousand feet AGL [above ground level], as I was getting ready to use those guys. Those planes were carrying five-hundred-pound air-burst bombs, which leave a pretty big footprint, plus they were armed with that big 30 mm Gatling gun. It would have been great to run them in from west to east, along the finger of the ridgeline, but that was just not how the mountain worked. In order for them to accomplish the CAS [close air support] we needed, they would have to come in, pop up, and see the target pretty much all at the same time. It would have been difficult, to say the least, so they were put in a holding pattern.

"The A-10s were loitering overhead, and the Apaches were off station, but I still had the two Black Hawks. They came on the radio, saying, 'Hey, if you need us in there, let me know.' I was like, 'Yeah, come on in . . . we can use you.' The Black Hawks have door gunners on either side of the helicopter, and as they come in, they can start firing on the enemy. As we moved down the hill, we were talking to the UH-60, who observed some ACM fighters and engaged them while we continued moving down the hill.

"We were moving down the eastern finger of the ridgeline, and we got to this large rock outcropping. The route around the north side was really steep and rocky, while the other side was not so bad, so Dave decided to move down that side. A couple of things happened while we were at that position. First, down in a wadi, I saw a guy take off, running. He ducked behind a bunch of trees, and I just waited for him to pop out the other side. He popped out the other side, and I shot him a couple times.

"Second, at the same time, Dave started maneuvering down along the right. He came down and around the outcropping, and linked up with me. As soon as he got abreast of me, another ACM appeared. He was about thirty feet away, hunkered down behind a tree, just waiting for us. At this point, Dave and I started engaging this guy. With that guy eliminated, Dave continued to maneuver and yelled over to me, 'Hey, if you're going to stay over there, you better find some cover.' So I backed up a couple feet, looking for something—and there was nothing. And right about that time, the whole hill erupted in fire. There were a half-dozen ACM who had been following the fight as it was coming down the hill toward them. Now, Dave and I were caught as they started laying down some fire. They had a PKM machine gun, RPGs, regular grenades, and AK-47s—all those kinds of weapons.

"I'd been getting shot at all the while I was moving down the hill, though I never really felt like I needed to get down or I needed to find some cover. Now, this was the first point [at which] I felt, 'it's time.' I could feel the rocks and dirt kicking up, hitting my legs and lower body. I lay down and got as small as I could. I looked down at my whole body—what was covered, what wasn't covered. My feet were sitting on top of each other—they were exposed. There was just no other place for me to put them, and then BANG . . . a round went through my right foot.

"I pretty much decided this was not the place to be. I knew what had just happened. I just flipped over, threw myself over a small cliff, landed on my feet, and headed to the tree where Dave was positioned. I lay down next to the ODA team sergeant and said, 'Okay, Dave, I'm hit.' And he replied, 'Yeah, I am, too.' Though both of us had taken hits, he was hit worse than I was. I looked at him, and he had taken round from kneecap to kneecap, and his whole groin was covered in blood. It looked like he had multiple entry and exit wounds. He had a round lodged in one of his M-4 magazines in his armor plate carrier. Then, he set down his helmet and laid it next to him, and I knew he was pretty much out of the fight from that point.

"I got on the radio. I was still on the air, and I let them know what was going on. I also informed the team, bringing them up-to-date on our situation. The team was following us down the hill, but when the firing erupted, it stopped them and isolated us. So for a while, about thirty minutes, it was just Dave and me—no one was coming down to our position. During that time, the two fighters that were following me were off to the side, in a position where they were not taking any fire. I kept yelling over to them to try and get them to open up on the nearest guy. The nearest ACM was about fifteen feet away. I was next to Dave, behind this tree, on my knees; the terrain was such that I could get down and he could not shoot at me. But if I popped up, he had a clear shot at me and he'd get me. So I was trying to get these guys to shoot at him, 'cause they were behind me. And, finally, they started capping off a couple of rounds. Every time they shot, the ACM would return fire because he was in a great position. Finally, they did it enough times that he focused his attention on them, and I popped up as high as I could and shot the guy.

"I was working the aircraft, shooting the ACMs, and in between I was taking stuff out of his [MSgt Hooper's] med kit and tending to his wounds. MSgt Hooper [Dave] had asked several times that he needed me to help him stop the bleeding. The round went through the back of his right leg and snapped his femur, exited, and then hit his left leg and kind of filleted his leg open. I placed a tourniquet on one leg, a pressure dressing on the other leg. I gave him his morphine, took his weapon, and charged it, making sure it was ready to go. I was already halfway through my combat load of eleven magazines; if the engagement was going to last much longer, I would have to begin using Dave's rifle or his magazines.

"At this time, the Black Hawk made contact, telling me [that] there were five ACMs moving toward my position. The shooting had stopped, and they were coming up to find out what had happened. The helicopter came down to take a look, but he got shot up pretty good, so he had to back out, try to observe from a distance, and then come in a little closer. I got on the radio and said, 'Hey, I need you in here right now! These guys are maneuvering up the hill. I need you right now.' The pilot acknowledged my call and responded, 'Okay, put me between you and the bad guys.'

"The helicopters were a conventional unit out of Germany, so the UH-60s were equipped with M-60s. [Our Chalk 2 helo] came in across our position at about fifty feet, and both of its door gunners were standing up on their machine guns, engaging the enemy from both sides of the aircraft. You could see the rounds hitting the helicopter's rotors—it took thirty rounds in the fuselage, alone. His crew chief was shot twice in the chest by an AK-47, but fortunately he had his plates on. The AC [aircraft commander] got on the 'comm' and told me he was shot up pretty good, the crew chief was hit, but he had no problem coming around again. He flipped it around, came back in, engaged, and killed about three more guys. His actions really saved both Dave and my lives, because by this time, these guys would have been on us, five to one.

"Also, while this was happening, Chalk 1 landed in the same spot we were [in]. They began their maneuver, but they were going more slowly than we were, and they got to where the first ACM had been positioned. Instead of going down the eastern finger, they went to the southern region, thinking maybe they could open up a flank. From that flank they could see these five ACMs maneuvering toward Dave and me. While this was happening, Emitt Knight, the 18D [Special Forces medical sergeant] who was with the other team, which was pinned down, finally worked his way down the ridgeline, all the way to Dave and me—this was about thirty minutes into the fight. I can't tell you what a great feeling that was—because he *was* a medic. First, he was going to take good care of Dave, and second, he was not shot or any-thing, so he was another shooter, if needed. Emitt put a tourniquet on Dave's right leg and bandaged up the wounds better than I had done while we were under fire. He was the guy who really started profes-sional care on Dave. He was so attentive to the wounded teammate that I had to reposition him about four or five times. At one point, I pushed his helmet down and said, 'Emitt, you're going to get your head shot off. They're still shooting at you.'

"The fire being directed at us had lessened, for a couple of reasons. For one thing, we had gotten the helicopter to come in a couple times, which suppressed the fire, actually engaging a couple of the ACM fighters. Second, the rest of the team was now firing on the guys, too, so we were defiantly not taking as much incoming fire as we had been. With Emitt now in our position treating Dave, I continued working the air. I got the A-10s, which had been loitering overhead and two more Apaches to come out. After I worked the UH-60s, they were so shot up they had to RTB [return to base] because they were starting to have systems failure. I started working the Apaches. I got two more A-10s to come out, and they sat up at seventeen thousand feet. I did a fighter check-in with them to let them know what was going on.

"We were waiting for a helicopter to pick us up, but there was physically no place for a helo to land. So we called in a MedEvac heli-copter equipped with a hoist. By the time that helicopter arrived, we had been in that position for about three hours—me, Emitt, and Dave. No one was able to make their way down to us, until the MedEvac helo got there. When the helicopter came in, I coordinated a couple things. One, the team and Apaches were going to unload on the enemy position; and two, the medic helo could hoist out Dave.

"He came in and lowered down a dude on a jungle penetrator. This guy threw out a Skedco roll-out litter and placed Dave on it. He hoisted Dave up, came back down, recovered me and Emitt, and they got out of the area. That was it: everyone [ACM] was dead. These ACM were smart fighters—they had dug fighting positions and they had fall-back positions. There equipment was suited for the fight—good radio gear and armored piercing rounds. And they worked in three- to four-man teams.

"When we arrived back to Salerno [FOB], they took off the tourniquets. Of course, Dave crashed; he took seven units of blood. They put a titanium rod in his left leg and he's now back on status. I was hit on the top of the foot, and it exited right below the ankle; the round broke the metatarsal, severing tendons to my toes. I remember [that] I jumped down on that foot and ran a short distance. Emitt did not have to treat me. I was sitting on my foot, and I knew it would fall asleep, so the pain was minimal."

Silver Star

Both MSgt Dave Hooper and TSgt Brad Reilly are back on operational status. For his heroic actions that day, TSgt Bradley Reilly was awarded the Silver Star. The following is the citation to accompany the award.

Technical Sergeant Bradley T. Reilly, United States Air Force, distinguished himself by his exceptionally valorous actions as the Combat Controller from 23rd Special Tactics Squadron assigned to Operational Detachment Alpha 163, Advanced

Operational Base 160, Forward Operational Base 12, the Combined Joint Special Operations Task Force-Afghanistan in support of Operation Enduring Freedom VI on 11 April 2005. The detachment responded to a no-notice air Quick Reaction Force (QRF) in direct support of an Anti Coalition Militia (ACM) ambush. The target was General Khil Baz, the new Border Battalion Commander.

The Khowst-Gardez pass (ambush site) is extremely rugged terrain and is an historical ACM ambush site. The detachment loaded two UH-60 aircraft; TSGT Reilly was in the second aircraft. Upon arrival at the ambush site the detachment was pointed in the direction of ACM egress. Once the aircraft flew over the area, the detachment was able to identify the suspected ACM. TSGT Reilly's' aircraft landed and immediately began receiving a high rate of effective machine gun and small arms fire. The detachment returned fire and assaulted uphill to the enemy position, again while under heavy effective enemy machine-gun fire. The detachment overran the enemy machine gun position through the use of small arms, fragmentary grenades, and 40 mm grenade fire. Once the detachment secured the enemy position, they began to receive an additional high rate of effective fire from three sides. The ACM forces were extremely close, well supplied, well trained, and dedicated allowing them to sustain effective fires against the detachment. The majority of enemy fire was coming from down an extremely steep cliff. Immediately MSGT Hooper and TSGT Reilly assaulted down the cliff in the direction of fire.

During the assault, MSGT Hooper was critically wounded in both legs and TSGT Reilly was hit in the foot. Both were hit by enemy machine gun fire. The enemy machine gun fire was so intense and effective that MSG Hooper and TSGT Reilly were pinned down approximately 100 meters down the cliff and isolated from additional detachment members. Even though TSGT Reilly was shot, he continued to return fire. During the lulls in the heavy machinegun fire, TSGT Reilly treated MSG Hooper's wounds, saving his life, and continued to control the rotary wing and fixed wing aircraft, control fires against the enemy forces (2 x AH-64's, 2 x A-10's, and 2 x UH-60's).

After the AH-64's departed the area, the still motivated enemy attempted to overrun TSGT Reilly and MSGT Hooper's position. TSGT Reilly, additional detachment members, and a UH-60 provided suppressing fire to the advancing enemy forces, forcing them to retreat to cover ending up approximately 50 meters from SSG Knight, MSGT Hooper, and TSGT Reilly's position. TSGT Reilly, provided life saving medical care, controlled aircraft fires, and provided suppressive fires for approximately three hours while being wounded. Throughout this time, they were still receiving effective machine gun fire. At one point, he was willing to have all other USSF move back up hill and call in A-10 ordnance danger close to his position (200M) to save others lives.

Due to the stand-alone actions of TSGT Reilly, his medical expertise, marksmanship skills, and proficiency for controlling aircraft, MSGT Hooper is alive today. The distinctive and life saving actions of Technical Sergeant Reilly reflects great credit upon himself, the Combined Joint Special Operations Task Force-Afghanistan, and the United States Air Force.

Dragons over Iraq

MSgt Justin Rogers, 3rd SOS Predators*

The Air Force Special Operations Command (AFSOC) reactivated the 3rd Special Operations Squadron on October 28, 2005. The 3rd SOS is the first unmanned aerial system squadron in AFSOC and is known as the "Dragons," its name derived from the Vietnam-era AC-47 "Puff the Magic Dragon" gunships. Since its reactivation, the 3rd SOS has become one of the most sought after air assets in Operations Enduring Freedom and Iraqi Freedom. By deploying the MQ-1 Predator unmanned aerial vehicle (UAV), it brings all elements into play as special operations forces (SOF) teams hunt down a wary and elusive enemy. The Predator allows the acquisition of real-time target data, transmitted back and forth between the UAV, Command and Control, the Special Tactics Squadron (STS) on the ground, and or-biting AC-130 gunships or other close air support (CAS) platforms.

Master Sergeant Justin Rogers was one of the original eleven

*Name changed for security reasons.

AFSOC personnel who volunteered for the Predator unit. He gave a brief overview of the history of the 3rd SOS: "In 2005, Lieutenant General Wooley, the AFSOC commander, was able to get an AFSOC permanent squadron—rather basically, being able to build one. Most of the Predators are run by the intelligence community. At that time, manning was pretty low and the intel community could not support a lot of the manning that Lieutenant General Wooley needed. So he saw fit to stand up a unit for combat operations. And also, knowing the enlisted aircrews very well, he spoke highly about [how] he wanted to build his unit from the ranks, for the flight engineers, gunners, operators from AFSOC units.

"We started doing operations even before that [time], with ACC [Air Combat Command] units, flying their assets and using their control stations. [Based on] the success of some of the stuff we did, the Air Force is now pushing to have enlisted aircrew members fly the Predators. Just for a simple fact, we are able to react quicker when situations develop, falling back on training we . . . had prior to coming to the UAV unit."

The MQ-1 Predator is a medium-altitude, long-endurance, remotely piloted UAV aircraft. The MQ-1's primary mission is interdiction and conducting armed reconnaissance against critical, perishable targets. The Predator provides the SOF area of operations with a continual reconnaissance, surveillance, target acquisition and strike capability without risking a manned aircraft. Operational control of the UAV can be performed in theater or operated from within the continental United States. The basic crew for the Predator is one pilot and one sensor operator. They fly the aircraft from inside the ground control station via a line-of-sight data link or a satellite data link for beyond line-of-sight flight. Officially called the Mobile Ground Control Station, it is affectionately known as "Dumpster." All members of the Predator control and support team are assigned to AFSOC. The personnel who operate the Predators are called pilots—and, yes, there are women on the Predator team.

The Predator UAV is much more than an airplane; it is a war-fighting system. An operational system includes four UAVs (with sensors), a ground control station, and a Predator primary satellite link. The Predator is equipped with a color nose camera that is generally used by the pilot for flight control, a day variable-aperture TV camera, a variable-aperture infrared (IR) camera used for low- light and night viewing, and a synthetic aperture radar (SAR) that allows the crew to observe through smoke, clouds, or haze. The cameras produce full-motion video while the SAR produces still-frame radar images.

The Predator UAV also includes an ARC-210 radio; an APX-100 IFF/SIF with Mode 4; and an upgraded Rotax 914F four-cylinder engine, turbo-charged engine providing thrust of 115 horsepower. The latest upgrade is the addition of a low-light TV (LLTV) and the ability to "fuse" sensors into one image; this allows the sensor operator to overlay a LLTV image or digital television (DTV) image over an IR picture.

The MQ-1 Predator UAV provides the Special Tactics team an extra set of eyes on the target. The UAV allows the acquisition of real-time data that can be transmitted between the Predator pilot and the team on the ground, as well as to other CAS aircraft, such as an AC-130 gunship. In addition to the intel, the UAV is a capable ordnance platform. *Courtesy of the U.S. Air Force.*

The MQ-1 Predator is a "killer scout" as well; the system is fitted with a multi-spectral targeting system with inherent AGM-114 Hellfire missile targeting capability. It integrates the electro-optical, infrared, laser designator, and laser illuminator into a single sensor package. This aircraft can employ two laser-guided Hellfire anti-tank missiles with the multispectral targeting system (MTS) ball.

The latest UAV coming on line with AFSOC is the MQ-9 Reaper. While the MQ-1 was a reconnaissance UAV turned hunter, the MQ-9 was born and bred as a "hunter killer." That is, the Reaper is designed to hunt down high-value targets and destroy time-sensitive targets with persistence and precision. The MQ-9 is a completely different aircraft twice as fast, it can also fly twice as high and can carry fifteen times the external payload. The primary mission of the Predator is armed reconnaissance; though the full combat load of a MQ-9 will vary depending on the munitions selected, it will carry up to fourteen AGM-114 missiles, as well as laser-guided bombs such as the GBU-12 Paveway II.

The introduction of the UAV has brought an additional level to the vertical battlespace—that is, joining the B-52s, AC-130s, helicopters, and close air support. The Predator team explained: "De-confliction with manned aircraft is a top priority. In theater, we communicate with [the] Control and Reporting Center and are assigned altitudes, just like any other aircraft. If necessary, we can move to allow strike aircraft to engage targets."

The commander of the 3rd Special Operations Squadron, Lieutenant Colonel Paul Calitgirone, stated: "The unit has been involved in more than three hundred operations and provided persistent intelligence coverage for more than four hundred objectives, resulting in over eleven hundred enemies [being] detained or killed in action, sixty-three of whom were high-value individuals. In 2006, with an average of only fourteen line crews and two borrowed aircraft, the 3rd SOS flew as many combat hours as the rest of AFSOC combined." As a result, plans include significant expansion of the Predator operations for the coming years, and some of that support will be dedicated to

SOF operations. AFSOC, as the air component of USSOCOM, maintains a close relationship with the command's SOF ground components. This personal level of relationship is an important ingredient for effective operations. Fielding a Predator force structure within AFSOC represents the quickest, most cost-effective, most supportable, and most sustainable means of providing full motion video (FMV) support to SOF units on the ground.

MSgt Rogers described the process of flying a Predator: "The actual UAV is physically located at an air base in theater—for example, Afghanistan or Iraq. There, it is maintained by a crew. They launch the aircraft and then I grab it through the satellites. The airplane is flown from Nellis AFB in Nevada through satellite control. Worth noting, the 3rd SOS is moving to Cannon, and will be there by the time this book is published. All my missions were flown from Nellis, using satellites—very few of the missions are flown by people who are actually in the theater. We have control stations—we call them 'trash dumpsters' because that is about what they look like. Each one of them controls an airplane, and we all have a command structure that is on the location, which we work through. Every Predator can be armed, but not every UAV is armed."

"The 'crew' is a pilot and a sensor operator, which is my assigned task. One of the things about the Predator right now is that it is not a major weapon system, so you do not have people on a career path as you would in an F-16 unit. For example, when they come out of the Air Force Academy, they get assigned to an F-16 squadron, get trained, and stay with the squadron until they want to change out. You get volunteers and people who 'get volunteered' to fly Predators, and they do it for three years, maybe four maximum, then they go back to whatever they were flying before. Right now, that in itself creates its own dilemma—having an all-volunteer force that gets smart, experienced, and then moves on to a new assignment. We pass along good info, and it's actually working out well, and the Air Force is adjusting accordingly.

"The [Predator] can fly for almost an entire day, so you never have one crew flying the entire mission. If there is a raid ongoing, and it is time to swap out a crew, the original crew stays on until the new crew no longer requires the expertise of the first guys. . . . Most of the time you can swap out, and there is not a problem.

"The UAV is in the theater, and the pilot and sensor operator is flying it from CONUS; which brings its own problems. [Say,] you are flying the mission when you have to kill a bunch of people and then have to go home to your family. When you are overseas, there is that buffer between combat and home. You have stuff channeled and compartmentalized; you have time to decompress. [But] operating stateside is different—you know you have to go home and deal with the lawn, work on the car, or take the kids to daycare, and also have to focus on the mission. Its one of the few jobs in the Air Force for which you really need to have a light switch to turn it on and off, [to switch] between combat work and home life. A lot of people say UAVs are the future, [but] they are not the future, they are now. And this has been happening for a while. I do everything the same [here] as I do when I am actually flying—the only difference is [that] my butt is on the ground. I still have to have battlespace awareness—I have to keep the aircraft away from other aircraft. I still have to make sure the good guys are in the right spot, and that the bad guys I'm about to kill are actually bad guys and not good guys. You interject a whole new group of issues when you are seven thousand miles away, flying an unmanned aircraft. It is an unmanned airplane, but it is *not* an unmanned system. You still have aircrew flying it."

Regarding that vertical battlefield, or airspace, that MSgt Rogers mentioned, he added: "We actually work with a number of systems. When you are flying the airplane through a satellite link, it is just like flying the plane there, in the theater. It is true [that] I cannot look out the window, but most of the time [when I'm actually in a plane], I can only look at the target because we are busy with what is going down with that target. [So, this way, too,] I am not able to physically look out for airplanes, but I *am* able to look at them electronically—the radar returns and systems like that. We get a lot of info from radar down range through the Internet's figuring out where other aircraft are positioned. We also have the radio that works on the UAV. That is just like being in the aircraft itself. When I talk, my voice is transmitted through the airplane and I can talk to any other agency, just as if I were in the airplane. So, if there is an STS team or Special Forces ODA on the ground, I can communicate with them. From seven thousand miles away, it sounds like I am directly overhead. My voice is, but I'm not."

✫   ✫   ✫   ✫

The Predators of the 3rd SOS are making an impact on the war against terrorism, as MSgt Rogers recounted one of his missions in support of Operation Iraqi Freedom: "This was in the spring of 2006. One of the things the Predator is really good at is keeping a watch for the bad guys. You always hear the coined phrase of the 'unblinking eye,' and that kind of stuff. We are really good at this, as the airplane can fly for an extremely long time. We can sit on top of someone's house and see who comes and goes—the types of vehicles and that kind of stuff. If we can figure out where somebody lives, we are able to get a lot of intel. This can provide information that will determine whether we want to raid a house or not.

"We were going on a lot of raids because we had intel that led us to a particular house. Tracking insurgents is kind of like hunting drug dealers. You can capture a drug dealer on the side of the street, but you really want to capture the guy he is talking to. Once we found a couple of bad guys, we then kept eyes on them and saw who they were talking with—who came and talked with them. We could not get into too much detail, but we were able to start discerning whether that guy's house needed to get raided, or whether we needed to wait and follow that individual.

"With all of the raids we were doing, a pattern began [to emerge] whereby afterwards we kept going to this one house. Now, this place was out in the middle of nowhere. There was a canal running beside it, and every time we went to this house after a raid, we would never see anything. Never saw any people, dogs, cats—nothing . . . and that's not normal; it's not normal to not see anything going on in a house. We sat on that house for a long time—probably over a month. Every time we went on a raid, we would go [back] to that house; after a while, it became a joke. During one op, we had been supporting a unit on the ground. Toward the end of the mission, they seemed not to know what to do with us. We still had a few hours of fuel left, so we joked—'Okay, they don't know what to do with us so they are sending us to the "penalty house." [As if they were saying,] 'You guys go stare at that house and we're going to go eat lunch.' We still took the job seriously, still even if was just observing this house, but it got to a point when, you are not even seeing a cat wandering around the building, you start to wonder, 'Okay, really, how important is this house?' A long time went by and we were still staring at this house. It was just going to be one of those days, we called it; the raid was over, so we knew where we were going, and—sure as hell—that is where we went.

"I was on this house for about five minutes, and we saw a rabbit running around; we think, "Wow, that was a big deal.' We actually called some people over to come take a look, because everyone had been sent to this house—it was not just me and the pilot, but pretty much just about everyone in the squadron had been sitting over this house. It was a running joke. So when we saw the rabbit, we got a big kick out it.

"Then, about five minutes later, an elderly gentleman and about a seven-year-old girl showed up with about a half dozen sheep. So, then we were really ecstatic because there *was* something going on. A big open field was on two sides of the house. The guy sent the sheep out to the field, and sent the little girl into the house. The house had a wall that covered two sides of the yard. After a while, the older gentleman also went in and then came back out. He and the girl gathered up the sheep and left. That was one of the things we thought was pretty odd. We had not seen anything, and then we see all kinds of activity. The fact that he had sent the little girl in, and then he went in to check the place out and then leaves—this was out of the norm. About twenty minutes later, a number of cars showed up. A couple of guys got out of the vehicles and went in the house. They came back out and opened the trunks of the cars and began taking things out.

"At some of the ranges we fly we cannot make out everything, because we do not want the insurgents to know we are there. There are times when we stand off far enough that they cannot hear us but we can see them. [This was one of those times.] We saw that they were moving a lot of stuff, but we could not make out what it was. Now, a Toyota van showed up and the same thing started up again. Guys started to pile out of the van. They started opening all the doors and the hatch on the back of the van. Another car showed up, dropped off a couple guys and some other items as well. That car ended up leaving, but we stayed on the house.

"At that time, the unit that we had been supporting thought that these events were important enough to carry out a raid on this house, too. They started getting everything together to conduct the raid. I believe by now that there were seven bad guys at this house. When we started watching, they were stuffing a lot of objects into the van. They were carrying quite a few heavy objects and putting them into the back of the van. At the time, it was thought that they were trying to make a vehicle-borne IED [improvised explosive device]."

A vehicle-borne IED, or VBIED, is an improvised explosive device that uses a car, van, truck, or other vehicle as the conveyance of a bomb. For example, a compact car may contain up to five hundred pounds of explosives, a van can contain up to four thousand pounds, and a large semi-trailer truck can hold upwards of sixty thousand pounds of explosives. These explosive devices have also been found in donkey carts and emergency vehicles, and have been used to attack U.S., coalition, and Iraqi forces.

MSgt Rogers continued with his story: "What we found out later was that this was actually a safe house that the bad guys were using to help make IEDs. Prior to this, nobody was one hundred percent positive that the building was being used for that. There was some information regarding this location—that's why we kept going back there. It was supposedly being used as a base of operations to retaliate against coalition forces—to strike back [periodically]. We were still watching the house as the unit we were supporting was getting their helicopters together.

"In the very beginning, we did not have a good working relationship with the supported unit. They had been working a lot with the other Predator units (from other government agencies), and so they did not know how much they could trust us. So a lot of information was not being passed on to us; we usual found things out as the information unfolded in front of us. We had found out pretty late in the game that U.S. helicopters were going to show up at the house. [In fact,] the supported unit told us about five minutes before they got there that the helicopters were coming.

"We helped those guys a lot, making sure they would go directly to the house. The radio plays an important role in these types of missions. If something happens, we can communicate with the friendly forces to ensure they are going to the right house. Normally, we hardly ever have to say anything. On this particular incident, there were a lot of houses, but they were scattered—all looked alike and most of them were near a canal. It was not that the pilots were confused, but the first group of helicopters flew by the house. We knew something was happening when we saw the people at the house start running around and bumping into each other when they heard the helicopters coming.

"We zoomed out on the video and saw the first group of helicopters pass by. We got on the radio and told them, 'Hey, you're flying by the house . . . it is going by the right side.' What we did know was that there was a second group of helicopters [coming]. And what was funny, if you can call it that; was [that] the bad guys did *not* know there was a second group of helicopters coming in on them. Two guys ran, trying to get away from the house. One of the helicopter pilots heard the radio call, saw the bad guys running around in the open, and was able to make an extremely hard turn, then strafe those guys in the open and kill them. [We came] to find out later [that] the two guys were wearing suicide vests.

"The first helicopters came back and the team actually did a raid on the house. They went in and cleared the house of the other five insurgents. Two more of the guys were also wearing suicide vests, so you have four out of seven guys fitted with suicide vests, preparing to head out. What you see is [that] they go to a large gathering, a marketplace and such, and blow themselves up—that is their way of retaliating. So we got four guys there, and we found out from the team on the ground that the van was indeed rigged as a VBIED.

"The team on the ground decided [that] they were going to level the house, and [they] prepared to set demolition charges inside the building. There had been a bunch of kids running around, but they never had gone into the house. There was another house that we knew had kids nearby, about three hundred meters. That was where those two bad guys were running toward when they ware strafed. The fact those guys had suicide vest on—well, the whole nature of the situation is you do not want to mess with a guy wearing a vest with a lot of explosives on it.

The unit on the ground placed charges on the bodies to ensure that all the ordnance on the vests was expended. This [meant] that no one else could use the vest, as well as making sure [that] there would be no collateral damage from the vests. We got word that the team was going to level the house, and to be prepared to see a big explosion. The house was leveled, and the bodies with the suicide vests blew up in the field five seconds later.

"The next matter at hand was the explosive-packed vehicle. At first, we were going to shoot the van, but there was concern with the amount of explosives—that it might damage the helos as it detonated. So it was decided we would shoot the van with a Hellfire. The helicopters flew in and strafed one of the cars. The car blew up, hitting the van, which in turn blew up the van, which [landed] in the canal about forty feet away. So, as it turned out, we played a major role in making sure those guys did not harm any civilians that day. . . . We did not have to watch that house anymore."

| C H A P T E R |
12

Spectre, Owning
the Night

Major Colin Duer, 16th SOS

The AC-130H Spectre gunship, which is armed with a 40 mm Bofors gun and 105 mm howitzer cannon, can deliver precision firepower in support of close air support (CAS) missions. This includes
alternate missions: air interdiction; armed reconnaissance; airbase,
perimeter, and point defense; land, water, and heliborne troop escort;
drop, landing, and extraction zone support; forward air control; limited airborne command and control; and combat search and rescue
(CSAR) support.

Heavily armed, the AC-130H incorporates port-side-firing
weapons integrated with sophisticated sensor, navigation, and fire-
control systems to provide surgical firepower or area saturation during extended periods, primarily at night and in inclement weather.
Included in the sensor array are low-light television (LLTV) and infrared (IR) sensors. The H-model is also equipped with radar and

electronic devices that give the gunship a positive Identify Friend/Foe (IFF) to distinguish between supporting friendly ground forces and efficient delivery of ordnance on hostiles during all weather conditions. Navigation devices include an inertial navigation system and GPS.

The AC-130H is powered by four Allison T56-A15 turboprop engines that provide the aircraft with a thrust of 4,910 in equivalent shaft horsepower, giving the gunship a speed of 300 miles per hour. It has a range of approximately 2,200 nautical miles, or unlimited miles with the capability of aerial refueling, and has a ceiling of 30,000 feet. Unlike the newer U-model gunship, the AC-130H is not pressurized, which means that the crew is required to use oxygen—or, as they call it, "sucking on the hose."

The Spectre gunship has a crew of thirteen, which includes five officers (pilot, co-pilot, navigator, fire control officer, and electronic warfare officer) and nine enlisted (flight engineer, LLTV operator, IR

The AC-130H gunship known as the Spectre. The twin 20 mm chain cannons have been removed from the H-model, as can be seen in the space located just aft of the crew hatch. The aircraft still retains the 40 mm Bofors and 105 mm Howitzer cannons. *Courtesy of the U.S. Air Force.*

detection operator, four gunners, and a loadmaster). Major Colin Duer is the fire control officer on an AC-130H Spectre gunship with the 16th Special Operations Squadron (SOS) in support of Operation Enduring Freedom, Southwest Asia.

Major Duer described his role: "I am responsible for the geometry of the aircraft and its orbit. In terms of altitude, I am in charge of directing the sensor operators' getting the proper gun on the proper target with the proper ammunition. I have the best situational awareness as the offensive coordinator of the aircraft 'cause I am the one directing all the visual sensors and the gun crews as to what sort of ammunition we should use. There are a number of checks and balances on the aircraft, so no one person can just 'go rogue' and shoot the round off. What happens in the main mode of shooting is called 'automatic trainable.' That gun will train or move as that particular sensor is looking at it. For example, I can 'marry up' the 105 with an infrared sensor or the 40 with a TV sensor, or vice versa, and the guns will move where that sensor is looking."

☆   ☆   ☆   ☆

Major Duer related two interconnected operations that took place in the spring of 2006, while his squadron was deployed in Afghanistan: "We were tasked to support some forces going in to capture a high-ranking Taliban commander. In the initial op, there was a small team observing an area; [the area] was a compound with about eight buildings. To the south, about two hundred meters, [was] a dry riverbed; toward the north, right next to the compound, was a large wall with a road and a big line of trees. Also to the north were a lot of fields, hedgerows—a typical agricultural area.

"The small team of operators called us in as soon as they were on the ground to get eyes on the objective. We were the only asset that night for this op. Initially, we observed fifteen to twenty individuals in the compound. There were several people in sleeping bags; others were walking back and forth from building to building. The team called us in immediately to provide them with fire support. They were positioned to the east of the objective, and they had just come under heavy machine-gun fire. We observed [that] they were taking fire from the eastern side of the compound. We saw a lot of personnel whom we had identified to the team earlier; the enemy was running around, and it looked like they were setting up some positions one hundred to two hundred meters south, adjacent to the riverbed. Initially, we thought the team was going to call us in to fire on those personnel, so we loaded a 'prox round' into the 105 mm." The major explained that a 'prox,' or proximity round, is designed for anti-personnel. Basically, it is ammunition that explodes above the ground, dispersing large amounts of shrapnel. It is what is used to take out soft targets. They also had high explosive (HE) rounds that explode on contact, and some that were designed especially to destroy buildings.

He continued with his story: "We loaded a 'prox round' into the pipe, thinking that was what the team was going to request. Then they shifted our fire to a small shack—just a little bit bigger than an out-house—that they had been taking heavy machine-gun fire from. I did not want to take the time to switch out the round, so we just shot the 'prox round' since we had seen four individuals right next to the shack on the western side. We took them out, and then we swapped out to a round that destroyed the building.

"At this point, there was a lot of activity on the ground. They [U.S. commanders] were going to send in a couple of helicopters full of SOF [Special Operations Forces] personnel to assault the compound and try to capture the Taliban commander. The helicopters were coming in from the south, but the landing zones were too hot, so they passed overhead of the objective. The helos eventually landed just to the north, so [that] their personal were coming in from the north, going to the south through the field and hedgerows and on to the objective.

"By now, it was obvious chaos on the ground. We were calling out the position of enemy personnel that we saw on the ground, as well as monitoring the friendlies coming in from the various directions. The team tried to set up positions to cordon off the area but when they were coming down, one of their guys on the northern side of the compound was shot in the leg. All this time we were trying to cover them, but they were now in close proximity to the enemy forces.

"While all this was playing out, we got an urgent call from some of our guys on the ground just to the north, saying that they were taking fire. They were behind a wall orientated north-south; they were positioned on the eastern side, taking fire from the west. When we got overhead, we heard their frantic calls coming in over the radio; they were screaming, yelling, and shooting their weapons, all at the same time. We picked up some heat signatures twenty-five meters from their position. Normally, they would mark it with some type of laser pointer or similar device mounted on their weapons, but this was so close that they marked it with a fragmentation grenade. What we did [was try] to eliminate any collateral damage after they called us for a 'danger close' fire mission of twenty-five meters."

As Major Duer explained, "danger close" is when the rounds are so close that the [troops] are willing to accept the risk of any collateral damage that might occur from our weapons." Calling in a fire mission as "danger close" can be done by the team on the ground; other times, though, the call may be made by the fire control officer on the gunship. Major Duer explained: "The team may have eyes on somebody who is really close, and they might immediately call for 'danger close.' But oftentimes we can identify the team and the enemy position and tell them how far away the enemy is from them, and then let them know if that is 'danger close' or not."

"At this point, we caught heat signatures twenty-five meters away, which I can tell you is very, very close. The team needed the fire, so what we did was, I shot with the 40 mm. I walked the rounds in from the opposite direction as safely as possible, and that way we could also make sure the rounds were going to be on target. Sometimes we put rounds down just to break contact, but this time they were so close we put rounds in all around that area twenty-five meters from them. They were able to protect themselves somewhat by hiding behind the wall.

"After we had taken care of that target for those guys, they wanted to make a hasty exfil from that hot area. We noticed, and had been calling this down all night, that there were a large group of enemy personnel from the objective who were massing up and heading toward the north. The team was still taking some sporadic fire from the buildings as they were trying to exfil. They were setting up a landing zone just to the east from where they originally were when they came onto the objective. So, they called us in to do fifty-meter 'danger close' fire missions on the buildings with the 105. We figured that that was too close and asked them to push back some. We loitered until we were out of gas, taking care of the rest of the buildings in the compound, as requested by the ground party. [Then] they could do a safe exfil and get their wounded out of there—that was it for *that* night."

☆   ☆   ☆   ☆

A couple of nights later, the aircrew of the AC-130H Spectre gunship would be on station again for another night operation. Major Duer continued: "The Task Force decided they wanted to send in another ground team or another ground force to take care of the Taliban in the area and the compound from where they were operating. They wanted to take care of those forces that were being track by various assets.

"At this point, they had been tracking this column that had nearly a hundred personnel—all bad guys. The op was set up. We were all loitering, and then they sent in the A-10s for a couple of gun runs on the enemy column. The A-10s got a few of them, and then they called in the two gunships. We flew in formation with each other, both using our dual-target attack capabilities." The fire control system provides the capability whereby two targets up to one kilometer apart can simultaneously be engaged by two different sensors, using two different guns. Dual-target attack capability means that the gunship is able to track both the 40 mm and the 105 mm projectiles and return pinpoint-impact locations to the crew for subsequent adjustment to the target.

The major explained: "Picture two gunships overhead, both firing 105 and 40s. We pretty much took care of all of those forces that had scattered. All the while we were overhead, engaging targets, the enemy ground forces started shooting up at us with whatever weapons they had. Nothing touched us, but they did start shooting at us. Our scanners identified incoming fire from the enemy ground forces. So, our aircraft peeled off to go get some gas, while the other aircraft prepared the landing zone with some pre-assault fire to make sure it would be clear for the helicopters to land and infil the Special Forces ground element." According the AFSOC sources, the AC-130H would RTB [return to base] where it would be refueled and rearmed, if necessary. The ground crews had their routine down pat and performed a quick turn-around, getting the gunships back on station.

Major Duer continued: "We came back on station, and were overhead just as the SF team was setting up all its positions around theses compounds, so as to clear out all the Taliban. At this time, the other Spectre went off station to go refuel. As we arrived overhead, the SF personal had set up in five different positions, and had started taking fire from the buildings and enemy personnel in the fields. Let me just say that it was chaos on the battlefield there. We immediately started taking these fire missions and interdicting the enemy personnel that the teams were requesting. We were called in to destroy several buildings and some compounds from where heavy fire was originating. Right in the middle of the battlefield, there were people running everywhere. We identified a couple of those running as a family; we could tell from our sensors that it was two adults and a child in the middle. We ascertained that they were not doing anything hostile—they were just running to get out of there. We marked their position with one of our laser pointers and identified them. We then called down to the SF team, telling them what we had, what we saw, and we directed that team to the family so they could get them out of there safely. In the middle of the fighting and chaos, we were able to get this family out of harm's way, and that made us feel pretty good.

"We continued taking the calls for fire from the SF team. At one point they wanted to destroy a building with some A-10s that was really close to one of their positions. We thought that was pretty close to be dropping bombs, so we voiced our opinion, [indicating] that [we thought it] would be too close, which could result in possible fratricide [considering] the type of munitions they were carrying; instead, we put ourselves out there and said we would destroy the building to maximize the safety of friendly ground forces. We destroyed that position for them and things started to quiet down.

Major Duer explained: "The SF teams were trying to conduct some SSE [sensitive site exploitation] when they encountered sporadic gunfire, but [it was] nothing they could not handle." Sensitive site exploitation, or SSE, involves a related series of activities performed inside a captured site to exploit personnel documents, electronic data, and material found at the site, while neutralizing any threat posed by the site itself or its contents. In application, this is a source of on special military, diplomatic, economic, or information that is helpful for the United States. The sites include factories with technical data on enemy weapon systems, locations of war crimes, critical hostile-government facilities, areas suspected of containing persons of high rank in a hostile government or organization, terrorist money-laundering operations, and document storage areas for secret police forces. These activities exploit personnel, documents, electronic data, and material captured at the site, while neutralizing any threat posed by the site or its contents. While the physical process of exploiting the sensitive site begins at the site itself, full exploitation may involve teams of experts located around the world.

"The SF team did direct us near the end of the op, right before the helos were suppose to come in for their exfil. During the middle-of-the-night ops there was a lot of fire going on. We kept ten of our 105 rounds in reserve just in case, since we were running low on ammo, as was the other AC-130H with us. At the end of the op, the team decided we should start shooting the ammo and arms cache. They had found a bunch of enemy weapons, explosives—you name it, and it was in there. We started to put rounds down, and they called for a ceasefire because the helos were coming in. One of the most important things we can do is protect our helicopters when they are coming down.

"As the helos were landing, we noticed a large number of Taliban reinforcements coming out of a building adjacent to the arms cache. We called info down, and immediately our guys on the ground said destroy it, as they did not want the helo shot down when they were packed full of people. We were the only aircraft left with 105s, so we went in with our dual-target attack capability and destroyed all of those enemy reinforcements and the arms cache together.

"Upon the exfil, the helos got out okay, with zero friendly casualties. We had also managed to get some civilians out of there. That night, we had conducted twelve fire missions and used up every round of ammunition; as did the other AC-130H gunship. By the end of the night, the SF team had attributed approximately forty to fifty enemy

KIA [killed in action] to our crew's [work], and we destroyed six enemy compounds."

The McKay Trophy

The OpTemp (operational tempo) is always high among AFSOC
units, and the gunship aircrews are no exception. For their action during this mission, the crew of Major Duer's AC-130H was nominated
for the McKay Trophy, which is presented exclusively to flying crews
of the U.S. Air Force. The award is for the most meritorious flight of
the year, and they won it at the AFSOC command level for 2006.

13

Operation Medusa

MSgt Mike West

Operation Medusa was a NATO operation whose mission was to remove the Taliban threat and provide stability in the Panjaway district of Kandahar. In September 2006, Special Forces joined with NATO International Security Assistance Forces (ISAF) that included the Royal Canadian Regiment Battle Group, a company from the U.S. Army 10th Mountain Division, and a battalion from the Afghan National Army (ANA). The ISAF deployed to an area just west of Kandahar that was heavily controlled by the Taliban. Intelligence reports estimated a Taliban force of about a thousand fighters in the area. Having just taken over the operations in Afghanistan, it was the wish of NATO to clean up the area. Panjaway had become a safe haven for the Taliban, and it was known to be a staging area from where the Taliban could launch attacks on Kandahar. The enemy would make its hits and then move back to the safety of this area. It was a very important and strategic place for the Taliban, and it was necessary for the U.S. and coalition forces to clean it up.

The SOF mission called for the Regional Command South to isolate and disrupt Taliban activity in the vicinity of Zahre-Panjaway in order to maintain freedom of movement on Highway 1 and the security of the city of Kandahar. The plan called for NATO conventional forces to sweep through the Panjaway area, moving west to east. U.S. special operations forces (SOF) would be positioned in the southern part of the area. There were three Special Forces Operations Detachments Alpha (ODAs 326, 331, and 336) and a command detachment of the 3rd Special Forces Group (Airborne) tasked for this mission. Combat Controller MSgt Mike West of the 23rd Special Tactics Squadron, AFSOC, would be responsible for providing close air support (CAS) for these SF teams.

MSgt West and the ODAs inserted into their area of operations using the SF ground mobility vehicle (GMV). This is a modified version of the HMMWV, outfitted with enhanced features that make it suited for SOF missions. For example, it has an improved helicopter transportability and extended range, and some models are equipped with auxiliary fuel tanks. The GMV is also fitted with a multipurpose rack for mounting communications equipment. It can provide a DC power system as well as an on-board 115 volt AC power inverter. The vehicle has GPS navigation, air compressor, optimized equipment stowage, extra-rugged tires, and skid plates. Adding to crew survivability, the GMV has been modified with rolls bars, side bars, and a smoke-grenade launching system.

Additional offensive modifications to the GMV have included installation of several weapons mounts to the vehicle. These multiposition mounts provide the SOF personnel with greater firepower and lethality, making the vehicle capable of deploying a large variety of weapons (for example, the M2 .50 caliber machine gun, M240B 7.62 mm machine gun, MK19 grenade launcher, AT-4 and LAW antitank weapons, and the Carl Gustav 84 mm anti-tank weapon). This GMV now bristling with an assortment of weapon systems has earned a new moniker, the "gun truck."

Regarding these gun trucks, MSgt West explained: "We drive the GMV and the ANA drive their Ranger-type pickup trucks. We drove from the base and rallied with the other ANA team, and then roadmarched to the mountain. We have a lot of latitude on equipment and placement; most of it is personal preference. Your area on the gun truck is *your* area, so ten guys will set it up ten different ways although there are some things we do like to keep standardized. The SF team leader would say, when carrying sensitive items or med gear, that it goes specifically here or there; that was SOP, so that when training together with the SF, we know where the other guy's blowout kit, etc., is located. I always had water stacked up next to me in the truck. I did use a Camelback, which I had attached to my vest. If I knew I was going to do some dismounted stuff, I'd fill it up; but normally, working out of the truck, I just had a bunch of water bottles stacked up beside me.

MSgt West provided a picture of his setup: "I sat in back of the vehicle and manned the M240B. With me were my personal weapon, radio 'ruck,' and twelve hundred rounds of 7.62 for the M240B. There was a Carl Gustav sitting next to me, which I could quickly hand the gunner. All of the weapons and ammo were readily accessible. My M4 sat in the gun truck, 'round in back behind the M240. There was a time

MSgt Mike West, of the 23rd Special Tactics Squadron, takes his assigned position on the Special Forces gun truck. Attached to the ODA to provide CAS, MSgt West is part of the team and has carried out other tasks in addition to his role as combat controller— such as pulling security. *Courtesy of the U.S. Air Force.*

when I had to shoot the M240, and another engagement when I shot almost a thousand rounds of that thing because I had no air support at the time—it all depends on what is going on at the time.

"My primary weapon is the radio. I carried a 117 and I had two hand-held PRC-148 MBITR radios in my vest. When I was walking around the mountain, I used one to talk with the aircraft and the other to talk with the team leader; in case we got separated. It was very important that I communicated with the aircraft and with my team. One, it gave me the picture of what was [happening] on the ground, hearing everybody including the team leader, if I need to talk with him. Two, it was my responsibility to brief him on how to utilize the aircraft and it's the team leader's ultimate decision on how to use the aircraft. Being able to communicate with him, twenty-four hours, seven days a week, is very important. Most of the time, I was next, to him. We were joined at the hip, doing things; but if not, if I was in the back of the vehicle, then we [would] talk on the radio.

"Some guys carry one [radio]. I was a big fan of two, because I [would] carry two on a vest which made me more mobile. I could have one to talk with an aircraft that is right above me and one to talk with the team. Or use both to talk with the aircraft. Having two radios was great—if one started to die or the battery went dead, I just switched over to the other in a couple of seconds. My sidearm was usually tucked in my back pack. I normally did not carry it with me, as I wanted to be more mobile. When I did carry the pistol, it was attached to my vest, where it was more accessible when I was in the vehicle, plus I didn't like [having] things hanging on my hip. Occasionally, I liked to have the gun on, so I could look down and see it. Another useful item attached to my vest was the viper light, IR and green light, which could be steady or blinking."

MSgt West related his part in the operation: "Our position for the three ODAs was to sit in the south part of the area of operations to wait while the NATO forces swept across. We were there to keep the Taliban forces from retreating south. [That is,] we were a sitting force, not so much a battle force; we were there to support the NATO troops. My position with the teams was as the Joint Terminal Attack Controller (JTAC) to support the forces with all CAS. The CAS included all types of aircraft: Predators, B-1 bombers, A-10s, F-16s, Apaches, any coalition aircraft, which included the GR7s—the GR7 is a variant of the RAF Harrier II Jump Jet. It didn't matter which aircraft was on station; I was there to offer them any type of air support. That was my job, and I always kept an eye on that, especially at night when we worked with the AC-130 gunships.

"On September 2, 2006, we began the operation. The NATO forces were to start their operation, but they ran into a lot of trouble, a lot of resistance with improvised explosive devices [IEDs], heavy machine-gun fire, and small arms, and they were stopped in their tracks. Their vehicles were taking hits, and they had a lot of casualties from attacks by the Taliban, who had been laying in wait for them. The NATO forces were forced to pull back.

"At that point, we were going to take more action in our area in the south and move a little bit farther north into the area of operations. As we wanted to go north, the Taliban were watching us, too. They had successfully stopped the NATO forces and they wanted to stop us as well. So we decided to move north. There was a small hilltop that we wanted to get up on, [from] which . . . we could see over the entire AO, which was fairly flat. This hilltop is known as Sperwan Ghar, located forty miles southwest of Kandahar. It was a great advantage; we could oversee the area and see what was going on. As we were moving toward the hill, we received contact and were forced to retreat to a stronghold to refit/recover and analyze the situation.

"On September 5, we decided to take the hill. We rolled up to the hill, which was still in the southern part of the AO. The ODA-326 went up the southwest side, ODA-331 drove up the center, and ODA-336 was at the end of the convoy. At the base of the hill was the SF command detachment, where Major Jared Hill, 3rd Group, was in command of the SF element. As we rolled up to the hill, [I] and three Special Forces soldiers and one Afghan National Army (ANA) platoon-size team dismounted and went on up the hill to clear it. I had two A-10s overheard, and as we [climbed], we came upon a building. We cleared the building. The building itself was rather insignificant— it had been built by UNICEF and used as a school, but it was abandoned and taken over by the Taliban. There were a lot of writings on the wall, lots of pictures of helicopters and vehicles.

"We were determined to walk up to the top of the small hill just outside of the school, to take a look around. Once [we were] on top of the hill, one of the ANA soldiers who had been standing beside me stepped on an anti-personnel mine. The initial blast put me to the ground, but after I realized what happened, we heard the screams of the injured ANA soldier. The team leader and I ran over, and noticed he was missing half of his leg. We applied a couple of tourniquets just above the wound, and made the decision to get off that hill. I still had radio contact with the A-10s and was communicating the situation on the ground. Little did we know we were completely surrounded.

"After hearing the explosion, one of the gun trucks started coming up the hill and inadvertently ran over a double-stacked IED pressure-plate mine hidden under the small path. The vehicle exploded right in front of us, with all our teammates on it. Most of the guys were either burned or blown out of the vehicle; the bottom of the vehicle stayed intact. No was killed, but a lot of guys were beat up. The blast pushed the vehicle up and caught on fire. A SF sergeant, positioned in the turret of the gun truck, was banged up pretty bad.

"This IED was a trigger for the Taliban. They immediately opened up on both sides of the mountain, with a lot of small arms and RPGs [rocket-propelled grenades] at our positions. While our team was retreating by foot from the hill, we had numerous 7.62 rounds land in the vicinity of our position. My job was to get the situational awareness and relay it to the air support above us. The hill gave us the advantage, and I could see the muzzle flashes. The team leader was yelling at me to take cover, but we needed suppression ASAP. We had multiple casualties, a burning vehicle, and all the Special Forces gun trucks were returning fire.

"I had two A-10s overhead, which I immediately put into action. On the west side of the mountain I called a 'danger close' gun run, bringing in thirty millimeters into the treeline. After about two or three more gun runs, and the Taliban were stepping out behind the treeline into an open field. I requested a five-hundred-pound airburst and authorization from the team leader for an additional 'danger close' mission. On the A-10s inbound, I had the whole team duck behind cover until after the explosion. The bomb did a number on the bad guys, for the moment, and I shifted fire to the east, where there was still shooting and sporadic RPG fire. The A-10s continued on the east until they were empty of bullets and were relieved by another set of A-10s. I later learned that they stayed on station until their fuel level hit a critical point and then they landed at a contingency base for emergency fuel. The Taliban were very determined and they continued to fight. We could even see more reinforcements coming from the north, and the fighting continued throughout the day.

"I emptied the A-10s, which is referred to as a 'Winchester,' denoting the aircraft had expended all of its ordnance. I had a number of aircraft supporting me, both U.S. and coalition planes. I had more A-10s, GR-7s, Predator, and four Dutch Apache AH-64s, all checking in at the same time to support our teams. . . . I had one other JTAC, a junior JTAC, with me up on the mountain. With the number of aircraft checking in and the number of enemy contacts on both sides of the hill, I decided to separate the aircraft. I put the four Apaches on the east side with the other JTAC, and I had the two A-10s and two GR7s on the west side—all simultaneously suppressing the enemy around the mountain. While working the CAS, we de-conflicted the aircraft with the inbound MedEvac helicopters." We continued the fight through the day. I still had a Predator on station that was watching the bad guys all running around us, and we would engage it every time we found them.

"I had a Predator supporting me just about every day almost—twenty-four hours. They were always up, sometimes there were two. When the Predator is above, it is like having a second set of eyes looking around you. Twice, I used the Predator's ordnance to destroy the enemy. On one mission, the Predator followed four Taliban that were engaging our position, but Winchester ammo, and there was a lull in aircraft support overhead. I requested the SF team to use the 84 mm mortars, and with the Predator watching, we worked the mortars onto the enemy's fighting position.

"Once night fell, I had an AC-130 check in, and they immediately found enemy positions around our position. As the first aircraft called in Winchester, we got a second AC-130 on station who I continued to engage enemy personnel through the night. By early dawn all the fighting had stopped. At that point we were able to refit and recover. There continued [to be] a small amount of fighting throughout the week, and we had a few minor contacts each day with the enemy, but nothing significant.

✫ ✫ ✫ ✫

"The most significant [point] was when the bad guys came up [the hill], having decided to put everything they had into taking back that mountain. On September 9, teams both on foot (owing to the terrain) and in vehicles had been tasked by the ground forces commander to search the surrounding treeline and houses in the vicinity of the hill. We were on vehicle patrol southeast of the hill when we heard on SATCOM that a team was surrounded by the enemy. It was four ODA guys and an ANA team of platoon size, [and they were] pinned inside a house just west of the hill. The Taliban, while maneuvering toward the hill, inadvertently came across the SF team after they had entered one of the farmhouses, and no one realized it until the last minute. They were all in very close-combat engagement, and the team got on the radio and was screaming for help—specifically, for my help. My team was ordered by the ground forces commander to get over and support those guys.

"In the confusion of where the team was pinned down, we drove up right into the middle of the gunfight. The Taliban fighters were literally forty to fifty meters off the front of our vehicles in a treeline, and we opened up a barrage of gunfire with the enemy. At the same time, I had two F-18 Hornets checking in, and we needed a gun run ASAP. I had couple of F-18s check in, too. I quickly talked them onto the all-friendly positions—ours and the additional team pinned down. Once I was assured the Hornet pilots had everybody identified, I requested a 'danger close' mission with twenty millimeter guns into the treeline, off the front of our vehicles. The team leader gave me the OK, and within seconds the first F-18 executed a run immediately in front of us and appeared to be very effective.

"It almost seemed [that] the fighters were at the point of retreating. I requested a second gun run and I didn't like the run axis. The aircraft was lined up on the treeline, but the aircraft was directly behind us, so I aborted the first run and requested [that] they realign parallel to the treeline. I pushed about four to five more gun runs into the treeline, until the enemy pushed out into the open field on the other side, and then I requested one five-hundred-pound bomb onto their position. All the enemy either were killed or fled the engagement. The gunfight was over and all friendlies were recovered with no injuries."

✯   ✯   ✯   ✯

According to reports from the U.S. Navy:

> Aircraft assigned to Carrier Air Wing (CVW) 1, stationed aboard USS *Enterprise* (CVN 65), for five consecutive days provided support to International Security Assistance Force (ISAF) troops on the ground as part of Operations Medusa and Enduring Freedom near Kandahar, Afghanistan. Coordinated with coalition air forces and ISAF troops on the ground, *Enterprise* aircraft provided close air support for ISAF troops encountering resistance from Taliban extremists in multiple locations around Kandahar on Sept. 6 and Sept. 7. F/A-18F Super Hornets from the "Checkmates" of Strike Fighter Squadron (VFA) 211, based in Virginia Beach, Virginia, expended Guided Bomb Unit (GBU) 12 bombs to destroy Taliban extremist fortifications west of Kandahar on Sept. 6. The GBU-12 is a general-purpose, laser-guided 500-pound bomb.
>
> On Sept. 7, at the request of ISAF ground troops, a "Checkmate" Super Hornet conducted a strafing run using the aircraft's M61A1 20 mm Gatling gun. F/A-18C Hornets from the "Sidewinders" of VFA-86, based in Beaufort, South Carolina, expended both GBU-12 and GBU-38 bombs in attacks on both fortifications and Taliban extremists operating against ISAF ground forces. The GBU-38 is a general-purpose, Global Positioning System (GPS) guided 500-pound bomb, also known as the Joint Direct Attack Munition (JDAM). *Enterprise*-based aircraft have focused their efforts on protecting ISAF ground forces near Kandahar and have flown 103 sorties over the last

five days and delivered nearly thirty precision weapons against extremists in support of Operations Medusa and Enduring Freedom.

MSgt West continues: "Once back at the mountain, intel reports stated [that] the Taliban wanted to make another push to chase us out of there, and we were ready. This last gunfight was just west of the hill, and there were a number of enemy spotted both north and west. We had additional F-18s checking in to include a Predator and a B-1 bomber on station. Each time the enemy would engage, we could quickly counter and destroy the enemy. In some cases, we were able to find and confirm enemy positions, therefore destroying them before they could get a shot off.

"This all continued throughout the night, where I again had two more AC-130 gunships show up, and we continued to use them both. Just after checking in, I had them engaging targets around the hill, and were able to work them farther out to develop a parameter." The AC-130s performed the first ever FARP [forward arming and refueling point] site at Kandahar, where they refueled and refitted ammo instead of having to fly back to their home station. This significant event kept the aircraft on station all night.

"This all pushed through most of the night, until early in the morning, when things began to slow down. Before checking out, I believe the gunship estimated seventy enemy KIA around our position. My team members commented that when the gunship and I were working all night, it gave some of them the [sense of] security they [needed so they] could get a little sleep and be ready for the next day.

"By the 10th of September, we saw things significantly slow down. Intel had reported that a majority of the Taliban were either KIA or had retreated to the valley to the west. The whole area was just like a ghosttown. By the 11th we started to see the civilians returning to their homes and farms. The civilians were very friendly; they would tell us anything we needed to know. They knew we were there to help.

"Working with the three SF teams and three ANA teams, we [were] all side by side. We lived together, slept together, and ate together—sometime we even ate what they ate. They loved cooking goat; if they were ever stressed out after a gunfight, we would buy them a goat to re-motivate them. In summary, my team was originally a blocking force for the operation, [but as the] NATO forces had to pull back twice, due to being hit and taking casualties, NATO was almost ready to cancel the whole operation. . . . But due to the success in the south with U.S. and coalition forces and the large number of Taliban forces that either were KIA or fled the area, the NATO forces called it a success and moved into the area by September 12."

✫   ✫   ✫   ✫

During a NATO briefing on September 20, 2006, U.S. Marine General James L. Jones, NATO's supreme commander at the time of Operation Medusa, reported: "Offensive operation in southern Afghanistan killed at least a quarter of the former Taliban regime's fighters, and possibly more." Accolades continued from the commander of Regional Command South, who stated: "[Operation Medusa was] the single most important and successful combat operation conducted in Afghanistan since 2002." From Apache helicopters to B-1 bombers, coalition GR7s, to carrier-based F/A-18s, over fifty thousand pounds of ordnance and fifteen thousand rounds of ammunition rained down on the Taliban, courtesy of Combat Controller MSgt Mike West, one of the "quiet professionals" of AFSOC.

14

Synergy of Command

Captain Paul Stewart, Special Tactics Officer*

Of all of the operators under the command of the U.S. Special Operations Command (SOCOM), the members of AFSOC's Special Tactics Squadrons (STS) are indeed unique. Consider that among Navy SEALs, all are SCUBA qualified but not all are trained in high-altitude, high-opening (HALO) operations. Among Special Forces ODAs, there exist unique teams that specialize in SCUBA or HALO operations. but not all SF troopers receive training in these areas. However, the men of the Special Tactics Squadron receive training and are proficient in both of these skills, as well as other skills. Special Tactics Squadron teams operate with members from the other special operations forces (SOF) units on a regular basis; and at times, they are on site prior to the arrival of their sister units. These highly trained and dedicated operators make up the core of the Special

---

*Name changed for security reasons.

Tactics Team (STT): combat controllers, pararescuemen, and special operations weather teams.

To lead such a collection of highly motivated specialists, AFSOC has created the Special Tactics Officer, called an STO. His leadership role, as stated by AFSOC, is to:

> Provide assault zone reconnaissance and assessments, terminal control, and personnel recovery (PR) and surveys, establish, and control the aerospace surface interface in objective areas. Deploy as team member, team leader or mission commander as a direct combatant or to command and battle staffs to provide subject matter expertise to plan for and manage command and control for special reconnaissance, terminal control and PR operations.

The extensive training that each STO receives is described in the AFSOC Special Tactics Officer Selection packet:

> STOs receive the same initial training as enlisted combat controllers, a process that takes approximately eight to ten months, followed by twelve months of AST [Advance Skills Training]. The entire training program includes eight schools. Training consists of the following schools: Combat Control Orientation Course: two weeks, Lackland AFB, Texas; Combat Control Operator/Air Traffic Control Officer Course: fifteen weeks, Keesler AFB, Mississippi; U.S. Air Force Basic Combat Survival School: two and a half weeks, Fairchild AFB, Washington; U.S. Army Basic Airborne School: three weeks, Fort Benning, Georgia; Combat Control School: thirteen weeks, Pope AFB, North Carolina; Advanced Skills Training: Hurlburt Field, Florida, for a year of follow-on training; U.S. Army Combat Diver School: five weeks, NAS Key West, Florida; U.S. Army Military Free Fall Parachutist School: five weeks, Ft. Bragg, North Carolina, and Yuma Proving Grounds, Arizona.

Captain Paul Stewart, of the 720 Special Tactics Group, 21st Special Tactics Squadron, was one of the first STOs deployed as a Joint Terminal Attack Controller (JTAC) in support of Operation Enduring Freedom. Regarding his vanguard assignment, he related: "Historically we have not put officers down at the JTAC level to deploy in a field position. It was not seen as the right role for a young officer. For a long time, it was very difficult because the training priority was given to the NCOs. It was difficult to define a position for a young officer. ... I was the first to serve a whole rotation whose deployment was in that capacity. Early on in OEF/OIF, there were some officers who were prior-enlisted, who already had that experience, who were employed as such, but not for the entire length of the deployment.

The captain described his service: "Going back to the fall of 2006, it was the southern part of Afghanistan. The country was split up into different regions of control [RC]. I was in the region known as RC South, in the Uruzgan Province, which is located north of Kandahar. My mission was to provide the whole realm of combat control capability: close air support (CAS), assault zone, helo work, DZ [drop zone] work for a variety of coalition and U.S. special operations forces that were operating in RC South.

"We had Canadian, British, Dutch, and Australian and U.S. forces that were all working together in that area. As it was a coalition, and not an alliance, everyone had his own mission. Because we were all in the same battlespace, there was a requirement to work together. Certainly, there were times when we all fought together against the Taliban–AQ [al-Qaeda] force as well.

"My chain of command was the Special Forces ODA I was with. They were not the only players in these kinds of operations. The Dutch 'owned' Uruzgan Province and were overall in charge of what went on there. Everything we did was coordinated with them and coordinated with the Afghan Army. We always had Afghanis with us; and we almost always had Dutch operating with us. There were also Australians and Canadians working that area. It was truly a coalition. The reality was, we would welcome anyone who wanted to help—that was more for us, more on our team. Because it was a coalition, there were challenges [, however]. Different countries have different philosophies of how the mission should be prosecuted; it was definitely an interesting scenario to be in with them.

"We would attend the mission planning. You had the Dutch

officers, who thought we should do it this way, the American officers who thought it should be done another, and the Canadians, who thought it should be done yet another way—and then the Afghani, who had their input. It was almost democratic [the way] we settled on our courses of action, in the way to operate. It was certainly unique, unlike anything I had experienced before. Normally, you get your orders and then decide how you are going to do the mission. There were a lot more factors to consider, and at the same time we did not want to disenfranchise any of those players, and make them think they were being marginalized or that their opinions were not valid. Because we did want their support—the Dutch had great artillery, they had great rotary-wing gunships, [and] we wanted that support. So we always had to do a little compromising. We could not just say 'It's our way or the highway' because then we would be left on our own. I think that is a metaphor for a lot of the operations at large over there. Every nation has its own opinions, but we were all going for the common goal, which was a better Afghanistan—one where there was a viable economy, a stable government, and not a safe haven for terrorism.

"When I arrived, everyone else had already been there for a matter of months. I was rotating with another combat controller who was a senior airman. He was much younger in rank and [shorter] time-in-service than I was. This was a surprise to the ODA team leader there, who was the same rank as I was. This fact was presented to the SF captain, as we [the combat controllers] are in a critically manned career field and additionally we need to show from an officer perspective that we are capable and willing to accept the same challenges and risks as I daily ask of my enlisted troops. That was part of the issue.

"The other thing was, we [the AFSOC] needed to do a better job of keeping up with our Army and Navy peers, in that when I would go forward in my career to the ops level—for example, the major, lieutenant colonel level—those guys would actually be pulling from real-world experience in their decision making, whereas I would not be. Had I not had this experience, I would be mostly going by what I had been told, rather than drawing from actual experience.

"There are a lot of reasons I think this will continue in the future; it happens because we are short-manned. We are not taking a job away from an enlisted man who, by right, would be over there instead of me. There is enough work for everyone to do, and that is just how it has come down.

☆ ☆ ☆ ☆

"When I first arrived in Afghanistan, there was a hurried handover that included a lot of tactics, techniques, and procedures [TTP], especially with the Dutch forces. I had to work out these TTPs fast. Within three days of hitting the ground, we were in contact with the enemy in southern Afghanistan. We went in by ground and were using some of the host-nation guides to help us navigate. The big concern was the suicide attacks, so we were pretty pragmatic about picking our routes to and from the target. We were also very conscious that many of the movements had been compromised, to the extent that they were able to be ambushed by small arms and other ways. We knew we were being watched—that every time we moved through any town, the people were reporting on our positions. Considering this, we tried to be as unpredictable as possible.

"One of the tactics I used with the Dutch Apaches was to 'recon' the routes ahead of our line of travel. We would use their systems to detect what could be IEDs [improvised explosive devices] or possible ambush sites. We did not want the helos to necessarily attack them, as we did not want to get ourselves into a position where we were not sure if these were militia or civilians. We did not really know, but we wanted to keep an eye on what was going on, [so as] to make informed decisions even if our mission was not to attack people along the way.

"After two days, the distance we traveled in the Humvees was substantial. In some of the locations we were moving to, it was close to one hundred miles. The area we traveled through was desert, as we stayed away from roads due to the IED threat. We were limited a great deal by the Afghanis, because they did not have a good night-fighting capability, [and] we would be at a higher risk of having a fratricide incident. Because of this, we did much of our operating during the daylight. Our intended purpose was to help support and establish a better indigenous Afghan fighting capability. We were there primarily as a supporting arm, providing the fire support from the air, mortars, arty, etc. Much of the war on terror is about advising and training host-nation forces to better conduct their own operations."

☆   ☆   ☆   ☆

The Humvees used by the Special Forces are highly modified and are referred to as gun trucks. Operating as a JTAC, Capt Stewart was attached to an ODA. However, he was not just along for the ride—the SF soldiers put him to work, as he related: "You are in that vehicle and there is only so much space. You are going to have a gun, you are going to be holding security and a lot of the other tasks, as well as the SF guys. It is upon that individual combat controller to develop a relationship with his ground commander so that he knows when things start getting bad, and [if] he needs air support, he can be counted on as much to do all these other functions. I spent my time on shift at night, holding security while some of the other guys were sleeping. It is a busy job, and it does not just pertain to talking to air. You are not always talking to air, as you don't necessarily have 24/7 air support."

Captain Stewart was assigned to man the M240B machine gun in the rear of one of the vehicles, and he was responsible for the rear security of that vehicle. The M240B medium machine gun is the replacement for the M60 family of machine guns. Manufactured by Fabrique Nationale, the twenty-four-pound M240B medium machine gun is a gas-operated, air-cooled, linked belt-fed weapon that fires the 7.62 x 51 mm round. The weapon fires from an open-bolt position with a maximum effective range of 3,725 meters. The cyclic rate of fire is 750 rounds per minute [low rate] and 950 rpm [high rate] through an adjustable gas regulator. It features a folding bipod that attaches to the receiver, a quick-change barrel assembly, a feed cover and bolt assembly enabling closure of the cover regardless of bolt position, a plastic butt stock, and an integral optical sight rail. In this case, it is vehicle-mounted to the gun truck. While it possesses many of the same characteristics as the older M60, the durability of the M240 system results in superior reliability and maintainability. Captain Stewart commented: "It [the M240B] was good when using tracer fire to mark targets that aircraft could see, so I could simultaneously direct them based on fire from the gun."

In addition to manning the M240B, the captain had his M4 and his primary weapon, his "comm" gear. Near his side was the AN/PRC-117F, which the captain called his "long-haul radio" owing to the SatCom capabilities. Along with the 117 he carried two AN/PRC-148 MBITR smaller inter-team radios that had some of the capabilities of the larger 117, but not nearly the amount of power output. Besides the "comm" gear, he carried laptops that would be used to store information pertaining to the mission. The laptops were the Panasonic Toughbook, which is specially designed and manufactured for environment that battlefield airmen operate in. These laptop computers are housed in a magnesium-alloy casing that ensures exceptional protection from the elements. The hard drives are mounted in special shock-absorbing compounds that insulate the disks from vibration and shock, thereby protecting the operator's mission-critical

Captain Paul Stewart, a Special Tactics Officer of the 21st STS mans the machine gun in the rear of a SF gun truck. The team is on patrol in the Uruzgan Province, north of Kandahar, Afghanistan. *Courtesy of the U.S. Air Force.*

data. The laptops are designed especially to withstand the rigors of being tossed around and transported in the back of a gun truck.

Stewart continued to describe the mission: "I was sitting in the back of the gun truck along with two interpreters. We moved into a very narrow valley; the way was difficult, as there was only one road in and out. That . . . really raised the hair on the back of my neck; a lot of other patrols had operated in this area and many people had been ambushed and killed. Intel placed about five medium-value individuals, and even a couple of high-value individuals, in the area. There was a command and control facility working with direction from higher levels in al-Qaeda, as well as a lot of money and weapons caches. We had signals intelligence, imagery, and a number of things to support [the premise] that there was some serious activity going on in there. Due to the distance of the valley from the nearest firebase, the enemy had plenty of warning whenever we were moving in. We needed to move quickly through a lot of the choke points in the valley. During this time we traveled mostly at night, again limited by the fact [that] our Afghani counterparts had to travel with white lights. We set up right as dawn was breaking, when we initiated our search of the first compound."

The Department of Defense defines a high-value target, or HVT, as "a target the enemy commander requires for the successful completion of the mission. The loss of high-value targets would be expected to seriously degrade important enemy functions throughout the friendly commander's area of interest." A medium-value target, or MVT, could be an enemy of lesser rank but, nevertheless, one involved in operations against U.S. and coalition forces, whose capture would lead to follow-on action. Signals intelligence, or SIGINT, is described by the National Security Agency (NSA) as "technical and intelligence information derived from the exploitation of foreign electronic emissions which is comprised either individually or in combination of communications intelligence (COMINT), electronic intelligence (ELINT), and foreign instrumentation signals intelligence (FISINT)."

"Our mission was to capture these guys, kill [them] if need be. But we wanted to capture them because we thought it would be better intelligence . . . also, because the risk of collateral damage in this area was so high. These compounds were so cramped, [so on top of] each other, that there was a lot of legitimate business—such as farmers—[who might be affected, and] so we were very concerned about collateral damage. We wanted to do as little bombing and as much capturing as possible. However, the enemy 'gets a vote'—as soon as we moved into the first target, there was resistance. The team dismounted, and the Afghani infantry led the patrol. Things tend to work better when Afghanis are searching [the] Afghanis' homes rather than Americans.

"They interviewed a couple of people and found out [that] the HVTs we were looking for were not there. We got a lot of intelligence from our interpreters' talking with the locals, narrowing down where these leaders were. Some of them had lived in that valley for over twenty-five years; some of those guys were part of the Taliban 'old guard.' They made it known [that] they were not going out without a fight, so we quickly packed up our gear and continued to move north into this valley. That was when we stared to receive fire, which picked up quickly from three different sides. We were stuck in many ways, due to the terrain; the rivers going through the valleys are choked with green vegetation.

"That is one of the hardest parts of being a JTAC. You could drop ninety-nine good bombs, and [the] one bad bomb would ruin everything—that is, fratricide, or collateral damage. Situational awareness was my number one job that day, based on the fact [that] we had a lot of dismounted friendlies. [That is,] we had a lot of enemy fighters whose positions were not completely known, and they were moving around through the trees. All I could see as I was moving down into the trees was fire everywhere. There was not a lot of coordination [on our part]; it is a challenge with the Afghanis, as . . . many of them . . . are new to our tactics. They operate much better in smaller groups than in larger groups, [but] we had an entire company of Afghani infantry pushing into this valley. That equates to almost a hundred soldiers, [and] it is very difficult from the command-and-control perspective.

"At the beginning of the firefight I [had] experienced some target difficulty. I was using a hand-held laser rangefinder to designate for a B-1 bomber that was coming in with two-thousand-pound bombs.

Unbeknownst to me, just a few minutes earlier, when I had bumped the rangefinder on the side of the truck, it lost its calibration. The first laser return I got when I directed the first set of four two-thousand-pound bombs came down five hundred meters off. That shocked me because, up till that time, we had no [problems] using the equipment. Now, here I was; these were my first bombs I was controlling in a combat environment. Having never worked with a B-1 before, there were a lot of firsts. Just being in country for three days [made] all [this] a bit of a blur. Not having slept for about two days prior to this mission, due to mission planning and travel time, as well. That was a big shock. It was, 'Hey, what just happened?'

"I immediately realized [that] the rangefinder was bad, and I shifted to a radar beacon that I had in my backpack. Using my compass heading off that radar beacon, the bomber put the bombs down and then we got some good effect. For the next twenty-one hours I had air overhead, dropping bombs and engaging everything from bomber, fast movers, helicopters, and Predators. At the end of the day, we had taken zero friendly casualties, which is good. We had zero collateral damage, no fratricide, and there were seventy confirmed enemy KIA, including fifty percent of the leaders we [had been] looking for, including most of their bodyguards and their own little squads.

"That night, we continued to travel. I had an AC-130H from the 16th SOS overhead escorting us. The next day, we set up a RON site [rest overnight]; everyone was exhausted. All we did was listen to our intelligence cells talking over the long-haul radios for the intel they were getting about what had occurred that day.

"We did work with Predators in the battlespace. What you want to do in these situations is to maximize every platform's capability synergistically with the other platforms that you have. What you do *not* want is to have a bunch of airplanes sitting over your head just burning gas, waiting for their turn to drop bombs or look at a target. Part of our tactical dilemma as controllers is—based on where their friendly positions are, where the bad guys are, [and] based on how the terrain is—to put these aircraft in different orbits in different ways so [that] they can all work together rather than just sequentially.

"Primarily, we would have the Predator exploiting its capacities to conduct reconnaissance—to 'recon' targets to track different vehicles or individuals moving around. We would use the strikers [fighters] that have a lot less gas available and are a lot heavier; they do not have the capability to stay over any one target very long, so we want to get those bombs off, get them back to the tanker, and send them home to get more bombs and ammo on board. Then you have the AC-130 gunships, which are good for the surgical purposes, escort, and tracking a lot of friendly positions at one time. They are a stable platform versus the fast-moving aircraft that come in, catch a glimpse, push out, turn around, and then come back; [those] are not nearly as effective for tracking and watching specific points.

"Helicopters are very good for chasing individuals, as well as 'reconing' our routes in and out of an area. Marking targets for some of the heavier aircraft, I found it to be very effective to use an Apache helicopter in conjunction with the B-1. The bombers were unable to actually see the target, but the Apaches could. The helicopters had a lot of systems that could give me good target information, which I then passed on to the bombers, thus maximizing their time in the air to get their bombs off quick.

"What we determined was [that] there was a lack of clarity [among] some of the village elders in the area as to why we had come and what we were doing. Our higher leadership determined [that] it would be in everyone's best interest [if], the next day, [we] woke up early [and] had the team leadership meet with some of the village elders and some of the religious leaders in the area. [They would] talk about why we were in the valley and make them fully aware [that] we were not concerned with any of their day-to-day operations—the running of their society. [That we were] strictly going after these Taliban guys [who] were finding a safe haven in their village. [That] we were there to support the locals and their government, but [that] we were not going to accept the enemy's being there, whether they were being supported actively or [whether] their presence was condoned.

"We conducted a MEDCAP [medical civic action program]. This

is when we gather a bunch of humanitarian supplies—a lot of food and medical stuff. We go in [and] set up in the middle of the village, and [we] let people come to us. We had requested PJs [pararescue jumpers] to assist with this; however, due to other tasking, they were not available to us at this time. For the MEDCAP, we were using the 18D [SF medical sergeant] on our team and also some of the coalition medics who traveled with us on occasion. The benefit of the 18D was that he had the cultural training, whereas the PJs have a background in rescue missions. We had not sold it to the leadership [that] they would be the best, even though I believe, having worked with many pararescuemen, [that] they would have been perfect for this kind of op.

"During a MEDCAP, the medics treat the folks, talk about any issues they are having, hand out some portable radios, blankets, and things like that. They just listen to how the people are dealing with it [the situation] and see upfront that the Afghani soldiers with us are there, [acting] in their best interests to try and make the village a safer place. Several of the [residents] were actually thankful for [our] scaring the Taliban out of the village. Through intelligence, we later learned [that], for the first time in twenty-five years, the Taliban were abandoning this particular area as a base for [its] operations. On subsequent patrols, we found [that], indeed, this was the case. The enemy had not returned to rebuild any of its command-and-control bunkers. That was a success story for us that ended up leading to a relatively quiet winter.

"Winter can be quiet, for a variety of factors. Many of these people are very rugged, but they do not have very much in the way of cold-weather gear. They tend to spend a lot of time indoors, so there are not a lot of things going on outside. These al-Qaeda/Taliban guys no longer had the winter haven they were counting on. They had retreated farther south toward Kandahar and, we expected, across the border [into Pakistan] as well. Ironically, the biggest engagement [took place] within a few days of my getting in country.

"The rest of my time in Afghanistan was spent supporting some of these other units—supporting similar missions. This was a success story for us—so much so that our team was relocated to other places because the leadership felt we were not needed in that area anymore."

Captain Stewart offered the following suggestions for future STOs: "I have a couple guys who I am working with now to do these kinds of missions. What I say to them is [to] be bold. Don't be intimidated; don't be too concerned about what you think someone would do in that situation. Try it the way you think it *should* work, and it just might. I found the rank to be very helpful, especially with some of the European and other armies with whom we work. For them, rank is much more of a factor. When we work overseas among Americans, rank is important, but [it] is your message and experience, and where you fit in and your job, [that are] also important.

"For example, when getting the hand-over from a senior airman, I found [that] the Dutch Air Force Apache folks were much less interested in what [the earlier guy] had to say, even though he had been in country for many months and had a lot more experience in that area. Yet, [when] I came in for three days, they were much more interested in what I had to say because of my rank. So, the rank thing was a help. A lot of the other coalition forces have officer JTACs—the Canadians, Australians, and Dutch. They all had officers, so I found myself fitting in a lot better. What I would say to [those] following me is to develop good relationships. Remember that influencing someone is usually more effective than coercing them to do things your way or in a specific manner.

"Remember, [also, that] at the end of the day it is your name on those weapons that are coming off of that plane. Do not let anyone convince you to bomb something unless you are [sure] that it is the right target and that it is defiantly hostile. There were a couple of situations when it would have been easier to take some bad advice, and get into the bad situation of killing friendlies and also civilians.

"There were some concerns before I went [into country] that [there would be] chain-of-command [problems] because, on the ODA, the Army captain is the only officer and then there is a team of NCOs that work for him. There were some concerns that I would upset that balance. [But] that was not found to be true. I developed a very solid relationship with both the team sergeant and the captain. I fit in fine—there were no rank issues. They understood what I was there to provide—not necessarily battlefield leadership, but a technical skill—and that's what I did. However, at the same time, I think I did make a good case for Air Force officers in general, because these SF guys never get to see them. They never get to work with them; they do not interface with them. They only know our NCOs, so now they got to see a little bit about what the Air Force flight-level leadership is like, and I think that was good. I think that was good exposure that will help us out in the long run."

The Lance P. Sijan Award

For his actions in support of Operation Enduring Freedom, Captain Paul Stewart was awarded the Lance P. Sijan Award. This award recognizes the accomplishments of officers and enlisted members of the Air Force who have demonstrated the highest qualities of leadership in the performance of their duties and the conduct of their lives. The closely evaluated criteria for the award include scope of responsibility, professional leadership, leadership image, and community involvement.

All in the Family

SSgt Scot Nichols,
9th Special Operations Squadron*

For SSgt Scot Nichols, being part of AFSOC was a family matter. His father had thirty years under his wings with the Air Force, including flying into Desert One. Indeed, his father was one of the founding fathers of AFSOC. SSgt Nichols carried on the family tradition as a crewmember with the 9th Special Operations Squadron (SOS), flying MC-130P Combat Shadow aircraft. Concerning the Shadow, he commented: "We do everything the Talons can do and then some!"

Primarily, the MC-130P Combat Shadow extends the range of special operations helicopters by providing air refueling. Operations are conducted primarily in formation, at night, at low level, to reduce the probability of visual acquisition and interception by airborne

---

*Name changed for security reasons.

threats. These operations are carried out as part of clandestine, low-level missions into politically sensitive or hostile territory. The Shadow is a visual flight rule (VFR) aircraft and would be used only when the pilots can see the ground, although penetrations are often aided by radar. The MC-130P may fly in a multiship or single-ship mission to reduce detection.

The secondary mission of the Combat Shadow includes the delivery of special operations forces. Small teams, assorted gear, equipment, Zodiacs, and combat rubber raiding craft (CRRC) are a few of the specialized items conveyed by the aircraft and its crew.

The Combat Shadow has a fully integrated inertial navigation (IIN) system, GPS, and night-vision goggle (NVG)-compatible lighting for the interior and exterior. This allows the crew to use NVG-compatible heads-up display (HUD) to fly the plane. It has Forward Looking Infrared Radar (FLIR) missile and radar warning receiver to alert the crew of threats; countermeasure devices include chaff and flare dispensers. Its communications include satellite and data-burst technology. In addition, the MC-130P has in-flight refueling capability as a receiver.

Originally designated the HC-130 N/P, these Air Force special operations aircraft were redesigned in February 1996 to correspond with all other M-series special operations aircraft. The aircraft has a crew of eight: four officers (pilot, copilot, primary navigator, and secondary navigator) and four enlisted (flight engineer, communications operator, and two loadmasters).

Flying with the 9th SOS in support of Operation Iraqi Freedom, SSgt Nichols has been on a wide variety of missions. "We did a lot of humanitarian stuff over in Iraq. One of the biggest impacts we had was around Christmastime in 2004. We did a psychological operation [PsyOp] whereby we pretty much papered a portion of Iraq with leaflets in support of Iraq's first democratic election. The wording was basically [to] encourage the people to go out and vote in their first free election in over fifty years. One of translators described the leaflets as a call to support the new government and move away from dictatorship.

"It was during one of the leaflet drops that something humorous happened. The other loadmaster ended up dropping his helmet [along] with the leaflets. [That is,] his 'comm' cord got wrapped around one of the static lines, pulled the helmet off his head, and [shot it] right out the back of the airplane. I was standing there, pulling the static lines back in, and something went rushing by my leg. I turned back and saw my partner lying on the ramp with his arm extended, trying to grab his helmet before it went out of the plane. But no such luck—so some Iraqi got an incentive along with the leaflet.

"Later on, we received feedback on the drop: the area we had papered had the highest turnout of voters in the country. Which is interesting—the Iraqi people will go out to vote even though they are getting shot at and persecuted, while here in America, we have a hard time getting the citizens out to vote for presidents, etc. That was one of the biggest contributions we made."

Flying PsyOp missions is just part of the job; SSgt Nichols recounted a humanitarian mission during the Christmas of 2006: "We carried in clothes, toys, food, and things of that nature—anything you can think of for the children. We helped move those items around the country to show the Iraq people our support. Most of the items were delivered to area chaplains, who then distributed them to the people." These are the 'hearts and minds' types of missions. We gain [the] support of the Iraqi people [by helping them] and [hope that they will] point out all the bad people to us. All of the feed back we have gotten from the ground forces is that this is having an impact on [the] country."

On a more tactical level, the aircrews of the 9th SOS also do their fair share of insertions and extractions of U.S. SOF units. Nichols explained: "We do a lot of insertions—pull them [SOF teams] in, bring them out. Take them back home, and get them out of the field so they can [have] a decent meal. Then a week later or so—it depends—we put them back in. Every crew member is armed with a least a 9mm pistol, and the enlisted personnel carry M4s. We have been fired upon a few times; usually the rounds do not get up as high as we are flying. During my first trip to Iraq, it was like the Wild West. When I first arrived, I used to think getting shot at would be cool; now, not so much—there are times when the pucker factor can get very high."

Other than getting shot at, SSgt Nichols explained that one of the most dangerous missions they do is helicopter aerial refueling (ARF). "What makes this maneuver dangerous is the fact that we are flying low and slow; since the helos cannot get up as high as we can. This makes us a very easy target. The MC-130P has to throttle down, and the helo has to throttle up to match air speeds. The helo is pushing max power, and we are sitting there right above stall speed; trying to get these guys gas so that they can go accomplish their mission. Flying slow is not a whole lot of fun. 'Low and slow' in Iraq is not conducive to long life . . . you are a huge target. Not only do you have to watch the helicopter, but you also have to watch the ground to make sure there is nobody shooting at you.

"We [the loadmasters] are positioned at the side paratroop doors, watching the helicopters and watching the surrounding area as well. [We are] making sure nothing is being launched up at us and [we are] watching that the helo does not strike the airplane.

An MC-130P Combat Shadow serves as the platform for aerial refueling for SOF helicopters. Here an MH-53M Pave Low has connected its refueling probe into the trailing hose-and-drogue. This allows the helicopter to top off its fuel tanks and continue with it mission. *Courtesy of the U.S. Air Force.*

"We watch as they fit the probe into the basket. Most of the refueling probes on the helicopters extend beyond the rotors, though there is a helicopter that the probe does not extend out beyond the rotor; in that case, they have about three feet of their rotor that actually extends over the hose. If you are flying that type of helo, you definitely have to 'thread the needle.' There is a pucker factor, too, especially on the right side of the airplane. And refueling a big helo is not so good, [either]. All helos have the probe on their right side, so [that] when they are on the right side of our plane, their rotors are a lot closer to our tail. The pilots of the MC-130P can feel the rotor wash coming off the helo, down on the tail of the aircraft, when they are coming in to contact the drogue fuel basket."

Aerial refueling, insertions, extractions, humanitarian efforts, and PsyOps are all in a day's work for the crews of the 9th SOS. SSgt Nichols described what life was like back at the base: "We watch movies, play video games, check e-mails, and keep in touch with loved ones back home. We try to get plenty of rack time. There are times when we do a lot, and [other] times we are wishing for things to do. It's something to do, it pays the bills. I don't mind it. I get to go to strange places."

16

The Battle of Najaf

SSgt Ryan Wallace

When SSgt Ryan Wallace deployed to Iraq in support of Operation Iraqi Freedom, he knew it would be a hazardous assignment. What he did not know was that a handful of combat controllers, including himself, would play a crucial role in one of the largest sustained engagements by the U.S. and Iraqi forces of the Iraqi war—the Battle of Najaf.

Staff Sergeant Wallace and three other combat controllers were with the 21st Special Tactics Squadron (STS) at Pope Air Force Base, North Carolina, until they were deployed to Iraq. Originally they staged out of Balad Air Base and were tasked to U.S. Army Special Forces Operational Detachment Alpha (ODA). Two of the controllers went to Baghdad, another was sent to Kalsu, and SSgt Wallace headed to Al Hilla to work with ODA-563. Sergeant Wallace explained that his specific job at Al Hilla was to work for the ODA that was combat-advising the Hilla special weapons and tactics (SWAT) team: "They are like any other SWAT team around the world, but in this case a little more paramilitary.

"On the morning of the battle, our guys from Baghdad were actually down in the town of Najaf, having completed some highly sensitive target mission sets, and they were on their way home. Separated from them was an ODA who had been staying at their camp. Early on the morning of January 28, the Special Forces team leader of ODA-566, Captain Eric, received a call from the Najaf police chief, informing him that the Iraqis had had gotten ambushed and were under fire a couple miles north of Najaf.

"The area where the attack occurred was a large farming complex about two kilometers north of Najaf. The main farm and the enemy positions were all northwest of there. The farm building was now basically a stronghold, with ten-foot-high mounds of dirt and trenches surrounding it. It was occupied by a small religious sect who called themselves the 'Soldiers of Heaven'—basically [like Koresh's Branch Davidians in] Waco, [Texas] but in Iraq. There were a lot of crazies out there 'on their own page,' not playing by the same rules as any of the Shiites, Sunnis, Christians, or anybody else going by. They had vehicle-mounted machine guns . . . enough weapons for every guy in the compound to have three machine guns and a chest rig full of ammo. It was estimated [that] there were between five hundred and a thousand personnel just in this little farm area, running through all these trenches.

"They were [going] to mass their fighters and walk into Najaf during the Ashura pilgrimage. [During] this time of Ashura, you have people walking all over along the streets visiting the shrines and doing their Muslim thing. [They would] dress in civilian clothes and carry concealed weapons, explosives, etc. It was their [plan] to mingle with the pilgrims, to go into Najaf and create mass chaos, assassinate some religious leaders, and basically start a big fight. The intent was to bring about the coming of the thirteenth Imam. In their religion, there are only twelve Imams; [it] is disputed whether a thirteenth exists or not. For these guys, it was to bring him back by making the world so crazy that the Iman would show himself and make the world right again.

"When the governor of Najaf, Asad Abu Ghalal, heard about this, he went to the area with his security escort to investigate. They went out early in the morning, about 0700. It was then that they were ambushed and called for help. When the Iraqis got ambushed that morning, they abandoned their vehicles and ran over to a river that was east of their [earlier] position. Special Forces ODA-566 in Najaf responded to the call. On their way out of the gate, they ran into the other ODA team. That [second] team, which had two combat controllers with them, was on its way back to Baghdad. They had F-16s overhead to follow their route as they drove to their base, and were about five minutes from leaving when the first ODA, which had received the QRF [Quick Reaction Force] call, asked these guys to come along and help. They said, 'Sure,' and the SF teams along with their combat controllers rolled out together.

"The [teams] approached from the south and ended up about three hundred to four hundred meters from where the governor and his escort had been ambushed. As soon as they arrived on site, they immediately came under fire. The combat controllers (CCTs) were MSgt Bryan and SSgt David, who were the first ones to show up in the morning. MSgt Bryan immediately started to call in strafing runs with the F-16s that were overhead. After the first strafing runs, the enemy started firing mortars at them. Now, the enemy had them bracketed—meaning mortar rounds were landing to the left and the right of the combat controllers.

"SSgt David dismounted the SF gun truck and headed over to a trench to find these mortars. At the same time, MSgt Bryan was still calling CAS [close air support]. The ODA sent some vehicles forward to exfil the governor and his entourage. [Meanwhile,] the CCT started dropping bombs on the trench line and on about thirty hostile personnel on the other side of the trench. After putting a couple of bombs down, the enemy fire ceased long enough for them to extract those personnel. Overhead now were A-10s and F-16 fighters on station. The pilots were calling out [that] there were more enemy troops in the trenches. The controllers put a couple of bombs down in one trench, and then got a call of more enemy troops in another trench about two hundred meters from the first one . . . where upon they directed bombs in there.

"The team then began to receive some accurate sniper and machine gun fire [that was] originating from a mosque located across the street from the farm. The local Iraqi Army commander who was there with the team authorized the destruction of the mosque. MSgt Bryan called in a five-hundred-pound laser-guided bomb; the first one hit, but it was a dud. You can image all those guys in the mosque looking up at the big gaping hole in the roof and thinking [that] Allah has protected them from bombs, since nothing happened. Then a minute later, the second bomb came in and leveled the building, killing everyone inside.

"After that, SSgt David took over control, as he was now closer to the fight; MSgt Bryan was with the guys who were moving to support the exfil of the governor. At that point, the ground commanders agreed [that] they had everything they needed. They were getting low on ammo, as they had fired everything they had—the machine guns, truck weapons—so they had to return to camp. As they were leaving, SSgt David called in some additional strafing and bomb runs on [any] enemy personnel who were still in the trenches. They left that morning to go back to Najaf, where they would rekit, rearm, and take care of the wounded. The CAS for this part of the operation included four JDAMs, four GBU-12s, seven gun runs by the F-16s, and five runs with the A-10s. This was all in the morning, before noon."

All in a day's work for the combat controllers of AFSOC! However, the day was not over. On the contrary, the fight had just begun, and SSgt Wallace would soon be thrust into harm's way as the Battle of Najaf continued.

Sergeant Wallace recalled the activity of that morning: "The night before we had conducted a raid near our area, so I was sleeping in when all this was going on. My place was inside of a metal shipping contain—kind of like a Conex container, which is what we had to live in down there. The ODA team leader came into my "can," woke me up, and wanted me to set up the video ROVER so we could receive a downlink of the TIC [troops in contact] that was going on to our south." ROVER is short for remote operations video enhanced receiver. The system consists of a laptop computer configured with a specialized radio and antenna system. Cameras mounted on aircraft collect images and send them as full-motion streaming video to the systems carried by the Special Tactics teams. The real-time imagery provides the Air Force JTAC with an aerial view of what is happening in an area—before and after they call in close air support. With this system, JTAC teams are able to pull down real-time video from specially equipped aircraft flying over the battlefield.

Prior to development of the ROVER, video images from unmanned aerial vehicles and other reconnaissance aircraft were available only to command centers and the pilots flying the aircraft. Now, teams on the ground were able to have an additional set of eyes to help them see what is happening at the moment. That is, the pilot overhead and the JTAC on the ground see the exact same image. To make the system even better, the controller can circle targets or draw lines of attack on his screen, and that will be transmitted to the pilot, who then sees it on his screen as well. The system is an innovative tool for the battlefield airman, ensuring accurate target identification and CAS, while minimizing fratricide.

Sergeant Wallace continued his story: "I got up and tried to set it [ROVER] up, but it was too far away. I could not receive any video from the fighters, so I headed back to bed. I turned on my SatCom, so I could listen to the chatter going on, and I went back to sleep. About thirty minutes later, I got another knock on the door, [this time from] somebody else on the team telling me to kit up because we were going as a QRF and were leaving in five minutes.

"I grabbed all my stuff and threw it on the truck, and we took off. My position on the vehicle—and I was pretty adamant about that—was in the back. For one thing, I carry my radio on my back, so if I am in the truck, [my pack] has to be beside me. With the antenna out in the open, I cannot talk as well inside the vehicle, since it is surrounded by steel. Two, I like to sit in the back in case we hit an IED [improvised explosive device] or similar explosion; that way, I get ejected from the truck versus getting rattled around inside. I would rather go flying than stay with the vehicle and catch on fire.

"In the back of the truck I had my 117 beside me. I had an antenna mounted on the top of the truck that I could just plug into. I had a Toughbook sitting beside me, the ROVER video downlink systems, and a M240 machine gun. The gun truck was configured with a large bench in the back; usually there was another SF guy sitting back there with me. Normally, the SF guys would handle the machine gun; that way, I could man the radio and all the 'comms.' In Iraq, it is very 'comms' intensive, and the airspace is really dense, so there was a lot of talking to be done. I was usually busy with that instead of pulling security.

"We rolled into the town of Al Hilla and picked up about four companies of the Hilla SWAT; approximately two hundred personnel, riding in thirty-six vehicles. The convoy then traveled south to Najaf and rolled in from the north with all these Hilla SWAT guys. We stopped at the police checkpoint that was two kilometers from

Members of the Hilla SWAT team with U.S. SOF operators during the Battle of Najaf in Iraq. SSgt Ryan Wallace, along with several other combat controllers, was called upon to provide CAS during what would be the largest sustained engagement of the war in Iraq. *Courtesy of the U.S. Air Force.*

where the fight was going on, and we thought the fight was over. We were pretty sure because, the week before, we had done a QRF with the Hilla SWAT and we had gone out to this area and sat there for about eight hours. Basically, [we were] providing a presence while the local forces cleaned up the mess, and then we came home. So this time we were expecting to be greeted by the same circumstances and expected to be bored. We were convinced [that] the fight was over and we had missed out on everything.

"The SF ODA team leader dismounted along with the Hilla SWAT commander and they talked to the police chief, Iraqi Army general, and the governor. While they were talking with them, I waited in the back of the truck. There were some Apaches flying over my shoulder about two klicks northeast over that farm area. But at this time I did not know where the compound was or what had happened that morning. I called back on SatCom, trying to get a frequency for the Apaches. I got on my data network; I had the data through SatCom to a different channel, so I could send some text messages and they [could] send me back a bogus 'freq.' Finally, the ODA was able to call over to the other ODA who was stationed in Najaf, and we got a good 'freq' for the apaches.

"As I was programming the good 'freq' into my radio, I looked over my shoulder to see what the Apaches were up to. At that moment, I saw an airburst RPG [rocket-propelled grenade] blow up between the flight. There were two AH-64s flying together, and then this puff of black smoke appeared between them. Right after that, I got the 'freq' programmed into the radio and I was able to call them up, asking if they saw that RPG. They acknowledged in the affirmative, plus they also had observed some enemy personnel with machine guns and they were going to engage them in self-defense. I passed that information on to the SF team leader, who was motivated to load all the guys back into the vehicles and begin a movement to contact. We just hopped into the trucks and started driving toward the sound of the machine-gun fire.

"On the out way, moving to contact, I called up the Apaches and got them onto our position by using a signal mirror. Once they saw us, the two helicopters went back to engage enemy personnel. We drove to this area, referred to as the 'chicken farm,' and after we exited, we were in the large, open flat area surrounded by a high berm. Imagine an ant on a billiard table—that was what it looked like. You had that high wall surrounding you, and then flat for as far as you could see. This was really a bad spot to be in with a large convoy of vehicles and a bunch of potential bad guys on the other side of that berm.

"Our intent was to drive across this open space and get to a hardball road, and then turn north. As we were driving across, we saw a break in the berm. But when we got up to it, it was actually a ten-foot cliff, so we could not get across. We immediately made a left turn and pulled the vehicles up into the berm, and nudged right up to the base. Our vehicles were in a turret defilade position; the only thing sticking up over the berm was the turret of the HMMWV and top of the five-ton truck. All of the other SWAT vehicles were just little pickup trucks, which were not tall enough to see over the top of the berm. So, all of those guys dismounted and crawled up to the top of the berm.

"We were spread out about almost half a kilometer because we had so many vehicles. From left to right was about four hundred meters between the endmost vehicles. The western flank was now coming under machine-gun fire. I was on the eastern end with about two hundred and fifty meters between me and the other SF vehicle. From my position, [I could see] the guys in our truck looking over the berm, and they saw a vehicle with a machine gun in it. We also saw another empty vehicle, but we did not see any people moving. There was no smoke from the machine gun or any other evidence of the enemy.

"About halfway through this battlespace there was a lot of vegetation and trees. It was in those trees and the area to the left of them that the enemy with the machine gunner was positioned. The guys in my vehicle dismounted. The medic got out; he was armed with a Carl-G and he sent some HE [high explosive] down range to blow up the truck with the machine gun."

"Carl-G" is slang for the Swedish-made Bofors Carl Gustav multirole recoilless weapon. It is a direct-fire, man-portable, shoulder-fired weapon that uses a variety of 84 mm ammunition. Among this ammunition is an HE round. Sergeant Wallace continued: "At this time, I still did not know [that] the western flank was under fire. Those guys were busy taking cover, and they were not talking on the radio yet. I called up the Apaches to tell them, 'Hey, man, we have got nothing going on over here. We are just trying to blow up this truck. If you guys have targets, continue to engage over there.'

"The Apache pilot radioed back, informing me that he was in sight of some more bad guys in the back of a truck with a machine gun, and they were rolling in on it. I looked up over the treetops and saw the Apaches flying in at less than a thousand feet. As the first one rolled in, I could see his chin guns pointed down at a target beneath him. I thought he was firing, but it turned out he had sustained damage from machine-gun fire from the ground. The next AH-64 came in behind him, pointed at the same target, and then the rotors of that helicopter completely stopped and the helicopter fell out of the sky. It had taken too many machine-gun rounds or took a hit in a critical location that froze up the entire workings of the helicopter.

"After I saw the helicopter fall from the sky, I made a net call on the radio [to announce] that the Apache had gone down. I had an MBITR on my chest rig, and then I had my big radio on my back. I had a Peltor headset on, so I could plug into both radios at the same time and talk to both air and inter-team. I made the call on both the inter-team frequency, so all the SF guys knew, and on the air frequency, so that his wingman knew as well. His wingman had been in the lead, so he could not see what had gone on behind him."

The AH-64 Apache helicopter was shot down by enemy ground fire, which killed Captain Mark T. Resh "HHC" and Chief Warrant Officer Cornell C. Chao, B Company. The other Apache that had been flying in the lead was piloted by Chief Warrant Officer 4 Johnny Judd and Co-pilot CWO2 Jake Gaston. The soldiers were assigned to the 4th Battalion, 227th Aviation Regiment, 1st Air Cavalry Brigade, 1st Cavalry Division, Fort Hood, Texas.

"With the helicopter down, the ODA team leader started talking about making a move to the crash site. Because the western flank was under such heavy fire; it was accessed [that] they could not move or that they would get shot if they tried to move out of their position. The ODA made the decision to execute a right flank with us guys on the right half. We grabbed some of the SWAT guys and moved around to the right side, trying to flank the guys who were pinning down our guys down on the left flank.

"The team leader grabbed me and the SF medic who had the

Carl-G, and then we headed off to the east. It was just three of us Americans, our interrupter, and about fifty of the SWAT guys. We ran around the berm, jumped down that ten-foot cliff, and came back up on the other side. As we emerged from the berm we were near a collection of vehicles. These were the vehicles that had been shot up in the morning, which belonged to the governor and his security detail. When we came upon those vehicles, we observed about twenty Iraqi police officers hiding behind them. Not sure of their allegiances—if they were good guys, bad guys, or indifferent—we ended up leaving some SWAT guys behind to keep an eye on them and to watch our backs as we continued the advance.

"From that position, we came under machine-gun fire from a spot on the berm about two hundred meters away. The bad guys had the compound set up [so that there was] a flat field, then a ten-foot berm, then a twenty-foot drop into the bottom of a trench [that was] about one car-length wide. Then there was a twenty-foot rise to the top of the next berm and then a drop down ten feet again. To go through this thing, you had to go up ten feet, then down twenty feet, and then back up twenty [feet] and back down ten again. It was a pretty heinous berm system and it was really deep.

"It was also terraced; up at the top, they had a little walkway built [that was] about three feet wide. The rest of the berm was about chest high so [that] they could walk along, and if they wanted to take cover, they could jump down into the bottom of the trenches. The bad guys were on the top of the terrace with a machine gun.

"I had a second flight of Apaches to check on, then my first flight of F-16s to check on. I was able to talk the F-16s onto our position, and then I called the Apaches in for a gun run to provide suppressive fire so we could advance. At this time, the entire SWAT element on the western flank was not able to get up on line to provide suppressive fire for us, so we used the second AH-64 attack to set [the] conditions for our first advance.

"Right after the helicopters made their gun run, the SF team leader was up and running. The SWAT guys were following him and I was trying to keep up with all of them. We got about fifty meters, and this machine gunner pops up again. Now, in this situation he had the angle on us—where he could just hang over the berm and fire while we had nothing to hide behind. We had a berm on our left with an enemy behind that, and we had a flat open space to our right. We hugged the dirt and tried to melt into the sand while this guy was shooting at us. When we returned fire, this guy took cover behind the dirt. I got in the prone position and got onto my scope, setting the cross hairs of the reticle right above the dirt level. He popped his head up and I squeezed off a couple shots; they hit the dirt right in front of his face. He ducked back down again. I reset my aim and waited about twenty seconds, and the guy did not come back up in that spot. So I called in another AH-64 gun run on that position.

"The Apache came flying in and got only five rounds out of the gun, hitting on my side of the berm. It was not an effective way to engage the enemy personnel. I advised the SF team leader [that] we ought to use a bomb in order to set conditions for our next advance. It turned out that was exactly what he was thinking, too. We called in the F-16, which put a laser-guided bomb down, taking out all of the bad guys in that position. Now, we were about a hundred meters away from where that bomb had gone off. 'Danger close' for that bomb is three hundred meters; we were well within 'danger close' for that ordnance!

"We still had smoke rising and big clumps of dirt falling down on us from the bomb. The team leader was up and running, and I tried to keep up. We got to that [next] berm. The only guys who went over the berm were the three Americans; all the SWAT guys hesitated— they pulled security to watch our backs, but did not go over the berm. One of the SWAT guys did attempt to go over the berm, but as soon as he did, he was shot in the face and fell back down the berm.

"We came over the top of the berm and began to engage those [enemy] personnel positioned down in the trench. The bomb had been effective at killing the guys on the corner; however, about thirty meters down the trench, there were more bad guys. Though those guys were really freaked out; they were still armed and ready to fight. So the captain, the SF medic, and I engaged about thirty personnel anywhere from two to fifty meters.

"After that, the medic came off the line to tend to the SWAT guy who had been shot in the face. The ODA team leader came off the line and, using the interpreter, tried to motivate the SWAT guys to get back up on the line—to continue to hold security and press on the fight. With the captain and medic off the berm, I looked around and it dawned on me that I was the only guy with my head still above the berm. I should probably have been pulling security down the trench line. As I turned around, there was this guy who had been lying behind a dead body. I do not know if he had been knocked unconscious or was just playing dead, but he took the opportunity when I was looking away to sit up and aim his weapon at me. I turned around and saw him just in time to squeeze off a couple of rounds. They hit in the dirt right near him; he took cover behind that dead body again. I shot again, [and] this time I was able to shoot him in the leg. I called for the team leader to come up and help me engage the guy, because the captain could probably get a better angle on him. When he came up, he was asking for me to talk him onto the body, as there were a whole bunch of bodies in the trench—you could not tell which was the shooter. I had just finished my talk when the bad guy blew himself up with a hand grenade. After that I told the captain, "Well, sir, that was him, so you can go back to what you were doing."

☆ ☆ ☆ ☆

"Unbeknownst to us, the guys who had been there that morning had gone back to Najaf. But as soon as the helicopter crashed, they got word to respond and moved to secure the crash site. They had been in camp about five minutes when they got the call; [they needed] another five minutes to rekit, reload weapons, change batteries, and drive back out to the crash site. So, they had about ten minutes in their camp before they were turned around and heading right back out again.

"I was pulling security and I could see some guys way off to my north about three hundred meters. They were out on the berms and do not see me behind them. I was able to squeeze off a couple of rounds; I hit one guy in the butt and he fell back into the trench. Then I engaged the rest of those guys with the Apaches, doing rocket and gun runs. Right about the time he was beginning his gun run, this U.S. element [team] came in from the north and drove all the way around the farm, looking for the crash site. They had been given some incorrect grid coordinates for the location of the downed helicopter. So now they were traveling in the blind, just looking for the site. We did not have 'comms' with them, and we did not know they were coming until we heard their machine gun firing.

"Once we heard their machine-gun fire, and they turned around the corner, we could see them. They had mini-guns on the gun trucks—.50 cals, 240s, and all that stuff was going off. We knew it was our guys because the *brrrrrrpf* of the mini-guns is real identifiable. So, we held our position and waited for them to roll up. They linked up with us, we had a little face-to-face, and I met SSgt David. I did not even know [that] the other two combat controllers, David and Bryan, were down there in Najaf. They were down there on a different mission, so I did not know they were in the area. To see him was really surprising—we gave each other a high-five! I gave him some grid co-ordinates for the targets I knew about and told him what aircraft were on station. We had a couple of flights of F-16s up there, a whole bunch of Apaches were now on site; about three flights of AH-64s, and a Predator was there, [too].

"SSgt David then passed the data back to MSgt Bryan, who was in the back of the convoy with the ground force commander. Our SF team leader and SSgt David's team leader had a face-to-face talk about the game plan—who was located where, etc. They divided the battle-space, [discussing] where they thought the crash site was. The element loaded back into their vehicles and headed off to the north. They made a left turn, then another left turn, and ended up coming right down through the middle of the enemy farm. The farm area was about two square kilometers; right through the middle of it was a main paved road and a whole bunch of buildings. The bad guys had reinforced this area as well.

"In Iraq, [for] most of the fights we were going to at this point, especially after the invasion, the bad guys were few and far between. Rarely did you see a massing of more than twenty to thirty guys. On this morning, when they were getting reports of twenty to thirty guys in the trench and were bombing them, then getting a report of another thirty guys, it was a real surprise. When we came over that berm and saw all those bad guys in the trench, it was a real eye-opener. We thought maybe this was a lot bigger than we thought it was.

"It had not dawned on any of us, or the coalition guys, how many bad guys were really in this area. We [didn't] figure this out until after nightfall. The element made their turn and drove right through the middle of the village. They were now engaged in a near ambush, anywhere from one meter away from the trucks to out to fifty meters away. This went on for about three hundred meters. All of the American and some of the Iraqi HMMWVs were armored. Both of their mini-guns were shot, two of the .50 cals were shot and went down, three of the 240s got hit and went down. One of the SF guys was on the mini-gun when it went down, so he transitioned to his pistol and ended up killing two bad guys from his moving HMMWV. All of the truck tires were shot out, and one of the Iraqi gunners in the gun turret was killed. When it was all said and done, they made a right turn at the end of that trench line. As they were driving through the village, they could see the helicopter crash site off to their right.

"They made another right, then another right back up to the north and [onto] the next parallel road, which put them about two hundred meters from the ambush they had just driven through. Now, the crash site was between them and the enemy on the other side. All this time, the Apaches were engaging any enemy forces that were attempting to move on the crash site. About the time the American convoy made its final turn to approach the crash site, MSgt Bryan was able to establish communication and get a good talk on with the Apaches. He began engagement of everything along their route of travel to the location of the down U.S. helicopter. Everywhere they had gotten shot [at] from before now came under attack by the AH-64 helicopters. From 30 mm rounds to Hellfire missiles, the Apaches pounded the enemy positions.

"We had divided the airspace before they left, with MSgt Bryan taking the three flights of Apaches with him and me keeping the fixed-wing fighters on my side. We split the battlespace from the main road that they ended up driving on. Everything east of that was mine, and everything west of the road was covered by MSgt Bryan. As it turned out once, he got into heavy fire, all the focus went on him. Since there was not much [happening] on our side, we stayed quiet while he worked all his fires over on the western side of the battlespace. Through that engagement, none of the rounds actually penetrated their vehicles, but there was a lot of accurate fire into the windows; the enemy did have some armor-piercing rounds, so there was some pretty good damage.

They had some injured, three Americans and eight Iraqis killed, and all of their vehicles disabled.

"We had showed up about 1200 noon, so from 1200 to 1400, we were engaged in the fight. It was around 1430 [when the element] linked up with us and headed toward the crash site. They held that crash site until about 2000 hours. That afternoon was all rockets and Hellfires. A lot of it was 'danger close' for controllers Bryan and David. Then, before sunset, I engaged another five guys in the trench line with a bomb and then a re-supply Bongo truck that was moving from the trench line back to the village, traveling back and forth with supplies.

"Through the day we had multiple flights of A-10s, a couple of flights of GR4 Tornados, lots of flights of F-16s and Apaches. We had a Predator and a Shadow show up along with a Navy P3. All of this was in the air space at the same time, meaning we spent a lot of time just de-conflicting air space. A lot of kudos go to the A-10 FAC [forward air control], who showed up and actually de-conflicted a lot of that air space for me while I was running around fighting bad guys.

"Sometime just before sunset, a reinforcing Stryker Brigade from Baghdad came down. The Strykers were from the 4th Brigade Combat Team (Airborne) of the 25th Infantry Division, MiTT (Military Transition Team) 810, commanded by Lieutenant Colonel Stephen Hughes, the deputy commander, 4th BCT(A). They loaded up some of the SF ODA-566 troops, moved into the crash site, and secured the position. SSgt David and the ODA medic went in and secured the remains of the Apache—the helicopter had caught fire as soon as it hit the ground. They exfiled the wounded and the remains, and then the ODA left the battle, returning to the fire base in Najaf to facilitate the resupply. They had about sixteen to twenty flights of MH-60s Night Stalkers, which brought in a whole bunch of vehicle parts, ammunition, food, and water.

"The Strykers remained at the crash site. The Stryker commander was a colonel, and he took over control of the battlespace on the western flank. My team leader still had control of the eastern flank, and we were coordinating fires. It evolved into a free fire zone—anything east of that road and in that village. Anything that moved west of that road, we called him and let him know what they were. He then engaged them or authorized me to engage them with CAS.

"As sunset came, the Stryker commander sent some of his element over to link up with us on the southern side. We had got the battlespace flanked on the south end and the west side. When the Strykers showed up, we begin the hand-over of the battlespace to the Stryker commander and his JTAC. The JTAC with the colonel was a conventional TACP [tactical air control party] assigned to the Stryker brigade. At the same time, an AC-130 showed up.

"Just after sunset, all this stuff came into play, like all the pieces [of a puzzle]. We still had no 'comms' with the element that went to the crash site. We did not know anything about the ambush they had driven through or all of the stuff they did. I could hear the Apaches talking to him, but I could not hear him talking to the helos because of line-of-sight issues. When they got back to their base and sent in their report, Higher called us back and told us what had happened. Now, we found out [that] all of their vehicles had gotten shot up. We found out [that] they were in a three-hundred-meter ambush [going] through that village. We got word back from our SWAT guys, reporting that some of the captured Iraqi Army HMMWVs that were in that village had been shooting at the helicopters that morning.

"Then we got a report from one of the UAVs [unmanned aerial vehicles] that somebody was back at headquarters watching "Kill TV." They sent a report down to us that there were a hundred personnel in that village. All that came together. I called up the AC-130 gunship and told them, 'Hey, we are looking for a hundred personnel massing in the village.' He called me back, confirming [that] he had a hundred personnel in a trench line. That set off the engagement for the rest of the night. We had the AC-130 gunships overhead and worked it all night long, integrating fire with the A-10s.

"The A-10s perched in an orbit around the AC-130 gunship. The AC-130 engaged troops in the open, and then when it came to hard buildings, it marked those structures for the A-10s. The A-10s then went in and whacked them with bombs. We 'Winchestered' four AC-

130 gunships that night. The A-10s and F-16s were bombing all night long as well—both JDAMs and laser-guided bombs. The next morning, fire stopped, [but it wasn't until] right about sunset [that] we stopped engaging with CAS.

"We were still seeing bad guys pop up and run across the field, so until 0900, we were shooting at bad guys. The Stryker commander moved in from the west, and on the loud speaker he called for their surrender. We cease-fired and sent our SWAT guys and our Stryker elements around to the east. We pulled up to the berms and start calling for surrender on that side, too. Then guys started coming out of the village on the western side, toward the Stryker commander's element. He had the MedEvac coming in for those wounded personnel who were surrendering. On the eastern flank, it was open farmland, so we were just holding security.

"We started conducting a battle damage assessment [BDA] of all the stuff that went on that [previous] night. As we were going through,

A DShK mounted on a trailer at Najaf. The DShK is a Russian-built 12.7 mm heavy machine gun used by the Soldiers of Heaven during the Battle of Najaf. Note the vast, flat land of the compound in the background. *Courtesy of the U.S. Air Force.*

we saw a Bongo truck we had blown up. The [enemy had] captured three Iraqi Army armored HMMWVs, so we shot those with the Apache. They had some other captured American vehicles [as well]. Since the Iraqi invasion, the [enemy] had been amassing equipment, so they had a huge stockpile of vehicles and weapons. [There were] caches of ammunition and ordnance spread all over the farm.

"The enemy had captured three Iraqi army soldiers when they had abandoned their vehicles that morning, and executed them in the village. One soldier had committed suicide to prevent his capture. We estimated about two hundred and fifty extremists were killed, and over three hundred prisoners taken. We [also] neutralized ten heavy machine guns during the fight. We stayed until around noon doing the BDA, then loaded up onto the trucks and went back to Hilla."

The Silver Star

SSgt Ryan Wallace had called in close air support around-the-clock during this long battle. When the job description for a combat controller says it is a day's work, that often means the *full* twenty-four hours. Sergeant Wallace was awarded the Silver Star for calling in CAS continuously for more than twenty-four hours during the battle of Najaf.

Staff Sergeant Ryan A. Wallace distinguished himself by gallantry as a Combat Controller, 21st Expeditionary Special Tactics Squadron, 1st Expeditionary Special Operations Group, Combined Joint Special Operations Air Component, Special Operations Command Central in connection with military operations against an enemy of the United States near An Najaf, Iraq from 28 January 2007 to 29 January 2007. During this period, while responding to United States and Iraqi forces pinned down by more than 500 well-armed and disciplined fighters, Sergeant Wallace bravely maneuvered to contact with the enemy. Approaching enemy fortifications, his team was ambushed with deadly fire striking two United States Soldiers. Sergeant Wallace exposed himself to a staggering volley of fire and gained valuable targeting information as he directed air strikes from helicopter gun ships enabling the team to regain the initiative. During a subsequent attack, he was again pinned down by heavy machine gun fire, so using his signal mirror, Sergeant Wallace identified his position clearing AH-64 fire as a mark for an F-16 "danger close" GBU-12 strike within one hundred meters. Following the successful precision strike, he led his force over a defensive berm, killing seven insurgents in a heated exchange of gunfire. Again pressing the fight, Sergeant Wallace heroically exposed himself to a hailstorm of bullets, directing 500-pound bombs and strafing runs on enemy forces massing for a counterattack. As the fight raged into the night and next morning, he skillfully controlled 23 attack sorties and three AC-130 gunships, killing 150 well-trained and entrenched insurgents. His courage under fire and deft airmanship skills saved his team and proved decisive in enabling the Iraqi forces to defeat a major insurgent organization. By his gallantry and devotion to duty, Sergeant Wallace has reflected great credit upon himself and the United States Air Force.

17

Spooky, on Station

LTC Don Bellinghausen,
Operation Iraqi Freedom

The flagship of the U.S. Air Force Special Operations Command (AFSOC) is the AC-130U Spooky gunship. These aircraft are assigned to the 16th Special Operations Wing's 4th Special Operations Squadron (SOS). This high-tech gunslinger was designed with special operations forces (SOF) teams in mind. The primary mission of the AC-130U gunship is to deliver precision firepower in support of close air support (CAS) for both special operations forces and conventional forces. Operating in the shroud of darkness, the Spooky gunship can remain on station for extended time, providing accurate fire support and intelligence to the operators on the ground.

The business end of the gunship is found in three weapon systems. As you enter the AC-130U by way of the front crew hatch and turn right, you find the first weapon system—the GAU-12/U 25 mm Gatling gun, which is fully traversable and is also capable of firing

1,800 rounds per minute from altitudes of up to 12,000 feet. The 25 mm weapon system automatically ejects the spent brass into a holding area, where it is emptied out at a later time.

Moving on toward the rear of the aircraft, you find a 40 mm Bofors gun and the 105 mm Howitzer cannon. The 40 mm Bofors gun has been associated with the gunships since 1969. Once used on naval vessels as anti-aircraft guns, the weapons were stripped from their pedestal mounts and placed in the AC-130s. The 40 mm Bofors is mounted in the port side of the AC-130U, with the ammunition stored in a special rack on the starboard wall of the fuselage, behind the gun. The 40 mm is often preferred for CAS in "danger close" support of friendly forces, owing to its small fragmentation pattern. Just aft of the Bofors is the M102, a 105 mm Howitzer cannon. This weapon was derived from the U.S. Army field artillery M1A1 Howitzer. It has been modified to fire from an aircraft and is placed in a special mounting and is positioned also on the port side of the gunship.

Unlike high-speed fixed-wing aircraft (i.e., "fast movers"), which must have qualified forward air controllers (FAC) or combat controllers for ordnance delivery in close position to friendly forces, the AC-130U can be controlled by fire support officers, team leaders, or self-FAC. This unique capability makes the gunship user-friendly for the operators on the ground. These fire control officers are located onboard the gunship in the battle management center, or BMC. Here, they operate state-of-the-art sensors, navigation, and fire control systems in a work area protected by a composite armor of silicon carbide and Spectra fiber. The BMC, coupled with the trained eyes and skilled hands of its officers, enables the crew to deliver the AC-130U's firepower or area saturation with surgical precision.

A wide assortment of sensors fitted into this ultra-modern gunship include an all-light-level television (ALLTV) system, a laser illuminator assembly (LIA), and an infrared detection set. Multimode radar furnishes exceptionally long-range target direction and identification. This radar is also able to track 40 mm and 105 mm projectiles and to return pinpoint impact locations to the crew for subsequent target adjustment.

The fire control systems offer a dual-target attack capability. Engaging two different sensors and using both weapons, the 40 mm Bofors cannon and 105 mm Howitzer have been updated with improved electronics that allow the gunnery crew to simultaneous aim at two separate targets. As long as the two targets are within a mile of each other, the gunship can divide its fire with devastating accuracy. No other air-to-ground attack platform in the world offers this capability.

So who pulls the trigger? The final trigger pull—actually it is a button—is, in a normal mode of fire, done by the sensor operator; that is, whatever primary sensor the BMC operators are using actually shoots the weapon. However, there are degraded modes of fire whereby the pilot pulls the trigger, which does occur periodically. In fact, there is a whole procedure of safeguards built into the system, including arming switches at multiple spots throughout the aircraft, all of which must be "on" to fire the weapon. If anyone observes anything unsafe at any of those positions, he can kill the gunfire. The last step in the procedure is the pilot's consent switch, after which the sensor operator pulls the trigger.

The new AC-130U is fully pressurized, allowing greater speeds, increased range, and additional crew comfort owing to its ability to fly above, rather than through, adverse weather. Navigational features include the inertial navigation systems (INS) and the GPS. This U-model gunship is capable of operation in adverse weather, in poor visibility, using the APQ180 strike radar. The radar tracks fixed or moving targets or beacon offsets. Its defensive systems include a countermeasures dispensing system that releases chaff and flares to counter radar and infrared-guided (IR) anti-aircraft missiles. To shield the aircraft's heat signature from the engines, the AC-130U has infrared heat shields mounted underneath the engines, which dispense and hide the heat source from hostile anti-aircraft with counter-IR devices such as the Directional Infrared Countermeasures system, or DIRCM. The DIRCM fires a laser at incoming heat-seeking missiles, blinding their optics and ruining their ability to track the aircraft, causing it to miss.

☆   ☆   ☆   ☆

The flagship of AFSOC is the AC-130U model. The gunship is referred to as "Spooky," in reference to the original AC-47 gunships of Vietnam. In addition to the 40 mm and 105 mm cannons, it is fitted with a 25 mm chain cannon toward the front of the fuselage. *Courtesy of the U.S. Air Force.*

While close air support is the Spooky's primary mission, additional tasks it may be asked to perform include air interdiction, armed reconnaissance, airbase, perimeter, and point defense; land, water, and heli-borne troop escort; drop, landing, and extraction zone support; forward air control; limited airborne command and control; and combat search and rescue support. Especially, the AC-130 gunships were among the first AFSOC aircraft deployed to support Operations Enduring Freedom and Iraqi Freedom. Having the ability to loiter over the area of operations, the gunships were a force-multiplier by their ability to provide precision close air support.

Lieutenant Colonel Don Bellinghausen, who was assigned to the 4th SOS, deployed four times to Afghanistan and completed eight tours to Iraq in the last six years. Half of that time he served as a crewmember and the other half as the squadron commander. He still flies periodically to keep his finger on the pulse of what is going on. As the fire control officer of an AC-130U, he experienced a trilogy of missions during his deployment to southwest Asia in support of the Iraqi operations.

The first of these missions found him orbiting the city of Najaf. The Battle of Najaf was considered the biggest contact with the enemy since the early days of the Iraqi War. During the battle, there was heavy involvement of conventional Air Force aircraft as well as special operations aircraft. That battle would become known as the "Mother of all TICs" (troops in contact). Lieutenant Colonel Bellinghausen told his story: "On January 28, 2007, just north of Najaf, there was a compound full of enemy personnel. These people were actually members of a doomsday cult called the 'Soldiers of Heaven.' . . . The local political Iraqi figures and the Iraqi police had received some tips about the compound and went to investigate. On their way, they received fire from the cult personnel. The Iraqis withdrew, realizing [that] there were a lot of people in the compound [and they] requested assistance from the Iraqi Army [IA]. The IA realized that they were overwhelmed, too, and requested assistance from the American Army. The American Army requested assistance from the Special Forces." During the course of the ensuing battle, the United States lost an AH-64 Apache helicopter; the helicopter was shot down during a lot of close-in fighting that involved Iraqis and Americans fighting side by side.

The AH-64 crew had been recovered before LTC Bellinghausen's crew arrived on station, but there was more action to follow. The lieutenant colonel related his view of the action: "The combat controller had already used some fast CAS—for example, F-16s. By the time we arrived on scene, they were popping in assets to us and the friendly forces were getting a little confused. The "fog of war" was setting in a little bit.

"What an AC-130U gunship excels at is close-in fighting—sorting out the good guys from the bad guys. That is what we did. When we arrived, we quickly determined where all the friendly lines were. The combat controller started to use the gunship to work these targets. There were a lot of heavy weapons in the compound—DShKs mounted on Bongo trucks, mortars . . . just a lot of firepower." The DShK is a Soviet-made 12.7 mm heavy machine gun similar to the

M2 .50 cal Browning Heavy Machine Gun. A Bongo truck is the model name for the Mazda 1.25-ton truck. With its low-walled cargo box, the truck's name has become the generic term for any type of small utility truck.

"They [the enemy] had dug trenches all along the compound. These were [full of] entrenched troops. . . . The first gunship came in, sorted everything out, and then started shooting. It did not take very long [for him] to go through all of his ammunition—[what] we call 'Winchestering.' While the gunship was performing its fire mission, the SOF were able to let the gunship mark targets for all of the fast CAS—the F-16s, A-10s, Apaches, and numerous assets that were all coming in to deliver ordnance. The second gunship came in and took over; he also Winchestered. That evening, we ended up sending in four gunships over that target—that is, four individual gunships, not one and rearm and return—four separate AC-130s. They completely overwhelmed the enemy complex. The estimate was approximately two hundred enemy KIA. They also captured close to four hundred personnel.

"It was uncovered [later] what this religious cult had planned. During the Shiite holiday of Ashura, which is a religious festival they observe in Najaf, the [devoted] walk through the streets and flog themselves; they actually beat their bodies until you can see blood dripping down their backs. That festival was about to begin. This cult believed [that] they had [a direct line to] the twelfth [thirteen] Iman and that they were going to [summon] his appearance. They were going to [come into the village and] kill all the Mullahs, including Grand Ayatollah al-Sistani and some of the other very important [religious] leaders. If those guys had been assassinated, it would have been very detrimental to the country, but the Iraqis had uncovered this plot in the nick of time. . . . It was a good story of cooperation between the Iraqi and U.S. forces. . . . The TIC in Najaf was untypical, as we had mass troops. We do not see that now. What we are doing [now], day in and day out, is getting the bad guys by the twos and threes. The guys that come, they pop out with an RPG, shooting at our guys, and then duck back around the corner to reload. They never get a chance to reload because a gunship drops a 40 mm round on them."

* * * *

The next mission that stood out for LTC Bellinghausen involved the support of a direct action (DA) mission. He related: "We had multiple missions where we supported ground forces that were moving by air, landing by Pave Low helicopters. The helos began to receive ground fire by triple-A [anti-aircraft artillery]. Normally, we would immediately roll over the triple-A and eliminate the threat. But this particular mission was a DA. There were multiple targets spread out over roughly three miles. We were covering a target to the north; to the south, the ground party had completed its mission and was getting back aboard the helicopters to depart the area.

"The MH-53 helicopters arrived at the landing zone. The ground troops had boarded the helos and [the] lead [helicopter] took off. As he did, he received triple-A fire from a DShK on a Bongo truck. This helo was hit by one round; fortunately, it passed through the cabin—just the skin of the aircraft—[and] did not hit anyone or anything vital, [so] the helicopter continued on its way. But the second helicopter was pinned on the ground. Tracers from the DShK were flying over the second Pave Low. [Again] fortunately, the helo had landed in an indentation in the ground—it was not a wadi, just a low depression with a road next to it. The road was a lot higher. Had it landed on the road, the helo would have been much [more] vulnerable. The MH-53 was about eight feet lower than the rounds going overhead. The gunner manning the DShK in the Bongo could not depress the gun any further, so with the limited amount of travel the gun was shooting over the helicopter.

"The gunship pilot [overhead] had the 'God's eye view' of the battlefield. You can equate this to [using] our sensors [to look] through a telescope, but it is easier to spot the target you want to zoom in on with a wide-angle view. We were busy with the target to the north. So when the pilot saw the triple-A fire, he immediately [turned] the gunship around, kicked the rudder, and [brought] the plane over to where the source of the triple-A was located.

"In the meantime, the MH-53 on the ground was returning fire. You could see two streams of fire coming up, going over the respective

target. Over the radio, the '53 was calling for us, calling for our assistance. It was very easy for us—we knew exactly where he was located as
well as where the bad guy was. As soon as we rolled in, I fired the Howitzer and we dropped a 105 mm shell down onto the Bongo. The first
one missed just a little bit; but it was [close] enough that the enemy immediately stopped firing. Then the second shot was direct—right on
the guy. It totally destroyed the Bongo and the DShK.

"After the flight, the gunner of the MH-53 came to us and said,
'The pucker factor was pretty high there, but as soon as the first 105
came down, they knew the gunship [was] there and they yelled to the
pilot, "The gunship's here! The gunship's here!" When the second
round hit, he said, "The gunship's got him. Let's get outta here!"' He
came back afterwards and everyone was pretty stoked, telling the story.
The pilot took off and departed from the area. There were no friendly
injuries and everyone got out safely. A lot of our missions are like that.
It can be relatively boring or mundane, and then all of the sudden,
when you least expect it, the action starts."

The third mission involved a compilation of events. The LTC related:
"Some of the missions of the gunship could be lackluster. We might
find ourselves escorting ground parties who were doing their missions.
Whether they were driving in, were a ground assault force, or were in-
serting a helicopter assault force, we were really a big flying insurance
policy for those guys. They walked softly and we were their big stick.
Many missions went by when we were not needed or—better said—
we did not shoot our guns. There were so many missions that [the job]
may have seemed routine, that the teams came under fire, that they
were traveling fairly light and we were the protection for them.

"Especially in some of those urban areas, with the very low-yield
munitions we shot, we could put the round so close to them. Many
times in the city, they would be going on a DA mission, entering the
building to seize some enemy personnel. All of a sudden, someone a
block away would step around the corner and shoot an RPG [rocket-
propelled grenade] at the team or open up with a heavy machine gun.

The ground force would immediately take cover and we were right there. Two or three rounds of 40 mm were all it took and we eliminated the threat.

"Sometimes it was pretty dramatic. [On a] mission in Sadar City, the ground force was taking fire; they were really pinned down. It was coming in close, and they were requesting fire. We had 'danger close' distances, and we did not like to shoot any closer than that because [of the] risk to the ground party. But the team had given 'danger close' permission because of the seriousness of the situation. The gunship crew ended up putting a round seventeen meters away from the ground force, which is pretty dang close to the friendlies. The team members were barricaded, so they had some protection, but that was still pretty close. They were indeed hearing the whistle as the ordnance came in."

LTC Bellinghausen gave this overview of his missions: "The difference between a CAP [combat air patrol] and what we did is this: A CAP was when the [aircraft] were sitting around orbiting, waiting to be called in. [On the other hand,] what we did was be an armed escort of CAS. [The difference was that] we were much more involved in the operation . . . the gunship was actually assigned to the mission. In the future, the AC-130 will receive an upgraded sensor ball to replace the ALLTV; which will make us even more lethal. We are looking forward to using this new setup, to tagging things."

Urrah!

TSgt Jason Dryer,
Operation Enduring Freedom

The men of the AFSOC Special Tactics Squadron (STS) are indeed a unique breed. These battle-tested warriors have what it takes to dig down and drive on, regardless of the circumstances or challenges. Members of the STS have a word that describes that drive: *Urrah!* Technical Sergeant Jason Dryer, of the 22nd Special Tactics Squadron, was deployed to Afghanistan and assigned to a U.S. Army Special Operations Task Force in support of Operation Enduring Freedom. He exemplifies *Urrah!*

TSgt Dryer was working with an Army Special Forces detachment that had received special intelligence about anti-Afghani forces (AAF) in the region. These forces were setting up illegal checkpoints on a main highway that ran through the center of the city. Jason recounted his experience: "We headed out under the cover of darkness to establish a blocking point in order to prevent insurgent forces from setting up the checkpoints. The detachment and I pulled off to the side of the highway and established a 'hide site' approximately two hundred meters, from where a team of Afghan National Army (ANA) opened a checkpoint of their own. The ANA checkpoint's mission was to funnel local nationals through the area and limit the insurgents' freedom of movement. The ANA checkpoint remained open until around dusk, when we received word from our ANA of an illegal anti-Afghani checkpoint five hundred meters down the highway. We immediately mounted our vehicles to investigate the [report].

"As we entered the illegal checkpoint site, we drew fire from enemy positions on all sides. The insurgents attacked with small-arms weaponry and rocket-propelled grenades [RPGs]. The first three vehicles were heavily damaged from the initial onslaught of enemy fire. Luckily, all personnel inside the vehicles dismounted without casualties and the engagement ensued. Once we pushed through the kill zone, we immediately responded with heavy weapons, returning fire on numerous positions with .50 caliber, 240B, and MK-19 crew-served weaponry. At one point in the engagement an insurgent trained a rocket-propelled grenade at my position. I neutralized the threat with the 240B before he was able to accurately employ his weapon. The RPG fired off into the ground and skipped across the highway under my vehicle. It did not explode, due to the proximity of the target and his inability to arm it.

"That initial engagement seemed to last forever. Team members attempted to engage the enemy as bullets ricocheted around their positions. Meantime, I tried to establish satellite communications [SatCom] in order to get close air support [CAS] to aid us in our engagement. I noticed that my satellite antenna was destroyed by enemy fire, so I reconfigured it to use my portable antenna and [then I] called for immediate air support. Air assets were on their way, and I continued to engage insurgents with my 240B. My teammates and I neutralized multiple insurgent fighting positions, until the enemy began to withdraw [so as] to collect more weaponry for future attacks.

"I had one B-1 bomber and one AC-130 gunship checking in, so I described the situation to the aircraft and separated them geographically. [Then] I started to engage the enemy with CAS to clear the area for friendly dismounts [who would] pursue the AAF into a [nearby]

TSgt Dryer mans his position on the M240B 7.62 mm machine gun in the back of a Special Forces gun truck. Assigned to the SF ODA, he can provide covering fire with the heavy machine gun or call in CAS with his nearby radios. *Courtesy of the U.S. Air Force.*

orchard. I cleared the B-1 to drop one two-thousand-pound bomb on the enemy, [which had] established in new fighting positions 1.5 kilometers of our position. The sporadic enemy fire [soon] ended, enabling the team leader and his maneuver element freedom of movement through the orchard.

"I was positioned with the supporting element. We were in three HMMWVs [that would] follow the maneuver element at a distance through the enemy territory. I requested air assets to report on friendly progress and clear their route systematically. As the maneuver element proceeded farther into the enemy territory, they funneled into a large wadi, [a dry riverbed] formed by years of erosion. The wadi was approximately fifteen feet wide and six to seven feet deep in most areas. The enemy used these wadis as their rat lines, to get supplies or to gain tactical advantage. I requested the gunship to scan ahead, through the wadi. The gunship reported seeing enemy personnel take cover inside what appeared to be several caves. I advised my team leader of the situation, and I ensured [that] the maneuver element was identified visually before it engaged the imminent threat. I advised the team leader to hold his current location while I cleared the gunship to engage the enemy. The gunship unleashed a stream of 40 millimeter rounds on the caves, killing eight enemy fighters.

"While we maneuvered closer to the objective site, several insurgents were identified on motorcycles at the base of a mountain. They were riding [along], two to three to a bike, and [stopped to hold] up at what appeared to be a meeting location. After twenty minutes, the meeting [site] was filled with fifteen motorcycles and thirty-five anti-Afghani fighters, [apparently] reconstituting for a[nother] ambush. Once again I advised the team leader of the developing situation and requested that he halt the maneuver element while we neutralized the enemy. The team leader concurred, and soon after I cleared the gunship to fire 105 millimeter rounds, decimating all insurgents in that area. From that point until sun-up, a massive stockpile of enemy ammunitions burned, cooking numerous rockets, grenades, and belted 7.62s. This created a hazardous environment for friendly assets, for obvious reasons, and it confused the battlefield tracking, due to the constant noise of discharging enemy ammunitions.

"As the maneuver element crept farther along, the support element was halted by an enormous wadi. We needed to find another crossing point—this wadi was impassible with our vehicles, especially at night. At this time, I was engaging the enemy on the high ground, as they flowed [down] the mountainside to reinforce their positions. We positioned our vehicles on the edge of the wadi, to aid the maneuver element's navigation through the last bit of low ground. At the same time, I utilized air assets to find us a route and essentially to guide us to our objective.

"We were stationary for only a moment before enemy elements above us attacked. They took aim on our position and hailed a stream of fire on all three vehicles. We responded with heavy weaponry, and I simultaneously called the gunship in on them. I cleared the gunship for an immediate attack with 40 millimeter rounds, 'danger close' to our position. Rubble and shrapnel rained down on our heads while the gunship pummeled the enemy.

"For the remainder of the night we used air assets to guide us onto the objective area and link us with the maneuver element. Meantime, the maneuver element made its way up through the wadi to what remained of the arms cache. Several enemy [fighters] who survived the CAS came out of hiding to engage the maneuver element, to no avail— they were immediately neutralized. An hour later, all parties linked up and we destroyed the remaining enemy armaments. A few hours later, with the aid of F-15s, we returned to our forward operating base without further incident. When it was all said and done, this ended up being a nineteen-hour enemy engagement."

The Bronze Star Medal (with Valor)

For his heroic actions that day, TSgt Jason Dryer was awarded the Bronze Star with Valor. The following is the citation to accompany the award.

Technical Sergeant Jason P. Dryer distinguished himself by heroism as Combat Controller, 22d Expeditionary Special Tactics Squadron, 1st Expeditionary Special Operations Group, Combined Joint Special Operations Air Component, Special Operations Command central while engaged in ground combat against an enemy of the United Sates on 10 April 2007.

Sergeant Dryer and his Army Special Forces team were supporting Operation ENDURING FREEDOM when they were ambushed and heavily engaged for over 16 hours by enemy small arms fire and rocket-propelled grenades. When his primary satellite communications antenna and radio handset were destroyed in the initial attack, Sergeant Dryer and his team returned fire and fought through the ambush. Sergeant Dryer regained communication with an AC-130 and cleared the delivery of 105 millimeter rounds on enemy militia in a nearby ravine and cave complex. Within in minutes, the gunship delivered a savage attack, killing eight insurgents. When a second group of insurgents engage his team with additional machine gun fire, Sergeant Dryer directed an AC-130 reattack that killed the remaining enemy in the complex. Soon thereafter, a third and previously undetected enemy force engaged the team from a cave 70 meters from the friendly position. With the team pinned down, Sergeant Dryer directed 40 millimeter gunfire from an AC-130 against the cave complex, annihilating the cave and its inhabitants.

Throughout the engagement, Sergeant Dryer provided unprecedented terminal attack control that proved decisive to countering the enemy's lethal intent and subsequent destruction of 14 anti-Coalition militia and 15 vehicles with no loss of United Stated or Coalition forces. By his heroic action and unselfish dedication to duty, Sergeant Dryer has reflected great credit upon himself and the United States Air Force.

✯ ✯ ✯ ✯

Not very long after Sergeant Dryer deployed into Afghanistan, he and his team fell victim to an improvised explosive device (IED) incident, earning him and three of his teammates the Purple Heart. The team had set out on a combat reconnaissance patrol to confirm or deny the special intelligence report of IED cells operating in the region. Sergeant Dryer recounted that mission:

"Three days into the mission, none of us were able to get much sleep—maybe two or three hours each night. We were performing reconnaissance of the area, attempting to get a good hold up site and a little rest. Through special intelligence we were advised of possible enemy activity ahead of us. We cancelled looking for a hold up site and pursued in the direction of the enemy. We scouted ahead and called for close air support for imminent enemy engagement. When the aircraft checked on, they were far to low in altitude and the noise they generated spooked the enemy. The Taliban quickly escaped up a mountain pass on motorcycles. We had accomplished our mission, so we started our long return to base.

"There were highly used roads throughout the territory, but the threat [from landmines] was extremely high. We were limited to off-road travel until we arrived at an unnamed location close to the forward operating base. The terrain was very uneven, making it a very rough ride in a HMMWV. The endless number of wadis and drainage ditches also complicated our navigation back to base. We had been driving through this terrain for fourteen hours, to no avail. The leadership finally made the call to turn back and return to base the way had come.

"Everyone was getting is getting bumped around, so we finally said, 'Let's go back to our same route of travel and make our way back home.' We were making our way back on the same route we came in, and we came up to a wadi and road intersection, next to a village. The first three vehicles made it through because they were the smaller SUVs from the ANA. As we moved closer to the intersection, I looked back to my teammate and said, 'God, I wish this shit would end!' I turned [around] toward the rear of the vehicle, and all went black.

"The SF troops manning the vehicle behind us said that my body was thrown about fifty feet up into the air. All they could see was the black smoke coming out of the vehicle. We had two SF medics come up to my position, as I was the only one seriously injured from the explosion. The other four guys in the truck suffered mild concussions. They were a little disoriented, but were still able to function. The interrupter that was with me in the back of the gun truck suffered some head trauma and was knocked unconscious.

"I suffered a lot of shrapnel damage to my right leg, tore four tendons in my left knee, broke my shoulder, ribs, and both wrists. There was a piece of shrapnel right in the center of my helmet, and two more pieces in the lower lumbar of my armor. Wearing all of my armor definitely saved my life. I always kept my rifle right underneath my leg. My M4/M203 saved my leg because the weapon was cut in half. The explosion sheared the M240 right off of its mount. My rucksack with all the radio equipment, Mark 13, and all that stuff was completely shredded and thrown about two hundred and fifty yards from the vehicle. It took them a while to find all of my stuff, as it had been blown all over the place.

"The SF medics started to prepare me immediately; they gave me a 'lollipop' for the pain. I do not know what is in that, but it makes you feel pretty good. As the painkiller took effect, they began working on me to see where my injuries were and got the MedEvac on its way. The MedEvac, which was an SOF asset, showed up about an hour later came and picked me up. I was out cold for at least an hour. After the MedEvac arrived, the F-15s showed up, too, and they started circling the area to scare off any bad guys who were in the area.

"The actual IED was an anti-tank mine placed in the side of the wall. It was not in the ground. What had been in the ground was the trigger—it was a little doorbell that we rolled over. There was a minute chance that we would have rolled over the trigger. It was a trigger—not command detonated."

Sergeant Dryer spent the next four days in the hospital. His injuries were severe enough to rate him a trip back home. When given the option to return to the states or stay in the fight; TSgt Dryer grabbed that *Urrah!* spirit and chose to stay. He commented: "It is a large process to get someone out to replace you, plus I had just arrived and this was what

I had trained [for] most of my life to do, so I stayed. The only thing that sucked about this job was the fact that you were away from your loved ones most of your career." Disregarding his status [at the time], banged up and bandaged, he continued the tour, pressing the fight [against] the enemy with his team.

Before he returned home, TSgt Dryer and his team had completed one hundred combat reconnaissance patrols. Regarding his condition and mission he stated: "You just suck up the pain. It is few and far between, when you have trained your whole career to do this type of mission and then actually get to do it. You do what you need to do to get the reward at the end, and that reward is to actually prosecute the mission. I think the hardest thing was the broken wrist; every time we hit a bump, my hand fell off my 240 and smashed against an ammo can. My wrists could not be [set in] casts because it would have limited my dexterity and maneuverability. I eventually threw an Ace bandage around my wrists, put my glove on, and drove on."

Urrah!

| CHAPTER |
19

One Period of Darkness

CPT Paul Alexander and
MSgt Chad Ackman, 8th SOS CV-22

In the early hours of April 24, 1980, in an Iranian desert, all hope for a successful hostage rescue mission evaporated. One of the RH-53 helicopters had hydraulic failure; Delta Force needed a minimum of six aircraft to carry out their assault on the American Embassy in Tehran, but they were now down to five. It was game over; Operation Eagle Claw aborted. To punctuate the hard luck of this operation, as the men prepared to exfil from the area, one of the helicopters collided with a MC-130, sending a fireball into the night sky and destroying both the helo and the Hercules transport. What had begun as a courageous rescue mission ended in disaster, with eight men killed. It was a devastating blow to the United States in general and to the special operations forces (SOFO) in particular.

The tragedy of the failed operation became the catalyst for a new aircraft that addressed the Achilles' heel of Operation Eagle Claw. Born out of the ashes of Desert One would come the concept for the Osprey. Despite numerous attempts to shut down the project, this innovative aircraft would become an operational asset to AFSOC. Ironically, the CV-22 would be assigned to the 8th Special Operations Squadron (SOS)—the same SOS that had supported Operation Eagle Claw thirty years earlier. During that mission, five members of the squadron had lost their lives. The squadron received its motto "With the guts to try" from this operation.

The 8th Special Operations Squadron, known as the "Blackbirds," is one of nine squadrons in the 1st Special Operations Wing, AFSOC, at Hurlburt Field, Florida. The primary mission of the 8th SOS is the insertion, extraction, and resupply of special operations forces and equipment into hostile or enemy-controlled territory using air-land or air-drop procedures. To carry out these missions, the 8th SOS operates the newest addition to the AFSOC inventory, the CV-22 Osprey.

The Bell-Boeing CV-22 Osprey is a tilt-rotor aircraft that combines the vertical takeoff, hover, and vertical landing qualities of a helicopter with the long-range, fuel efficiency and speed that are characteristics of a turboprop aircraft. This versatile, self-deployable aircraft offers increased speed and range over other rotary-wing aircraft, enabling Air Force Special Operations Command aircrews to execute long-range special operations missions. Indeed, the CV-22 can perform missions that normally would require both fixed-wing and rotary-wing aircraft. That is, the Osprey takes off vertically and, once airborne, the nacelles (engine and prop-rotor group) on each wing can rotate into a forward position. The aircraft is equipped with integrated threat countermeasures, terrain-following radar, forward-looking infrared sensor, and other advanced avionics systems that allow it to operate at low altitude, in adverse weather conditions, and in medium- to high-threat environments.

Captain Paul Alexander is the CV-22 Branch Chief and evaluator pilot, 1st Special Operations Group, and an experienced MH-53 Pave Low and MH-47 Chinook pilot. Captain Alexander flew with the 160th Special Operations Aviation Regiment (Airborne) before he crossed over to AFSOC, with the expressed hope of getting behind the controls of the CV-22. MSgt Chad Ackman is the 8th SOS First Sergeant, Noncommissioned Officer in Charge of Standardization and Evaluation, and a CV-22 evaluator flight engineer. Both rotary-wing men have spent their time in service getting to the fight at half the speed they can now attain with the Osprey. For them, it is easy to look at this unique aircraft and see the niche that it will fill as AFSOC continues to prosecute its anti-terrorism missions.

Over the course of the Osprey's development, there was much apprehension about the CV-22; however, as it has become operational, it has been finding more acceptance with the SOF teams. Captain Alexander explained: "We did a big exercise in 2006 at Hurlburt with our weapons school guys. We were asked if we wanted to participate and [we] said 'Yes, we would love to.' It gave us the chance to integrate with the other AFSOC platforms and work with some customers to get feedback. That very event was a turning point for us.

"As I was standing before these guys, briefing them on the aircraft's capabilities, I could see the look of skepticism on their faces. I asked them who knew anything about the V-22. Everyone raised his hand. I picked one guy and asked what [he] knew and he replied, 'It's killed a bunch of people.' I laughed and said, 'Yeah. Do you know how many times a V-22 has crashed since it was brought out into development?' And he guessed ten times. I told him [that it was] four, and only three had fatalities. That is a pretty good record considering the technology.

"I gave them a couple comparisons with the development of other aircraft in history that hurt and killed a lot of people [before they were ready]. The WWII Corsair was called the 'Ensign Killer'; the Harrier . . . even the F-14 had a lot of problems. To get these guys to believe you were bringing something good to the fight was a tough pill to swallow. I told them I was not a salesman, I was not there to blow sunshine up their skirts. [I said,] 'You guys are going make a decision and I want

your honest feedback.' When we finished the exercise, luckily for us—
and unluckily for our Pave Low brethren, [as] they broke during one
mission and we picked up the entire mission and accomplished it. We
actually picked up a load from the landing zone that the MH-53 was
not capable of doing. We figured this out later, with the '53 pilots and
flight engineers who were also in awe of the CV-22's capabilities—and
that spoke volumes.

"You can brief this stuff all day long, but until you can go out and
actually demonstrate it; it's a whole different game. Most of the feedback we got was positive. Of course, we really got some good con-
structive [bad] feedback, too—it's too small, it cannot carry all the
gear I need to carry, there's no possible way to fit it in the airplane.
And, yes, those are limitations that the teams are going to have to accept and make the best of."

Captain Alexander elaborated on the Osprey's potential: "This
airplane certainly was not designed to put a Ranger battalion on a target en masse, like an MH-47. However, it will take a small group of
people or, using multiple aircraft, will take you in and out in one period of darkness, as advertised, a long, long way. I think that is how we
need to employ the airplane, and that is where we are going to earn
our pay.

"Our customer feedback has been better than expected," Captain
Alexander said. "Working with the aircraft has alleviated the original
concerns about size and maneuverability. We have briefed and briefed
the capabilities of the aircraft, but in the last year we have been able to
take the CV-22 out and do proof-of-concept missions. The biggest
thing that hits us in the head is the speed and range of the aircraft,
without the external support you would typically need for a helicopter mission—such things as aerial refueling (AR) support and
forward area refueling and rearming point (FARP) support to get
to the fight and get away from the fight. That is one of the biggest
advantages.

"There are a lot of naysayers out there who speak up about the
V-22 and what its capabilities truly are. [But] we are still learning
what those true capabilities are. In many aspects, the aircraft is performing much better than we expected. Performance charts continue
to change as little things are adjusted on the aircraft—such as software

modifications, etc. You end up with something better than you thought you were going to have in the first place. We have had nothing but positive response from all of the SOF teams we have worked with." We bring them in, brief them and tell them; here is what we know about the airplane. We are not here to sell it to you; we want the airplane to sell itself. We tell them the first thing you will notice is the CV-22 is smaller than a '53 on the inside; it is smaller than a Chinook. It will not be able to carry as much space-wise as those other larger helicopters. However, what we can do is get you there twice as fast and twice as far. The V-22 can get the SOF team in and out in one period of darkness, which we have been trying to do for years and years. Now, we can finally do it! This is not lip service! The most important thing we bring to the fight is speed and range! "When the V-22 was introduced to AFSOC, it was touted as the replacement for the MH-53 Pave Low, and even in some cases, for the MC-130. Since the CV-22 has become operational, it has established its unique niche. Captain

The CV-22 Osprey tilt-rotor aircraft has entered service with the 8th Special Operations Squadron. This revolutionary aircraft will serve as an insertion, re-supply, and extraction platform for U.S. SOF units, as seen here hoisting up a pair of Navy SEALs from helocast operations. The CV-22 is capable of carrying out its mission in one period of darkness, making it a valuable asset to AFSOC. *Courtesy of the U.S. Air Force.*

Alexander explained: "The drawdown of the '53 and the simultaneous buildup of the Osprey are coincidental. The program actually came to a screeching halt in 2000, then came back on line in 2003, or else we would have a lot more CV-22s sitting on the ramp right now."

☆ ☆ ☆ ☆

The majority of the CV-22 pilots have come from a rotary-wing background, though there are a few with fixed-wing experience. The first group of cadre members were pilots with experience flying terrain, following radar as a minimum. This saved time in teaching them how to fly the radar, as it is a critical part of what the CV-22 crews do during adverse weather conditions. After that initial group, the squadron opened the doors a little. Capt. Alexander stated: "We took in the first line pilot from the Air Force. He graduated from Fort Rucker a month ago, and has been selected for the CV-22. So we will see him in the next year . . . year and a half."

What people may not realize is how many V-22 aircraft are out there right now, flying. The Air Force has four at the schoolhouse at Kirtland AFB, the 8th SOS at Hurlburt Field currently has five, and the numbers continue to grow. The Marine Corps has about forty of the MV version sitting on the ramp at New River MCAS.

In September 2007, the Marines deployed an MV-22 with the Marine Expeditionary Unit (MEU) down range. That is, the CV-22 is the AFSOC version and the MV-22 is the Marine version. Captain Alexander described the main differences: "It is all in the avionics, defensive systems, and radios. We have multi-mode radar similar to that on the MH-47 flying with the 160th. Other than that, it is the same basic airframe. We have a little different symbol use in the cockpit, but if you saw them in the dark, you could not tell the difference—except that we have a few more antennas and a couple more "bumps" on the aircraft.

"Both versions are fitted with aerial refueling (AR) probes. In the helicopter world, the refueling MC-130 has to slow down to almost near stall speed for the helos to refuel. With the V-22, the MC-130 has to speed up and the CV-22 has to slow down to do the linkup. The

MC-130s are a lot more comfortable refueling the CV-22; especially in theater, where they are not hanging it out. Also, the MC-130s are a lot more efficient at these higher speeds.

"There are a lot of positive things [going for you] when you execute a mission in a CV-22. You do not require as much gas, or you do not require it as many times. In MH-53s, we [would do] two or three ARs in Afghanistan and Iraq just to get in and out of the target area. In the CV-22, we might see a tanker one time during a mission and sometimes not at all. This frees up those assets to support someone else's mission and also reduces the likelihood of being detected by the enemy."

For anyone who has had the chance to get into the cockpit of a CV-22, the immediate response is that it does not have the look or feel of a helicopter. Captain Alexander explained: "It is very airplane-like. It is also a more crew-friendly environment. We have always operated in airframes that did not have an environmental control system. When you are sitting in the cockpit on alert, on the ramp supporting Southern Watch, and it is 140 degrees on the tarmac, you are losing pounds just as you sit there and perspire. Now, you climb into the CV-22 and you literally have ice chunks getting blown on you. That really makes the mission a bit better on the crew; you do not have that fatigue wearing you down throughout the flight. You can take a seven-, eight-, ten-, or twelve-hour mission and still walk away feeling a lot more alert than you would have after sweating for twelve hours. I remember missions in a '53: we would get out of the aircraft and would be worn out. All we could do was to get the crew rested for the next mission."

"Concerning the avionics, our heads-down hover display is like flying a video game. It is similar to a few other rotary-wing aircraft; you have a velocity vector and a speed queue; you have your position, altitude, rate of descent, and ground speed; and basically are taking a circle and are trying to establish that circle in the middle of the display on a reference mark, and hold it in the same place while you maintain heading and altitude. In today's modern age, it is really true; you find [that] the folks who grew up playing video games do very well [with] stuff like that. Some of the older guys, like myself, kind of struggle with some of those things. But once you grasp what you are looking at, it makes it very easy to place the aircraft into a precision hover. Plus, the airplane will actually hover itself. You can couple it up and it will maintain that position. The same symbology is on our heads-down display as on the HUD that slips over a tube on your night-vision goggles. You can maintain a visual reference outside but still fly those symbols and easily transition your vision from inside to outside the cockpit. We use those symbols during brown-outs, similarly as we did in the '53 and the '47. When you do not have any visual reference, you can fly those symbols and still safely land the aircraft."

While speed and surprise are two dynamic features of the CV-22, what happens when the team hits a hot landing zone? Or, the bad guys are hot on the tail of the SOF team as they are trying to exfil? Captain Alexander addressed this issue: "The Marines have a tail gun placed on the ramp of the MV-22. However, that is not the answer we are looking for in AFSOC; though it is certainly a stopgap measure until we find a better solution. We are looking at a possible turret-mounted system, in which we remove the two cargo hooks out of the floor of the fuselage. In the aft location, we can place a turret-mounted system that will have 360 degrees of azimuth. In the forward hole, we can place a sensor for that weapon. It seems like the best solution at this time.

"There are many complications associated with putting a weapon on this particular aircraft, because when you bring the nacelles all the way down into the airplane mode, the blades are actually nine feet below the airframe. You have to have something that will not shoot your blades. It you try to put door guns on the aircraft, you have a very limited field of fire because of the close proximity of the prop-rotors. Furthermore, you cannot have weapons hanging out of the aircraft when you transition from helicopter mode to airplane mode." The AFSOC is currently testing the remote guardian system (RGS) developed by BAE Systems. This weapon system will provide a full 360 degrees of suppressive fire for the CV-22 aircraft. The RGS is designed to be mounted on the belly of the fuselage (in the cargo hook wells), and will be capable of delivering precise, sustained fire throughout the flight of the aircraft. Completely compatible with the Ospreys avionics, this system may be the answer to providing the aircraft with defensive weapons.

Captain Alexander, having had time in all three aircraft, is aptly suited to discuss the differences between the CV-22 and the MH-53 and MH-47: "The CV-22 operating ceiling is much higher than the MH-53 and MH-47; the CV-22 has been tested up to 25,000 feet. However, it is not a pressurized aircraft. If we are carrying any passengers, we have to have supplemental oxygen or stay at altitudes that do not put physiological stress on those guys."

MSgt Chad Ackman had his own impressions of the new aircraft: He particularly commented on the interior size: "There is not a vehicle that will fit in the CV-22 at this time. They are still working on a couple of versions, including one that looks like the old WW II Jeep. You can fit a couple of ATVs or motorcycles in the back. Our usable payload is better than a MH-53. The airplane sits at about 32,000 pounds and we can take off at 60,500 pounds. We tend to always 'cube out' before we 'gross out.' That is, we always run out of space before we run out of lift.

"The other beautiful thing about the airplane is [that], in a helicopter, if you over-gross it to where you do not have the power to hover, you are not going anywhere. If you do that in a CV-22, you can still take off without the power to hover by doing a rolling take-off: a short take-off, burn off some fuel en route, and land on the other end. It is one of those situations where you are filling a void [that you] never [knew you had, since you never] had that kind of capability before. We routinely take off without the power to hover and still make the mission.

MSgt Ackman continued: "As far as the maintenance goes, the

CV-22 is much easier. The Pave Low is an older airplane, a lot of steam gauges, a lot of numbers you had to remember; the CV-22 is color-coded green, yellow, and red: green is good, yellow means you need to look at something, and red is not so good. As long as you can tell colors, you're okay. The CV-22 is a much easier plane to operate from the flight engineer's perspective. The Osprey has what is referred to as a 'glass cockpit.'"

When asked about rotor wash between the regular helicopters and the CV-22, Captain Alexander expressed this: "It depends on what size of helicopter you are talking about. If it is a '47 or '53, then, of course, there are variables there, too. How heavy and how high are you? It is probably a little bit worse, based on the size of the rotor disk. The props on the CV-22 are a little bit smaller than your typical large helicopter rotor system, but then you have two. But because we have such highly loaded disks, the column of air that flows beneath the airplane is very concentrated.

"We have done some hoist training with guys in the water, and the feedback we got was: 'Yeah, it is tough; the higher you guys are the better.' We have a really good hoist on the tail of the airplane, so we find that from one hundred fifty feet and up, the downwash is more negligible to the guy in the water. If we have to go to a hundred feet or below, you pretty much beat up the guy in the water. We are assuming that if we ever have to do a rescue in the water, we will be equipped with PJs or some type of rescue swimmer who is going to go in there strong—someone who can withstand the downwash and help the survivor get on the hoist."

In June 2007, the 8th Special Operations Squadron completed another mission to verify and prove the tactics, techniques, and procedures of the CV-22 Osprey during a water operations exercise with Navy SEALs at Lake Jackson in Florala, Alabama. The mission was a three-part event, with boat deployment, helocasting, and live water-hoist operations. "The boat-deployment exercise is when we have a boat, called a 'soft duck,' in the cargo area and we are flying a 'low and slow' approach over the water," said MSgt Ackman. "When we're at the correct speed and altitude, we drop the boat out the back. The boat drop was made in helicopter mode, at a height of ten feet and a flight speed of ten knots. Helocasting is basically the same thing, except the team in the back of the aircraft jumps in the water right after the boat is deployed. The CV-22 is great in this role because it can fly farther and faster than a helicopter. We will use the knowledge gained during this validation exercise to create new training plans for all future aircrews [regarding] the best way to accomplish these types of operations."

Captain Alexander commented: "Flying ten feet above the water is not really a big deal. The unique characteristic of the CV-22 rotor design creates rotor wash off the nose and tail at a hundred knots per hour; this causes the water to move away from you so it appears as if you are flying backwards. That's why we again use a heads-down hover display, or HUD, as [that] helps us keep situational awareness of our actual position, such as velocity, drift, and altitude."

"The 'soft ducks' were partly inflated Zodiacs, as you cannot fit a fully inflated duck in the cabin—you just don't have the dimensions. We are just a little bit bigger inside than a CH-46. We have a roller system in the aircraft, and the SEALs we worked with had palletized the load and bundled it, [so] it went out of the CV-22 like greased lightning; it worked really well."

Captain Alexander related the experience he and MSgt Ackman had as the first trainers to land on a ship. This would be the first time the CV-22 conducted actual shipboard operations, done on the USS *Battan* in August 2007. "There was nothing really cosmic about this. Once you've landed a rotary-wing aircraft on a ship, and realize the fact [the ship is] moving, it is not really a big deal. However, the space you are used to with the rotors directly overhead is reduced, as now the [roters] are sitting out on the edge of the wings—there are some considerations there. We were able to do short take-offs from the ship, both day and night. There are some space issues, [such as] where you are on the deck [and] what pad you land on. It is really a stable platform—at a hover, this aircraft is exactly like a tandem rotor helicopter . . . just rock solid."

Considering the difference in getting the Osprey shipboard ready, MSgt Ackman elaborated: "The fold system is pretty good on the CV-22. It is quicker than the Pave Low. The fold system is more reliable, and it does fold up faster than the Pave Low did." Captain Alexander added: "The '47 is all manual. Folding a '47 takes a lot of guys and probably about forty-five minutes to an hour to get all the blades folded. With the CV-22, it is a one-button push, all done hydraulically; the wing folds ninety degrees, and you are done. From the time you shut down the engines till you fold it is definitely within five minutes. You can get below deck a lot quicker and, of course, with the reduction of space, you can get a bunch of them aboard a ship."

Considering the distinctiveness of this aircraft, its heritage, and its future, the question is, how will the CV-22 affect AFSOC capabilities in the combat situations ahead? What about this aircraft will help special operations forces stealthily get in and get out with a firefight? Captain Alexander answered: "As with any helicopter, once you are in the terminal area, the jig is up. It doesn't matter how quiet you were or how fast you got there. The aircraft's acoustical signature is very low in the airplane mode. Of course, you are flying higher and faster than a helicopter, so you are much harder to pinpoint. However, when you get down there, and you have a guy on a rooftop with an RPG or small arms, you are subjected to a possible shoot-down. We need something that will put the enemy's head down while we're at a hover, and will allow us to get our guys off or on the aircraft. In airplane mode—up high, you don't sound like a helo; when you return to the conversion mode, the laws of physics take over and you sound more like a helo again— however, it is a lot smoother than the traditional helo. The rotor RPM is faster and the blades are smaller than the typical helicopter. It is not a traditional *whomp, whomp, whomp* sound of a helo. It is more of a *purrrring* sound—very distinctive.

Also, "It does not sound like a traditional helo, so if the enemy is expecting a Chinook or a Pave Low, you will surprise them. In fact, we like to take our team guys out and drop them in a landing zone, and then do a high-speed pass over them so they can hear how quiet we can be. From their perspective, they hear what the enemy hears when we are inbound. They all are amazed 'cause they tell us, 'Man, we did not hear you until you were right on top of us, and then you were gone.' Conversely, as we are slowing down to come into the landing zone, at about a minute out you definitely know someone is coming. There is no hiding it at that point."

It is the consensus in the AFSOC community that, had the Air Force been involved in the design of this aircraft from square one, it would have been a different plane. Captain Alexander commented: "Yes, it would. Many times we struggle with the fact [that] we are a very small proponent of the V-22 program. We certainly feel like we are the most important proponent of the program, however. As the numbers speak, the Marines are supposed to get three-hundred fifty MVs while we are getting fifty CVs. Sometimes it is a fight to get our wishes into the airplane. However, I think the Marines are starting to come around. Because it is a joint program, if the Air Force and the Marines agree on a changes—say, in software or hardware—then it tends to happen pretty rapidly.

"There have been things that we have had to fight for, tooth and nail. As an example, when we [are going to have to] go to a software-change review board, where we rack and stack our wants, we can sit down with the Marine Corps beforehand and ask, 'Okay, what are your top ten?' And, 'Okay, here are our top ten.' And out of the blue, the 'top ten' are just about the same now. We are interested in what they are doing, and they are interested in what we're doing. It is good because [the two communities] can glean a lot of lessons [from one another]; we don't have to relearn lessons or make the same mistakes. We can streamline the process, as it were. We actually have the 8th SOS DO [director of operations] in theater, doing a staff job, but he is also taking a good look at what the Marines are doing with the aircraft, so he can capture lessons learned and bring them back to us."

The bottom line is that the CV-22 is self-deployable, quicker, and cheaper than other aircraft in our inventory. It has a greater un-refueled combat radius, which reduces tanker requirements, and longer un-refueled loiter times. Helo-fixed-wing transloads are reduced, and complex airfield seizures are decreased. Missions can be completed easier and quicker, reducing mission complexity. The CV-22 increases mission flexibility by conducting the missions formerly done by the MH-53 and MC-130. Indeed, the CV-22 is a most capable aircraft. It can and *will* accomplish all of these tasks in "one period of darkness."

Antiterrorism (AT). Defensive measures used to reduce the vulnerability of individuals and property to terrorism.

Battlefield airmen. Air Force Special Operations Command Special Tactics Squadron team members, combat controllers, pararescuemen, and Special Operations Weather Teams.

Battle rattle. Combat gear, from body armor to load-bearing vest and all related equipment carried by the Special Tactics Team members.

Chalk. A load of troops, grouped together and given a particular number, often written in chalk on the tarmac.

Civil affairs. The activities of a commander that establish, maintain, influence, or exploit the relations between military forces and civil authorities, including both governmental and nongovernmental, and the involving the civilian population in a friendly, neutral, or hostile area of operations. The goal is to facilitate military operations and consolidate operational objectives. Civil affairs may include performance by military forces of activities and functions that would normally be the responsibility of the local government. These activities may be performed prior to, during, or subsequent to military action, and may also take place, if directed, in the absence of other military operations.

Clandestine operation. Activities sponsored or conducted by governmental departments or agencies in such a way as to ensure secrecy or concealment. (This differs from *covert operations* in that emphasis is placed on concealment of the operation rather than on concealment of the identity of the sponsor.) In special operations, an activity may be both covert and clandestine, and may focus equally on operational considerations and intelligence-related activities.

Close air support (CAS). Air action against hostile targets that are in close proximity to friendly forces on the ground and that require detailed integration of the air mission with the fire and movement of those ground forces.

Collateral special operations activities. Collateral activities in which special operations forces, by virtue of their inherent capabilities, selectively may be tasked to participate. These activities may include security assistance, humanitarian assistance, antiterrorism, counterdrug operations, personnel recovery, and special activities.

Counter proliferation. Activities taken to counter the spread of dangerous military capabilities, and allied technologies or know-how, especially weapons of mass destruction and ballistic missile delivery systems.

Counterterrorism. Offensive measures taken to prevent, deter, and respond to terrorism.

Covert operations. Operations planned and executed to conceal the identity of or permit plausible denial by the sponsor.

Danger close. In close air support, artillery, mortar, and naval gunfire support fires, this is the term included in the method-of-engagement segment of a call for fire that indicates friendly forces are within close proximity of the target. The actual distance that determines close proximity depends on the weapons and munitions fired.

Direct action mission. In special operations, a specified act involving operations of an overt, covert, clandestine, or low-visibility nature, conducted primarily by a sponsoring power's special operations forces in a hostile or denied area.

Door Kicker. See *Shooter.*

Exfiltration. The removal of personnel or units from areas under enemy control.

Fast mover. Term used to indicate jet fighter aircraft.

Foreign internal defense (FID). Participation by civilian and military agencies of a government in actions taken by another government to free and protect its citizens from subversion, lawlessness, and insurgency.

Guerrilla warfare. Military and paramilitary operations conducted in enemy-held or hostile territory by irregular, predominantly indigenous forces.

Helo. Slang term for a helicopter.

Host-nation. A nation that receives the forces or supplies of allied nations or NATO organizations, which are located on, operate in, or transit through its territory.

Infiltration. The movement through or into an area or territory that is occupied by either friendly or enemy troops or organizations. The movement is made, either by small groups or by individuals, at extended or irregular intervals. When used in connection with the enemy, it implies that contact is avoided.

Insurgency. An organized movement aimed at the overthrow of a constituted government through the use of subversion and armed conflict.

Internal defense. The full range of measures taken by a government to free and protect its society from subversion, lawlessness, and insurgency.

Interoperability. The ability of systems, units, or forces to provide services to and to accept services from other systems, units or forces, or to use the services so exchanged to enable them to operate effectively together.

Low-intensity conflict. Political-military confrontation between contending states or groups below conventional war and above routine, peaceful competition among states. It frequently involves protracted struggles of competing principles and ideologies. Low-intensity conflict ranges from subversion to the use of armed force. It is waged by a combination of means employing political, economic, informational, and military instruments. Low-intensity conflicts are often localized, generally in the Third World, but contain regional and global security implications.

Military civic action. The use of indigenous military forces on projects useful to the local population at all levels, in such fields as education, training, public works, agriculture, transportation, communications, health, sanitation, and others contributing to economic and social development.

Mission. A statement of reason by an organization for its existence and what it wishes to accomplish.

National Command Authorities (NCA). The U.S. President and the Secretary of Defense, together or with their duly deputized alternates or successors. The term signifies Constitutional authority to direct the Armed Forces in their execution of military actions.

Nap-of-the-earth (NOE). Flight close to the earth's surface, during which airspeed, height, and/or altitude are adapted to the contours and cover of the ground in order to avoid enemy detection and fire.

Objectives. Specific actions to be achieved in a specified time period. Accomplishment of the objectives will indicate progress toward achieving the overall goals of a mission.

Operator. See *Shooter*.

Penetrometer. A device used to test the compactness of soil. Used to test an area where aircraft will land.

Rigging alternate method Zodiac (RAMZ, pronounced RAMS). Procedure for air-dropping a Zodiac raft.

Rubber Duck. Deployment of a Zodiac raft; deployment can be by parachute from a plane or by direct insert via helicopter.

Shooter. A special operations forces trooper, from U.S. Army Special Forces, U.S. Navy SEALs, U.S. Army Rangers, Delta Force, SAS (British or Australian), and so on.

Special reconnaissance (SR). Reconnaissance and surveillance actions conducted by special operations forces to obtain or verify, by visual observation or other collection methods, information concerning the capabilities, intentions, and activities of an actual or potential enemy, or to secure data concerning the meteorological, hydrographic, or geographic characteristics of a particular area. This includes target acquisition, area assessment, and post-strike reconnaissance.

Stick. A number of paratroopers who jump from one aperture or door of an aircraft during one run over a drop zone.

Strategy. The methods, approaches, or specific moves taken to implement and attain an objective.

Unconventional warfare (UW). A broad spectrum of military and paramilitary operations conducted in enemy-held, enemy-controlled, or politically sensitive territory. Unconventional warfare includes, but is not limited to, the interrelated fields of guerrilla warfare, evasion and escape, subversion, sabotage, and other operations of a low-visibility, covert, or clandestine nature. These interrelated aspects of unconventional warfare may be prosecuted singularly or collectively by predominantly indigenous personnel, usually supported and directed in varying degrees by (an) external source(s) during all conditions of war or peace.

A B B R E V I A T I O N S
U S E D   I N   T H I S   B O O K

AAA	anti-aircraft artillery
ACM	anti-coalition militia
AFSOC	Air Force Special Operations Command
AFSOF	Air Force Special Operations Forces
AGL	above ground level
AI	area of interest
ARSOF	Army Special Operations Forces
AO	area of operations
AOR	area of responsibility
AR	aerial refueling
AST	advanced skills training
BDA	battle damage assessment
BDU	battle dress uniform
C4I	Command, control, communications, computers, and intelligence
CAP	combat air patrol
CAS	close air support
CEP	circular error probable
CI	counterintelligence
CIA	Central Intelligence Agency
CinC	Commander-in Chief. This refers exclusively to the President of the United States.
CCT	combat control team
COA	course of action
COMSEC	communications security
CSAR	combat search and rescue
CT	counterterrorism
CQB	close quarters battle
CQC	close quarters combat

CRO	combat rescue officer
CWS	Combat Weather Squadron
DA	direct action
DZ	drop zone
E&E	evasion and escape
EMS	emergency medical support/services
EW	electronic warfare
FAC	forward air controller
FARP	forward arming and refueling point
FFJM	free-fall jumpmaster
FID	foreign internal defense
FLIR	forward looking infrared
FOB	forward operations base
FRIES	Fast rope insertion and extraction system
FTX	field training exercise
GPS	global positioning system
GWOT	Global War on Terrorism
GLTDII	ground laser target designator
HAHO	high-altitude high-opening
HALO	high-altitude low-opening
HE	high explosive
HEDP	high explosive dual purpose
HEI	high explosives incendiary
HUD	head-up display
HUMINT	human intelligence
HMMWV	high mobility multipurpose wheeled vehicle
IED	improvised explosive device
IFF	identification, friend or foe
IIN	integrated inertial navigation
INTREP	intelligence report
IPB	intelligence preparation of the battlespace
IR	infrared
JCS	Joint Chiefs of Staff
JM	jumpmaster
JSOTF	Joint special operations task force
JTF	joint task force
JTAC	joint terminal attack controller

LBE	load-bearing equipment
LZ	landing zone
MAC	military airlift command
MedEvac	medical evacuation
MEOW	mean effect of wind
METT-T	mission, enemy, troops, terrain, and time
MRE	meal, ready to eat
MTT	mobile training team
MiTT	military transition team
NOE	nap-of-the-earth
NOD	night optical device
NVD	night vision device
NVG	night-vision goggle
ODA	operational detachment Alpha
ODC	operational detachment command
OEF	Operation Enduring Freedom
OGA	other government agency—e.g., CIA
OIF	Operation Iraqi Freedom
OpTempo	operational tempo
PJ	pararescue jumper
PR	personnel recovery
PsyWar	psychological warfare
PAR	precision approach radar
PI	point of impact
PLGR	precise lightweight global positioning system receiver
PYSOP	psychological operations
QRF	quick reaction/response force
QRT	quick reaction team
R&S	reconnaissance and surveillance
RECCE	reconnaissance (pronounced REK-ee)
RST	reconnaissance and surveillance team
RATT	rapid all terrain transport
RTB	return to base
RF	radio frequency/response force
SEAL	Sea-Air-Land (U.S. Navy commandos)
SAR	search and rescue

SAS	Special Air Service (UK)
SASR	Special Air Service Regiment (Australian)
SatComm	satellite communications
SF	Special Forces (U.S. Army)
SFG	Special Forces Group
SIGINT	signals intelligence
SMU	special mission unit
SOAR	special operation aviation regiment
SOCOM	Special Operations Command
SOF	special operations forces
SOFLAM	special operations forces laser marker
SOG	special operations group
SOS	special operations squadron
SOW	special operations wing
SOWT	Special Operations Weather Team
SPIES	Special procedure insertion extraction system
SR	special reconnaissance
SSE	sensitive site exploitation
SST	SAR security team
STG	special tactics group
STO	Special Tactics Officer
STS	Special Tactics Squadron
STT	special tactics team
TAC	tactical air command/coordinator
TACAN	tactical air navigation
TF	task force
TTP	tactics, techniques & procedures
UAV	unmanned aerial vehicle
USACAPOC	U.S. Army Civil Affairs/Psychological Operations Command
USASFC	U.S. Army Special Forces Command
USASOC	U.S. Army Special Operations Command
USSOCOM	U.S. Special Operations Command
UW	unconventional warfare
VBIED	vehicle-borne improvised explosive device
VFR	visual flight rules
WMD	weapons of mass destruction

INDEX

227